Getting Started in

CURRENCY TRADING

SECOND EDITION

*Winning in Today's
Hottest Marketplace*

Michael Duane Archer

WILEY

John Wiley & Sons, Inc.

Library of Congress Cataloging-in-Publication Data

Archer, Michael D. (Michael Duane)
 Getting started in currency trading : winning in today's hottest marketplace /
Michael Archer.—2nd ed.
    p. cm.—(Getting started in)
 Includes index.
 ISBN 978-0-470-26777-6 (paper/website)
 1. Foreign exchange market.   2. Foreign exchange futures.   I. Title.
 HG3851.A739 2008
 332.4'5—dc22

                                                         2008019033

Printed in the United States of America

10 9 8 7 6 5 4 3 2 1

For my children, Brandy, Jonathan, Stephen, and Anthony

Contents

Acknowledgments   **xv**

Introduction   **xvii**

    About This Book   xvii

    How This Book Is Organized   xvii

    Disclaimer   xix

PART 1

THE FOREIGN EXCHANGE MARKETS

Chapter 1

The FOREX Landscape   **3**

    Introduction—What Is FOREX?   3

    What Is a Spot Market?   3

    Which Currencies Are Traded?   4

    Who Trades on the Foreign Exchange?   4

    How Are Currency Prices Determined?   5

    Why Trade Foreign Currencies?   5

    What Tools Do I Need to Trade Currencies?   8

    What Does It Cost to Trade Currencies?   8

    FOREX versus Stocks   8

    FOREX versus Futures   9

    Summary   10

Chapter 2

A Brief History of Currency Trading   **11**

    Introduction   11

    Ancient Times   11

    The Gold Standard 1816–1933   12

    The Fed   12

    Securities and Exchange Commission 1933–1934   14

    The Bretton Woods System, 1944–1973   14

    The End of Bretton Woods and Floating Exchange Rates   15

    International Monetary Market   15

Current Perspective   16
Arrival of the Euro   16
Summary   18

Chapter 3

Spot or Futures FOREX?   **19**
Introduction—Futures Contracts   19
Currency Futures   20
Contract Specifications   20
Currencies Trading Volume   21
U.S. Dollar Index   22
Summary   22

PART 2

GETTING STARTED

Chapter 4

The Regulatory Environment   **25**
Regulation Today   25
The Commodity Futures Trading Commission (CFTC)   26
National Futures Association   26
Commodity Futures Modernization Act of 2000   27
The Patriot Act   27
The CFTC Reauthorization Act of 2005   27
Summary   28

Chapter 5

The FOREX Lexicon   **29**
Currency Pairs   29
Major and Minor Currencies   29
Cross Currency   30
Exotic Currency   30
Base Currency   30
Quote Currency   30
Pips   30
Ticks   31
Margin   31
Leverage   32
Bid Price   32
Ask Price   32
Bid/Ask Spread   32

Quote Convention   32
Transaction Cost   33
Rollover   33
The Trader's Nemesis   33
Summary   34

Chapter 6

The Calculating Trader   **35**
Leverage and Margin Percent   36
Pip Values   36
Calculating Profit and Loss   37
Calculating Units Available   44
Calculating Margin Requirements   46
Calculating Transaction Cost   47
Calculating Account Summary Balance   50
For Futures Traders   52
Summary   53

Chapter 7

Selecting the Right FOREX Broker for You   **55**
Broker-Dealer Due Diligence   55
Demo Accounts   56
Market Maker, ECN, or IB?   56
Introducing Brokers   57
Platform Capabilities   58
Trading Tools   58
Order Execution and Accounting   60
News   60
Chat   60
Platform Stability and Backbone   62
Historical Data   62
Data Feed   63
Third-Party Offerings   63
Orders   63
Margin Requirements   64
Order Backup   64
Account Minimums   64
Pairs, Crosses, and Exotics   65
Deposits and Withdrawals   65
Transaction Costs   65

Trading Hours   66
Customer Service   66
Documentation   68
Requoting   68
Financials   68
Rollovers and Interest   69
FOREX Broker-Dealers   69
Popular Broker-Dealers   70
The Big Three   73
For the Professional   74
Fraud, Scams, and Off-Exchange   74
Summary   76

Chapter 8

Opening a FOREX Account   **77**
Account Types   78
Opening the Account: Steps   78
Summary   81

Chapter 9

Pulling the Trigger   **83**
Orders   83
Market Orders   84
Limit Orders   84
Stop Orders   85
Combination Orders   86
Specialty Orders   86
Order Placement Walk-Through   86
Order Execution   86
Order Confirmation   87
Transaction Exposure   87
Summary   88

PART 3

THE TOOLS OF THE TRADE

Chapter 10

Fundamental Analysis   **93**
Supply and Demand   93
Interest Rates   94
Balance of Trade   94

Purchasing Power Parity 97
Gross Domestic Product 98
Intervention 100
Other Economic Indicators 100
Forecasting 102

Chapter 11

Technical Analysis **107**
Overview 107
Bar Charts 108
Trend Lines 110
Support and Resistance 111
Recognizing Chart Patterns 111
Reversal Patterns 112
Continuation Patterns 113
Candlestick Charts 115
Point and Figure Charts 117
Charting Caveat—Prediction versus Description 119
Indicators and Oscillators 120
Relative Strength Indicator 120
Momentum Analysis 121
Moving Averages 123
Bollinger Bands 123
Indicator Caveat—Curve-Fit Data 126
Swing Analysis 126
Cycle Analysis 128
Advanced Studies 128
The Technician's Creed 129
Summary 130

Chapter 12

The Toolbox Approach **131**
General Principles 131
A KIS Toolbox 132
The Goodman Swing Count System 133
GSCS Rules 133
"3C" Stands for Carryover, Compensation, and Cancellation 136
The Nofri Congestion Phase Method 138
Pugh Swing Chart Formations 139
A Moving Average and Oscillator Battery 140
Contrary Opinion 142
Volume 142

Open Interest 142
Heuristics 143
Summary 144

Chapter 13

The FOREX Marketplace 145

Organizing Your Bookmarks 146
Cross-Category Services 147
Portals, Forums, Reviews 147
Charting and Technical Services 150
FOREX Education 152
Trading Signals and Software 153
News, Announcement Services, and Calendars 154
Live Data Streams 157
Historical Data 157
System Development Tools 159
FOREX Managed Accounts 161
Peter Panholzer 163
Odds and Ends 164
Summary 166

PART 4

THE COMPLETE FOREX TRADER

Chapter 14

Psychology of Trading 169

The Trading Pyramid 169
Fear and Greed, Greed and Fear 170
Profiling 171
The Attitude Heuristic 171
Characteristics of Successful Traders 172
Summary 173

Chapter 15

Money Management Made Simple 175

Breaking Even—The Belgian Dentist 175
Expectations 176
Trader Profiles 176
Parameters for Trader Profiles 178
The Trade Campaign Method (TCM) 179
Calculating TCM Profit and Loss 179

Stop-Loss Orders—A Brief Discussion 181
Selecting Markets 181
Summary 182

Chapter 16

Tactics and Strategy 183

Trending and Trading Markets 183
Market Environments (ME) 184
Directional Movement (DM) and Volatility (V) 185
Price and Time Rhythm (PR and TR) 185
Thickness (T) 188
Shape (S) 190
Pretzels (PZ) 190
ME Applications 190
The Three Chart System 193
The Dagger Entry Principle 193
Sitting on Your Hands 194
Time Filters 195
Trading the News 196
Going Against the Crowd 196
Trading Methods 197
The Flyer 197
Bathtub Analysis 198
Summary 198

Chapter 17

When and How to Regroup 199

Common Trading Errors 199
Performance Review 201
Heuristics Review 202
When to Say Uncle 202
Summary 202

Chapter 18

For the Record 203

Type of Records 203
The Rogers Method 205
The SnagIt Tool 205
Planning Records 206
Summary 206

PART 5

EXTRA FOR EXPERTS

Chapter 19

Options and Exotics   **209**
    Options   210
    An Options Primer   210
    Basic Options Terms   211
    The Pros and Cons of Options   212
    The Four Basic Options Strategies   213
    Purchasing and Writing Options   214
    Advanced Options Strategies   214
    The Retail FOREX Options Landscape   214
    Options for Trading   216
    Options for Money Management   216
    Exotics   218
    Trading Exotics   219
    Summary   220

Chapter 20

The Final Frontiers   **221**
    Rollovers   221
    Hedging   222
    Arbitrage   223
    Pros and Cons of Arbitrage   227
    Artificial Intelligence   228
    Complexity Theory Models   228
    The Trend Machine   229
    Automated Trading and Robots   229
    A Last Word   231

Appendix A   **233**
    How the FOREX Game Is Played   **233**

Appendix B   **237**
    **Retail FOREX Regulations—CFTC Reauthorization
    Act of 2005**   **237**

Appendix C   **243**
    List of World Currencies and Symbols   **243**

Appendix D 249
　　Major Currency Cross Rates 249

Appendix E 251
　　Euro Currency Unit 251

Appendix F 253
　　Time Zones and Global Banking Hours 253

Appendix G 255
　　Central Banks and Regulatory Agencies 255

Appendix H 259
　　Resources 259

Glossary 265

Index 277

Acknowledgments

I would like to thank those who assisted with editing, suggestions, and encouragement on this second edition of *Getting Started in Currency Trading*: Dawn Borris and Derek Ching of HawaiiForex (www.hawaiiforex.com), Frank Semone, and Jay Meisler of Global-View (www.global-view.com). Continued appreciation to Susan Cress and Gregory Morris, who contributed similar efforts on the first edition.

Introduction

About This Book

This book is intended to introduce the novice investor to the exciting, complex, and sometimes profitable realm of trading world currencies on the foreign exchange markets (FOREX). It also serves as a reference guide for stock and futures traders who wish to explore new trading opportunities. My primary focus is on the rapidly expanding and evolving online trading marketplace for spot currencies, generally referred to as *retail FOREX*.

From the very beginning I must emphasize currency trading may not be to everyone's disposition. The neophyte investor must be keenly aware of all the risks involved and should never trade on funds he or she deems necessary for survival. If you have some experience with leveraged markets such as futures or options, you owe yourself a look at FOREX. Those who have never traded will find it the "purest" of all speculative adventures.

How This Book Is Organized

There are six main parts to this book:

1. Part 1—The Foreign Exchange Markets

   The FOREX Landscape, A Brief History of Currency Trading, Spot or Futures FOREX?

   I open the book with a brief overview of the FOREX markets, a question-and-answer historical overview of currency trading, and the two primary methods for participating in the markets as a retail trader. I hope to dispel any myths the reader may have about FOREX.

2. Part 2—Getting Started

   The Regulatory Environment, The FOREX Lexicon, The Calculating Trader, Selecting the Right FOREX Broker for You, Opening a FOREX Account, Pulling the Trigger.

Every lucrative industry has its own gamut of highly specialized terms, and currency trading is no exception. You must thoroughly comprehend these terms before attempting to initiate any trades. With a little familiarization, the jargon of currency trading will become second nature.

I will assist the new trader in selecting a reputable online currency dealer and explain the steps involved in opening a trading account. The actual step-by-step processes of initiating and liquidating a live market order are examined in detail with a lengthy explanation of each order type.

Currency trading requires some minimal record keeping. The novice investor will be pleased to know that the mathematics of trading and calculating profit or loss involves nothing more than simple, four-function arithmetic—addition, subtraction, multiplication, and division—and that I have kept division examples to a minimum.

This section must be understood before the reader proceeds to the later sections.

3. Part 3—The Tools of the Trade

Fundamental Analysis, Technical Analysis, The Toolbox Approach, The FOREX Marketplace

Historically, there have been two major schools of thought in this endeavor: fundamental analysis and technical analysis. I explore the advantages and disadvantages of both schools in the chapters in this section. I offer ideas on selecting from these trading tools to assemble a basic, personal trading approach. The final chapter previews the wealth of FOREX products and services now available from third-party vendors.

4. Part 4—The Complete FOREX Trader

Psychology of Trading, Money Management Made Simple, Tactics and Strategy, When and How to Regroup, For the Record

In this section, I expose the trader to the psychology of trading and the stresses that may accompany same. I place much emphasis on money management and psychology—two key topics vital to success but often neglected in the search for the holy grail of trading methods. Tactics and Strategy proffers a potpourri of ideas from my own trading experience.

5. Part 5—Extra for Experts

Options and Exotics, The Final Frontiers

A single chapter covers options and exotics. A final chapter briefly discusses advanced strategies such as rollovers, hedging, and arbitrage, and proffers a speculative look at the future of FOREX.

This section is optional for the novice trader though investors with some trading experience will find it informative.

6. Appendixes

The appendixes are a ready reference of FOREX-specific information. I point you especially to Appendix A, How the FOREX Game Is Played.

The author's attempt has been to make *Getting Started in Currency Trading* an all-in-one introduction as well as a handy computer-side reference guide. Alas, only you, dear reader, may judge the level of my success therein and thereof.

Disclaimer

Neither the publisher nor the author is liable for any financial losses incurred while trading currencies.

Part 1

The Foreign Exchange Markets

The FOREX Landscape

Introduction—What Is FOREX?

Foreign exchange is the simultaneous buying of one currency and selling of another. Currencies are traded through a broker or dealer and are executed in currency pairs; for example, the Euro Dollar and the US Dollar (EUR/USD) or the British Pound and the Japanese Yen (GBP/JPY).

The FOReign EXchange Market (FOREX) is the largest financial market in the world, with a volume of over $2 trillion daily. This is more than three times the total amount of the stocks and futures markets combined.

Unlike other financial markets, the FOREX spot market has neither a physical location nor a central exchange. It operates through an electronic network of banks, corporations, and individuals trading one currency for another. The lack of a physical exchange enables the FOREX market to operate on a 24-hour basis, spanning from one time zone to another across the major financial centers. This fact—that there is no centralized exchange—is important to keep in mind as it permeates all aspects of the FOREX experience.

What Is a Spot Market?

A spot market is any market that deals in the current price of a financial instrument. Futures markets, such as the Chicago Board of Trade, offer commodity contracts whose delivery date may span several months into the future.

TABLE 1.1 Major FOREX Currencies

Symbol	Country	Currency
USD	United States	Dollar
EUR	Euro members	Euro
JPY	Japan	Yen
GBP	Great Britain	Pound
CHF	Switzerland	Franc
CAD	Canada	Dollar
AUD	Australia	Dollar

Settlement of FOREX spot transactions usually occurs within two business days. There are also futures and forwards in FOREX, but the overwhelming majority of traders use the spot market. I will discuss the opportunities to trade FOREX futures on the International Monetary Market.

Which Currencies Are Traded?

Any currency backed by an existing nation can be traded at the larger brokers. The trading volume of the major currencies (along with their symbols) is given in descending order: the U.S. Dollar (USD), the Euro Dollar (EUR), the Japanese Yen (JPY), the British Pound Sterling (GBP), the Swiss Franc (CHF), the Canadian Dollar (CAD), and the Australian Dollar (AUD). See Table 1.1. All other currencies are referred to as minors.

FOREX currency symbols are always three letters, where the first two letters identify the name of the country and the third letter identifies the name of that country's currency. (The "CH" in the Swiss Franc acronym stands for Confederation Helvetica.)

A FOREX transaction is always between two currencies. This often confuses new traders coming from the stock or futures markets where every trade is denominated in dollars. "Pairs," "crosses," "majors," "minors," and "exotics" are terms referencing specific combinations of currencies. I will discuss these in "The FOREX Lexicon" (Chapter 5). They are defined in the Glossary.

Who Trades on the Foreign Exchange?

There are two main groups that trade currencies. About five percent of daily volume is from companies and governments that buy or sell products and services in a foreign country and must subsequently convert profits made in foreign currencies into their own domestic currency in the course of doing business. This is primarily hedging activity. The other 95 percent consists of investors trading for profit, or speculation. Speculators range from large banks trading 10,000,000 currency units or more and the home-based operator trading perhaps 10,000 units or less. Retail FOREX, as much as it has grown in the past 10 years, still represents a very small percentage of the total daily volume.

Today, importers and exporters, international portfolio managers, multinational corporations, speculators, day traders, long-term holders, and hedge funds all use the FOREX market to pay for goods and services, to transact in financial assets, or to reduce the risk of currency movements by hedging their exposure in other markets.

A producer of Widgets in the United Kingdom is intrinsically long the British Pound (GBP). If they sign a long-term sales contract with a company in the United States, they may wish to buy some quantity of the USD and sell an equal quantity of the GBP to hedge their margins from a fall in the GBP.

The speculator trades to make a profit by purchasing one currency and simultaneously selling another. The hedger trades to protect his or her margin on an international sale (for example) from adverse currency fluctuations. The hedger has an intrinsic interest in one side of the market or the other. The speculator does not.

How Are Currency Prices Determined?

Currency prices are affected by a very large matrix of constantly changing economic and political conditions, but probably the most important are interest rates, international trade, inflation, and political stability. Sometimes governments actually participate in the foreign exchange market to influence the value of their currencies. They do this either by flooding the market with their domestic currency in an attempt to lower the price or, conversely, buying in order to raise the price. This is known as central bank intervention. Any of these factors, as well as large market orders, can cause high volatility in currency prices. However, the size and volume of the FOREX market make it impossible for any one entity to drive the market for any length of time.

Why Trade Foreign Currencies?

In today's marketplace, the dollar constantly fluctuates against the other currencies of the world. Several factors, such as the decline of global equity markets and declining world interest rates, have forced investors to pursue new opportunities. The global increase in trade and foreign investments has led to many national economies becoming interconnected with one another. This interconnection, and the resulting fluctuations in exchange rates, has created a huge international market: FOREX. For many investors, this has created exciting opportunities and new profit potentials. The FOREX market offers unmatched potential for profitable trading in any market condition or any stage of the business cycle. These factors equate to the following advantages:

- **No commissions.** No clearing fees, no exchange fees, no government fees, no brokerage fees.

- **No middlemen.** Spot currency trading does away with the middlemen and allows clients to interact directly with the market maker responsible for the pricing on a particular currency pair.

- **No fixed lot size.** In the futures markets, lot or contract sizes are determined by the exchanges. A standard-sized contract for silver futures is 5,000 ounces. Even a "mini-contract" of silver, 1,000 ounces, represents a value of approximately $6,000.00. In spot FOREX, *you* determine the lot size appropriate for your grubstake. This allows traders to effectively participate with accounts of well under $1,000.00. It also provides a significant money management tool for astute traders.

- **Low transaction cost.** The retail transaction cost (the bid/ask spread) is typically less than 0.1 percent under normal market conditions. At larger dealers, the spread could be as low as 0.07 percent. This will be described in detail later.

- **High liquidity.** With an average trading volume of over $2 trillion per day, FOREX is the most liquid market in the world. It means that a trader can enter or exit the market at will in almost any market condition.

- **Almost instantaneous transactions.** This is a very advantageous by-product of high liquidity.

- **Low margin, high leverage.** These factors increase the potential for higher profits (and losses) and are discussed later.

- **A 24-hour market.** A trader may take advantage of all profitable market conditions at any time. There is no waiting for the opening bell.

- **Online access.** The big boom in FOREX came with the advent of online (Internet) trading platforms.

- **Not related to the stock market.** Trading in the FOREX market involves selling or buying one currency against another. Thus, there is no correlation between the foreign currency market and the stock market. A bull market or a bear market for a currency is defined in terms of the outlook for its relative value against other currencies. If the outlook is positive, we have a bull market in which a trader profits by buying the currency against other currencies. Conversely, if the outlook is pessimistic, we have a bull market for other currencies and traders take profits by selling the currency against other currencies. In either case, there is always a good market trading opportunity for a trader. Fund managers are beginning to show interest in FOREX because of this noncorrelation with other investments.

- **Interbank market.** The backbone of the FOREX market consists of a global network of dealers. They are mainly major commercial banks that communicate and trade with one another and with their clients through electronic networks and by telephone. There are no organized exchanges to serve as a central location to facilitate transactions the way the New York Stock Exchange serves the equity markets. The FOREX market operates in a manner similar to that of the NASDAQ market in the United States; thus it is also referred to as an over-the-counter (OTC) market.

- **No one can corner the market.** The FOREX market is so vast and has so many participants that no single entity, not even a central bank, can control the market price for an extended period of time. Even interventions by mighty central banks are becoming increasingly ineffectual and short lived. Thus central banks are becoming less and less inclined to intervene to manipulate market prices. (You may remember the attempt to corner the silver futures market in the late 1970s. Such disruptive excess is not possible in the FOREX markets.)

- **No insider trading.** Because of the FOREX market's size and non-centralized nature, there is virtually no chance for ill effects caused by insider trading. Fraud possibilities, at least against the system as a whole, are significantly less than in any other financial instruments.

- **Limited regulation.** There is but limited governmental influence via regulation in the FOREX markets, primarily because there is no centralized location or exchange. Of course, this is a sword that may cut both ways, but the author believes—with a hardy caveat emptor—that less regulation is, on balance, an advantage. Nevertheless, most countries do have some regulatory say and more seems on the way. Regardless, fraud is always fraud wherever it is found and subject to criminal penalties in all countries.

- **Online trading.** Today you may select from over 100 online FOREX broker-dealers. While none is perfect, the trader has a wide variety of options at his or her disposal.

- **Third-party products and services.** The immense popularity of retail FOREX has fostered a burgeoning industry of third-party products and services.

Traditionally, investors' only means of gaining access to the foreign exchange market was through banks that transacted large amounts of currencies for commercial and investment purposes. Trading volume has increased rapidly over time, especially after exchange rates were allowed to float freely in 1971.

What Tools Do I Need to Trade Currencies?

A computer with reliable high-speed connection to the Internet, a small grub-stake, and the information in this book are all that are needed to begin trading currencies. You do not even need the grubstake to practice on a demo account.

What Does It Cost to Trade Currencies?

An online currency trading account (a "micro-account") may be opened for as little as $100. Mini-accounts start at $300. Do not laugh—micro- and mini-accounts are a good way to get your feet wet without taking a bath. Unlike futures, where the size of a contract is set by the exchanges, in FOREX you select how much of any particular currency you wish to buy or sell. Thus, a $3,000.00 grubstake is not unreasonable as long as the trader engages in appropriately sized trades. FOREX mini-accounts also do not suffer the illiquidity of many futures mini-contracts, as everyone feeds from the same currency "pool."

FOREX Versus Stocks

Historically, the securities markets have been considered, at least by the major-ity of the public, as an investment vehicle. In the last ten years, securities have taken on a more speculative nature. This was perhaps due to the downfall of the overall stock market as many security issues experienced extreme volatility because of the "irrational exuberance" displayed in the marketplace. The implied return associated with an investment was no longer true. Many traders engaged in the day trader rush of the late 1990s only to discover that from a leverage standpoint it took quite a bit of capital to day trade, and the return—while potentially higher than long-term investing—was not exponential, to say the least.

After the onset of the day trader rush, many traders moved into the futures stock index markets where they found they could better leverage their capital and not have their capital tied up when it could be earning interest or making money somewhere else. Like the futures markets, spot currency trading is an excellent vehicle for the pattern day trader that desires to leverage his or her current capital to trade. Spot currency trading provides more options and greater volatility while at the same time stronger trends than are currently available in stock futures indexes. Former securities day traders have an excellent home in the FOREX market.

There are approximately 4,000 stocks listed on the New York Stock Exchange. Another 2,800 are listed on the NASDAQ. Which one will you trade? Trading just the seven major USD currency pairs instead of 6,800 stocks simplifies matters significantly for the FOREX trader. Fewer decisions, fewer headaches.

FOREX Versus Futures

The futures contract is precisely that—a legally binding agreement to deliver or accept delivery of a specified grade and quantity of a given commodity in a distant month. FOREX, however, is a spot (cash) market in which trades rarely exceed two days. Many FOREX brokers allow their investors to "roll over" open trades after two days. There exist FOREX futures or forward contracts, but almost all activity is in the spot market facilitated by rollovers.

In addition to the advantages listed, FOREX trades are almost always executed at the time and price asked by the speculator. There are numerous horror stories about futures traders being locked into an open position even after placing the liquidation order. The high liquidity of the foreign exchange market (roughly three times the trading volume of all the futures markets combined) ensures the prompt execution of all orders (entry, exit, limit, etc.) at the desired price and time.

The caveat here is something called a requote or "dealer intervention," which we will discuss in a later chapter.

The Commodity Futures Trading Commission (CFTC) authorizes futures exchanges to place daily limits on contracts that significantly hamper the ability to enter and exit the market at a selected price and time. No such limits exist in the FOREX market.

Stock and futures traders are used to thinking in terms of the U.S. Dollar versus something else, such as the price of a stock or the price of wheat. This is like comparing apples to oranges. In currency trading, however, it's always a comparison of one currency to another currency—someone's apples to someone else's apples. This paradigm shift can take a little getting used to, but I will give you plenty of examples to help smooth the transition.

I must reiterate: There is always some risk in speculation regardless of which financial instruments are traded and where they are traded, regulated or unregulated.

Summary

- FOREX means "FOReign EXchange."
- The FOREX market is more than a $2 trillion-a-day financial market, dwarfing everything else, including stocks and futures.
- There is no centralized exchange or clearinghouse for currency trading.
- The FOREX market is less regulated than other financial markets.
- The top four traded currencies are: the U.S. Dollar (USD), the European Dollar (EUR), the Japanese Yen (JPY), and the British Pound (GBP).
- Access to the FOREX markets via the Internet has resulted in a great deal of interest by small traders previously locked out of this enormous marketplace.

Chapter

2

A Brief History of Currency Trading

Introduction

This material may not seem very relevant to trading currencies today, but even a modest, perspective adds substance and depth to a trader. "He who knows only his own generation remains always a child," George Norlin once said.

Ancient Times

Foreign exchange dealing may be traced back to the early stages of history, possibly beginning with the introduction of coinage by the ancient Egyptians, and the use of paper notes by the Babylonians. Certainly by biblical times, the Middle East saw a rudimentary international monetary system when the Roman gold coin *aureus* gained worldwide acceptance followed by the silver *denarius,* both a common stock among money changers of the period. In the Bible, Jesus becomes angry at the money changers. I hope His wrath was directed at the poor exchange rates and not the profession itself!

By the Middle Ages, foreign exchange became a function of international banking with the growth in the use of bills of exchange by the merchant princes and international debt papers by the budding European powers in the course of their underwriting the period's wars.

The Gold Standard, 1816–1933

The gold standard was a fixed commodity standard: participating countries fixed a physical weight of gold for the currency in circulation, making it directly redeemable in the form of the precious metal. In 1816 for instance, the pound sterling was defined as 123.27 grains of gold, which was on its way to becoming the foremost reserve currency and was at the time the principal component of the international capital market. This led to the expression "as good as gold" when applied to Sterling—the Bank of England at the time gained stability and prestige as the premier monetary authority.

Of the major currencies, the U.S. dollar adopted the gold standard late in 1879 and became the standard-bearer, replacing the British pound when Britain and other European countries came off the system with the outbreak of World War I in 1914. Eventually, though, the worsening international depression led even the dollar off the gold standard by 1933; this marked the period of collapse in international trade and financial flows prior to World War II.

The Fed

As an investor, it is essential to acquire a basic knowledge of the Federal Reserve System (the Fed). The Federal Reserve was created by the U.S. Congress in 1913. Before that, the U.S. government lacked any formal organization for studying and implementing monetary policy. Consequently, markets were often unstable and the public had very little faith in the banking system. The Fed is an independent entity, but is subject to oversight from Congress. This means that decisions do not have to be ratified by the president or anyone else in the government, but Congress periodically reviews the Fed's activities.

The Fed is headed by a government agency in Washington known as the Board of Governors of the Federal Reserve. The Board of Governors consists of seven presidential appointees, who each serve 14-year terms. All members must be confirmed by the Senate, and they can be reappointed. The board is led by a chairman and a vice chairman, each appointed by the president and approved by the Senate for four year terms. The current chair is Alan Greenspan, who has been chairman since 1987. His latest term expires in 2006.

There are 12 regional Federal Reserve Banks located in major cities around the country that operate under the supervision of the Board of Governors. Reserve Banks act as the operating arm of the central bank and do most of the work of the Fed. The banks generate their own income from four main sources:

1. Services provided to banks
2. Interest earned on government securities
3. Income from foreign currency held
4. Interest on loans to depository institutions

The income generated from these activities is used to finance day-to-day operations, including information gathering and economic research. Any excess income is funneled back into the U.S. Treasury.

The system also includes the Federal Open Market Committee, better known as the FOMC. This is the policy-creating branch of the Federal Reserve. Traditionally the chair of the board is also selected as the chair of the FOMC. The voting members of the FOMC are the seven members of the Board of Governors, the president of the Federal Reserve Bank of New York, and presidents of four other Reserve Banks who serve on a one-year rotating basis. All Reserve Bank presidents participate in FOMC policy discussions whether or not they are voting members. The FOMC makes the important decisions on interest rates and other monetary policies. This is the reason they get most of the attention in the media.

The primary responsibility of the Fed is "to promote sustainable growth, high levels of employment, stability of prices to help preserve the purchasing power of the dollar, and moderate long-term interest rates."

In other words, the Fed's job is to foster a sound banking system and a healthy economy. To accomplish its mission the Fed serves as the banker's bank, the government's bank, the regulator of financial institutions, and as the nation's money manager.

The Fed also issues all coin and paper currency. The U.S. Treasury actually produces the cash, but the Fed Bank then distributes it to financial institutions. It is also the Fed's responsibility to check bills for wear and tear, taking damaged currency out of circulation.

The Federal Reserve Board (FRB) has regulation and supervision responsibilities over banks. This includes monitoring banks that are members of the system, international banking facilities in the United States, foreign activities of member banks, and the U.S. activities of foreign-owned banks. The Fed also helps to ensure that banks act in the public's interest by helping in the development of federal laws governing consumer credit. Examples are the Truth in Lending Act, the Equal Credit Opportunity Act, the Home Mortgage Disclosure Act, and the Truth in Savings Act. In short, the Fed is the policeman for banking activities within the United States and abroad.

The FRB also sets margin requirements for investors. This limits the amount of money you can borrow to purchase securities. Currently, the requirement is set at 50 percent, meaning that with $500 you have the opportunity to purchase up to $1,000 worth of securities.

Securities and Exchange Commission, 1933–1934

When the stock market crashed in October 1929, countless investors lost their fortunes. Banks also lost great sums of money in the Crash because they had invested heavily in the markets. When people feared their banks might not be able to pay back the money that depositors had in their accounts, a "run" on the banking system caused many bank failures.

With the Crash and ensuing depression, public confidence in the markets plummeted. There was a consensus that for the economy to recover, the public's faith in the capital markets needed to be restored. Congress held hearings to identify the problems and search for solutions.

Based on the findings in these hearings, Congress passed the Securities Act of 1933 and the Securities Exchange Act of 1934. These laws were designed to restore investor confidence in capital markets by providing more structure and government oversight. The main purposes of these laws can be reduced to two commonsense notions:

1. Companies that publicly offer securities for investment dollars must tell the public the truth about their businesses, the securities they are selling, and the risks involved in investing.

2. People who sell and trade securities—brokers, dealers, and exchanges—must treat investors fairly and honestly, putting investors' interests first.

The Bretton Woods System, 1944–1973

The post-World War II period saw Great Britain's economy in ruins, its infrastructure having been bombed. The country's confidence with its currency was at a low. By contrast, the United States, thanks to its physical isolation, was left relatively unscathed by the war. Its industrial might was ready to be turned to civilian purposes. This then has led to the dollar's rise to prominence, becoming the reserve currency of choice and staple to the international financial markets.

Bretton Woods came about in July 1944 when 45 countries attended, at the behest of the United States, a conference to formulate a new international financial framework. This framework was designed to ensure prosperity in the postwar period and prevent the recurrence of the 1930s global depression. Named after a resort hotel in New Hampshire, the Bretton Woods system formalized the role of the U.S. dollar as the new global reserve currency, with its value fixed into gold. The United States assumed the responsibility of ensuring convertibility while other currencies were pegged to the dollar.

Among the key features of the new framework were:

- Fixed but adjustable exchange rates
- The International Monetary Fund
- The World Bank

The End of Bretton Woods and Floating Exchange Rates

After close to three decades of running the international financial system, Bretton Woods finally went the way of history due to growing structural imbalances among the economies, leading to mounting volatility and speculation in a one-year period from June 1972 to June 1973. At the time the United Kingdom, facing deficit problems, initially floated the sterling. Then it was devaluated further in February of 1973 losing 11 percent of its value along with the Swiss franc and the Japanese yen. This eventually led to the European Economic Community floating their currencies as well.

At the core of Bretton Woods' problems were deteriorating confidence in the dollars' ability to maintain full convertibility and the unwillingness of surplus countries to revalue for its adverse impact in external trade. Despite a last-ditch effort by the Group of Ten finance ministers through the Smithsonian Agreement in December 1971, the international financial system from 1973 onward saw market-driven floating exchange rates taking hold. Several times efforts for reestablishing controlled systems were undertaken with varying levels of success. The most well known of these was Europe's Exchange Rate Mechanism of the 1990s which eventually led to the European Monetary Union.

International Monetary Market

In December 1972, the International Monetary Market (IMM) was incorporated as a division of the Chicago Mercantile Exchange (CME) that specialized in currency futures, interest-rate futures, and stock index futures, as well as futures options.

Current Perspective

Until the arrival of the Euro in 2002 (see next subsection), the international scene has remained essentially unchanged for over 30 years, although the volume of transactions in foreign exchange has increased enormously. Electronic trading has made it possible to initiate instantaneous trades in the billions of dollars. That has introduced the fragile nature of technology with its lack of redundancy, but no fallout from that has yet to be seen. China's emergence as a world power has focused attention on its economy and its currency, the yuan, which at the present time is controlled and does not float. The author believes it will be impossible to continue the tight control over the yuan, and floating rates will be inevitable.

Arrival of the Euro

On January 1, 2002, the Euro became the official currency of 12 European nations that agreed to remove their previous currencies from circulation prior to February 28, 2002. See Table 2.1.

TABLE 2.1 European Monetary Union	
Austria	Schilling
Belgium	Franc
Finland	Markka
France	Franc
Germany	Mark
Greece	Drachma
Ireland	Punt
Italy	Lira
Luxembourg	Franc
Netherlands	Guilder
Portugal	Escudo
Spain	Peseta

The Euro was considered an immediate success and is now the second most frequently traded currency in FOREX markets. More details on the Euro can be found in the Appendix of this book.

Table 2.2 depicts the major events in FOREX history and regulation.

TABLE 2.2 Timeline of Foreign Exchange
1913—U.S. Congress creates the Federal Reserve System.
1933—Congress passes the Securities Act of 1933 to counter the effects of the Great Crash of 1929.
1934—The Securities Exchange Act of 1934 creates the beginnings of the Securities and Exchange Commission.
1936—The Commodity Exchange Act is enacted in direct response to manipulating grain and futures markets.
1944—The Bretton Woods Accord is established to help stabilize the global economy after World War II.
1971—The Smithsonian Agreement is established to allow for a greater fluctuation band for currencies.
1972—The European Joint Float is established as the European community tries to move away from their dependency on the U.S. Dollar.
1972—The International Monetary Market is created as a division of the Chicago Mercantile Exchange.
1973—The Smithsonian Agreement and European Joint Float fail, signifying the official switch to a free-floating system.
1974—Congress creates the Commodity Futures Trading Commission to regulate the futures and options markets.
1978—The European Monetary System is introduced to again try to gain independence from the U.S. Dollar.
1978—The free-floating system is officially mandated by the International Monetary Fund.
1993—The European Monetary System fails to make way for a worldwide, free-floating system.
1994—Online currency trading makes its debut.
2000—Commodity Modernization Act establishes new regulations for securities derivatives, including currencies in futures or forwards form.
2002—The Euro becomes the official currency of twelve European nations on January 1.

Summary

- Until the late 1960s the currency markets were extremely stable and very much a closed club. Things were about to change rapidly!
- Currency trading is probably the world's *second*-oldest profession!
- The Euro, introduced in 2002, is the official currency of twelve European countries: Austria, Belgium, Finland, France, Germany, Greece, Ireland, Italy, Luxembourg, the Netherlands, Portugal, and Spain.
- Key dates and events—1973, 1978, 1994, 2002

Spot or Futures FOREX?

Introduction—Futures Contracts

The overwhelming majority of currency trading volume is in the spot market. "FOREX" inevitably means spot trading to most participants. But it is possible to trade FOREX as a futures vehicle. The volume of futures FOREX has also increased. The primary advantage of futures FOREX lies in the fact that the futures markets are centalized and as such are more heavily regulated. A secondary advantage is that many popular technical trading methods use volume of trading and open interest. While aggregate volume is known in FOREX, daily figures are unobtainable because of the decentralized nature of the business. Attempts are under way, including those by the author, to synthesize spot FOREX volume and open interest statistics from other data using statistical methods.

A futures contract is an agreement between two parties: a short position, the party who agrees to deliver a commodity, and a long position, the party who agrees to receive a commodity. For example, a grain farmer would be the holder of the short position (agreeing to sell the grain) while the bakery would be the holder of the long (agreeing to buy the grain).

In a futures contract, everything is precisely specified: the quantity and quality of the underlying commodity, the specific price per unit, and the date and method of delivery. The price of a futures contract is represented by the agreed-upon price of the underlying commodity or financial instrument that will be delivered in the future. For example, in the grain scenario, the price of the contract might be 5,000 bushels of grain at a price of four dollars per bushel and the delivery date may be the third Wednesday in September of the current year.

Currency Futures

The FOREX market is essentially a cash or spot market in which over 90 percent of the trades are liquidated within 48 hours. Currency trades held longer than this are normally routed through an authorized commodity futures exchange such as the International Monetary Market. IMM was founded in 1972 and is a division of the Chicago Mercantile Exchange (CME) that specializes in currency futures, interest-rate futures, and stock index futures, as well as options on futures. Clearinghouses (the futures exchange) and introducing brokers are subject to more stringent regulations from the SEC, CFTC, and NFA agencies than the FOREX spot market (see www.cme.com for more details).

It should also be noted that FOREX traders are charged only a transaction cost per trade, which is simply the difference between the current bid and ask prices. Currency futures traders are charged a round-turn commission that varies from broker house to broker house. In addition, margin requirements for futures contracts are usually slightly higher than the requirements for the FOREX spot market.

Contract Specifications

Table 3.1 is a list of currencies traded through IMM at the Chicago Mercantile Exchange and their contract specifications.

TABLE 3.1 Currency Contract Specifications

Commodity	Contract Size		Months	Hours	Minimum Fluctuation		
Australian Dollar	100,000	AUD	H, M, U, Z	7:20–14:00	0.0001 AUD	=	$10.00
British Pound	62,500	GBP	H, M, U, Z	7:20–14:15	0.0002 GBP	=	$12.50
Canadian Dollar	100,000	CAD	H, M, U, Z	7:20–14:00	0.0001 CAD	=	$10.00
Eurocurrency	62,500	EUR	H, M, U, Z	7:20–14:15	0.0001 EUR	=	$ 6.25
Japanese Yen	12,500,000	JPY	H, M, U, Z	7:00–14:00	0.0001 JPY	=	$12.50
Mexican Peso	500,000	MXN	All months	7:00–14:00	0.0025 MXN	=	$12.50
New Zealand Dollar	100,000	NZD	H, M, U, Z	7:00–14:00	0.0001 NZD	=	$10.00
Russian Ruble	2,500,00	RUR	H, M, U, Z	7:20–14:00	0.0001 RUR	=	$25.00
South African Rand	5,000,000	ZAR	All months	7:20–14:00	0.0025 ZAR	=	$12.50
Swiss Franc	62,500	CHF	H, M, U, Z	7:20–14:15	0.0001 CHF	=	$12.50

Size represents one contract requirement though some brokers offer mini-contracts, usually one-tenth the size of the standard contract. Months identify the month of contract delivery. The tick symbols H, M, U, Z are abbreviations for March, June, September, and December respectively. Hours indicate the local trading hours in Chicago. The minimum fluctuation represents the smallest monetary unit that is registered as one pip in price movement at the exchange and is usually one ten-thousandth of the base currency.

Currencies Trading Volume

Table 3.2 summarizes the trading activity of selected futures contracts in currencies, precious metals, and some financial instruments. The volume and

TABLE 3.2 Futures Volume and Open Interest				
Market	*Sym*	*Exch*	*Vol*	*OI*
S&P 500 e-mini	ES	CME	489.1	377.9
Nasdaq 100 e-mini	NQ	CME	237.6	158.4
Eurodollar	ED	CME	93.9	772.5
S&P 500	SP	CME	59.3	531.4
Eurocurrency	EC	CME	49.5	112.9
Mini Dow	YM	CBOT	48.1	30.2
10-year T-note	TY	CBOT	43.1	676.4
Gold	GC	NYMEX	33.7	163.0
5-year T-note	FV	CBOT	29.6	582.8
30-year T-bond	US	CBOT	25.9	324.1
Japanese Yen	JY	CME	18.6	132.1
Canadian Dollar	CD	CME	18.0	64.2
Nasdaq 100	ND	CME	13.3	65.4
British Pound	BP	CME	12.2	58.3
Silver	SI	NYMEX	10.0	84.2
Swiss Franc	SF	CME	9.3	45.6
Mexican Peso	ME	CME	8.8	30.5
Dow Jones	DJ	CBOT	8.7	29.5
Aussie Dollar	AD	CME	7.8	55.7
2-year T-note	TU	CME	7.0	108.6
Copper	HG	NYMEX	4.2	32.8

Legend: *Sym:* Ticker symbol, *Exch:* Futures exchange on which contract is traded, *Vol:* 30-day average daily volume, in thousands, *OI:* Open interest, in thousands.

Source: Active Trader Magazine, January 16, 2004 (www.activetradermag.com).

TABLE 3.3 U.S. Dollar Index	
Currency	*Weight %*
Eurocurrency	57.6
Japanese Yen	13.6
British Pound	11.9
Canadian Dollar	9.1
Swedish Krona	4.2
Swiss Franc	3.6

open interest readings are *not* trade signals. They are intended only to provide a brief synopsis of each market's liquidity and volatility based on the average of 30 trading days.

U.S. Dollar Index

The U.S. Dollar Index (ticker symbol = DX) is an openly traded futures contract offered by the New York Board of Trade. It is computed using a trade-weighted geometric average of six currencies. See Table 3.3.

IMM currency futures traders monitor the U.S. Dollar Index to gauge the dollar's overall performance in world currency markets. If the Dollar Index is trending lower, then it is very likely that a major currency that is a component of the Dollar Index is trading higher. When a currency trader takes a quick glance at the price of the U.S. Dollar Index, it gives the trader a good feel for what is going on in the FOREX market worldwide.

For traders who are interested in more details on commodity futures, I recommend Todd Lofton's paperbound book, *Getting Started in Futures* (John Wiley & Sons, 2001).

Summary

Almost all retail traders prefer spot FOREX. But futures FOREX has its advantages: (1) a centralized exchange, (2) stronger regulation, and (3) availability of daily volume and open interest statistics.

Part 2

Getting Started

4

The Regulatory Environment

The foreign exchange market has no central clearinghouse as do the stock market and the commodity futures market. Nor is it based in any one country; it is a complex, loosely woven worldwide network of banks.

These two facts permeate every aspect of currency trading, especially the regulatory environment. It is difficult, if not impossible, to get a firm regulatory grip on such an entity. That cuts both ways. The market is very laissez-faire, but it is also a caveat emptor enterprise. If you wish to trade currencies, you must accept these facts from the beginning.

Regulation Today

The retail FOREX regulatory picture continues to evolve—slowly. Three years ago some broker-dealers proudly advertised they were not NFA members. Curiously one of those was REFCO, which failed soon thereafter. Today all of the major broker-dealers have joined the NFA (National Futures Association) and come under the watchful government eye of the CFTC (Commodity Futures Trading Commission). My first advice to you: Do not trade with an unregistered broker-dealer. Every broker-dealer should have his NFA registration number on the web site's home page.

Regulation is seldom proactive; it usually is the result of a crisis. An NFA spokesman confessed to me that their hands were somewhat tied until a crisis provoked additional legislation. The NFA does host a booth at most FOREX trade shows. If you attend one of these, you might want to ask questions or voice your concerns to the people staffing them. They seem to be good listeners and keep close tabs on the pulse of the FOREX marketplace.

Broker-dealers register as Futures Commission Merchants (FCMs). Currently, Introducing Brokers (IBs) can be covered by the FCM or register independently. As below, it is likely that IBs will all soon be required to register.

Appendix A, "How the FOREX Game Is Played," outlines many of the issues all parties—broker-dealers, traders, and regulators—are grappling with today.

The Commodity Futures Trading Commission (CFTC)

In 1974 Congress created the Commodity Futures Trading Commission as the independent agency with the mandate to regulate commodity futures and options markets in the United States. The agency is chartered to protect market participants against manipulation, abusive trade practices, and fraud.

Through effective oversight and regulation the CFTC enables the markets to better serve their important function in the nation's economy, providing a mechanism for price discovery and a means of offsetting price risk. The CFTC also seeks to protect customers by requiring: (1) that registrants disclose market risks and past performance to prospective customers (in the case of money managers and advisors); (2) that customer funds be kept in accounts separate ("segregated funds") from their own use; and (3) that customer accounts be adjusted to reflect the current market value of their investments at the close of each trading day ("clearing"). Futures accounts are technically safer than securities accounts because brokers must show a zero-zero balance sheet at the end of each trading session.

National Futures Association

The CFTC was originally created under so-called Sunshine Laws meaning that its continued existence would be evaluated vis-à-vis its effectiveness. As the futures industry exploded in the late 1970s, not only was its charter renewed but a separate quasi-private self-regulatory agency was created to implement the laws, rules, and regulations. Thus in 1982 was born the National Futures

Association (NFA). The NFA is the CFTC's face to the public and directs the regulatory and registration actions of the CFTC into the marketplace.

The NFA stipulates that members cannot transact business with non-members. So, for example, if your FOREX broker/dealer is an NFA member, it is not allowed to do business with nonmember money mangers (Commodity Trading Advisors or CTAs).

Commodity Futures Modernization Act of 2000

This was the first act by the CFTC pertaining to the then-emerging retail FOREX business. Beginning in the 1980s cross-border capital movements accelerated with the advent of computers, technology, and the Internet— extending market continuum through Asian, European, and American time zones. Transactions in foreign exchange rocketed from about $70 billion a day in the 1980s to more than $2 trillion a day two decades later.

The Patriot Act

A principal feature of the ubiquitous Patriot Act is the desire to limit money laundering so that large transactions might be followed, theoretically ensuring funds are not headed to finance terrorist activities. It is obvious such tracking will affect foreign exchange markets. You will see reference to the Patriot Act on broker forms when you open an account.

The CFTC Reauthorization Act of 2005

The most critical legislation of interest to U.S. traders is the CFTC Reautho-rization Act of 2005; it specifically addresses retail FOREX. See Appendix B, Section 101(a)(B)—"Agreements, Contracts, and Transactions in Retail Foreign Currency."

The primary thrust of the Reauthorization Act and legislation currently pending is to require retail brokers to meet minimum capital requirements. The new minimum will apparently be $5,000,000. If so, many small firms will either close, be absorbed, or face mandated euthanasia. At the time of this writing this is, in fact, already taking place.

The NFA is also enacting a Know Thy Customer rule for FCMs. This will require them to undertake a more proactive due diligence of prospective clients and their suitability for currency trading. One effect of this will probably be eliminating account funding options by PayPal and other electronic transfers except for bank wires.

Traders may wish to periodically check FOREX broker-dealer financials here: http://www.cftc.gov/files/tm/fcm/tmfcmdata0704.pdf.

Retail FOREX seems to be following a path parallel to retail futures in the 1970s and 1980s. If so, the next step will be to require Introducing Brokers (IBs) to either register or themselves meet some minimum capital requirements. Beyond that, expect mergers between the majors within the next two or three years as competition, smaller profit margins, and lower growth rates loom.

Similar slow-but-sure regulation of retail FOREX is occurring in other countries. Brokers not domiciled in the United States also should register with the NFA if they desire to prospect and accept accounts from U.S. citizens.

The Financial Markets Association (ACI) has suggested international foreign exchange regulatory standards. ACI's model code currently has regulatory standing in Australia, Austria, Canada, Cyprus, Hong Kong, Malaysia, Malta, Mauritius, the Philippines, Slovenia, and Switzerland.

Countries with specific agencies regulating FOREX: United Kingdom—Financial Services Authority (FSA), Australia—Australian Securities and Investment Commission (ASIC), Switzerland—Requires registration as a Financial Intermediary under Swiss Federal Law, Canada—Investment Canada, Federal Competition Bureau.

Summary

The FOREX forums are a good place to find updated regulatory information. Both the CFTC web site, www.cftc.gov and the NFA, www.nfa.futures.org web site are worth checking on a monthly basis.

"No central clearing exchange" means regulation in FOREX evolves slowly and will never be as strong as it is in the securities or futures industry. Caveat emptor.

The trend is toward more regulation of cash/spot currency markets. Traders should watch the actions of the Commodity Futures Trading Commission (CFTC) and its quasi-independent administration arm, the National Futures Association (NFA). Do not take regulation as an excuse for not doing your own homework!

The FOREX Lexicon

A s in any worthwhile endeavor, each industry tends to create its own unique lingo. The FOREX market is no different. You, the novice trader, must thoroughly comprehend certain terms before making your first trade. As your eighth-grade English teacher taught you in vocabulary class—to use them is to know them.

Currency Pairs

Every FOREX trade involves the simultaneous buying of one currency and the selling of another currency. These two currencies are always referred to as the currency pair in a trade.

Major and Minor Currencies

The seven most frequently traded currencies (USD, EUR, JPY, GBP, CHF, CAD, and AUD) are called the major currencies. All other currencies are referred to as minor currencies. The most frequently traded minors are the New Zealand Dollar (NZD), the South African Rand (ZAR), and the Singapore Dollar (SGD). After that, the frequency is difficult to ascertain because of perpetually changing trade agreements in the international arena.

Cross Currency

A cross currency is any pair in which neither currency is the U.S. Dollar. These pairs may exhibit erratic price behavior since the trader has, in effect, initiated two USD trades. For example, initiating a long (buy) EUR/GBP trade is equivalent to buying a EUR/USD currency pair and selling a GBP/USD. Cross currency pairs frequently carry a higher transaction cost. The three most frequently traded cross rates are EUR/JPY, GBP/EUR, and GBP/JPY.

Exotic Currency

An exotic is a currency pair in which one currency is the USD and the other is a currency from a smaller country such as the Polish Zloty. There are approximately 25 exotics that can be traded by the retail FOREX participant.

Base Currency

The base currency is the first currency in any currency pair. It shows how much the base currency is worth as measured against the second currency. For example, if the USD/CHF rate equals 1.6215, then one USD is worth CHF 1.6215. In the FOREX markets, the U.S. Dollar is normally considered the "base" currency for quotes, meaning that quotes are expressed as a unit of $1 USD per the other currency quoted in the pair. The primary exceptions to this rule are the British Pound, the Euro, and the Australian Dollar.

Quote Currency

The quote currency is the second currency in any currency pair. This is frequently called the pip currency and any unrealized profit or loss is expressed in this currency.

Pips

A pip is the smallest unit of price for any foreign currency. Nearly all currency pairs consist of five significant digits and most pairs have the decimal point immediately after the first digit, that is, EUR/USD equals 1.2812. In this instance, a single pip equals the smallest change in the fourth decimal place, that is, 0.0001. Therefore, if the quote currency in any pair is USD, then one pip always equals $\frac{1}{100}$ of a cent.

One notable exception is the USD/JPY pair where a pip equals $0.01 (one U.S. Dollar equals approximately 107.19 Japanese Yen). Pips are sometimes called points.

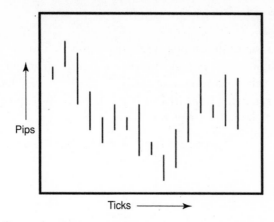

FIGURE 5.1   Pip-Tick Relationship

Ticks

Just as a pip is the smallest price movement (the *y*-axis), a tick is the smallest interval of time (the *x*-axis) that occurs between two trades. When trading the most active currency pairs (such as EUR/USD or USD/JPY) during peak trading periods, multiple ticks may (and will) occur within the span of one second. When trading a low-activity minor cross pair (such as the Mexican Peso and the Singapore Dollar), a tick may only occur once every two or three hours.

Ticks, therefore, do not occur at uniform intervals of time. Fortunately, most historical data vendors will "group" sequences of streaming data and calculate the open, high, low, and close over regular time intervals (1-minute, 5-minute, 30-minute, 1-hour, daily, and so forth). See Figure 5.1.

Margin

When an investor opens a new margin account with a FOREX broker, he or she must deposit a minimum amount of monies with that broker. This minimum varies from broker to broker and can be as low as $100.00 to as high as $100,000.00.

Each time the trader executes a new trade, a certain percentage of the account balance in the margin account will be earmarked as the initial margin requirement for the new trade based upon the underlying currency pair, its current price, and the number of units traded (called a lot). The lot size always refers to the base currency. An even lot is usually a quantity of 100,000 units, but most brokers permit investors to trade in odd lots (fractions of 100,000 units).

Leverage

Leverage is the ratio of the amount used in a transaction to the required security deposit (margin). It is the ability to control large dollar amounts of a security with a comparatively small amount of capital. Leveraging varies dramatically with different brokers, ranging from 10:1 to 100:1. Leverage is frequently referred to as gearing. The formula for calculating leverage is:

$$\text{Leverage} = 100/\text{Margin Percent}$$

Bid Price

The bid is the price at which the market is prepared to buy a specific currency pair in the FOREX market. At this price, the trader can sell the base currency. It is shown on the left side of the quotation. For example, in the quote USD/CHF 1.4527/32, the bid price is 1.4527; meaning you can sell one U.S. Dollar for 1.4527 Swiss Francs.

Ask Price

The ask is the price at which the market is prepared to sell a specific currency pair in the FOREX market. At this price, the trader can buy the base currency. It is shown on the right side of the quotation. For example, in the quote USD/CHF 1.4527/32, the ask price is 1.4532; meaning you can buy one U.S. Dollar for 1.4532 Swiss Francs. The ask price is also called the offer price.

Bid/Ask Spread

The spread is the difference between the bid and ask price. The "big figure quote" is the dealer expression referring to the first few digits of an exchange rate. These digits are often omitted in dealer quotes. For example, a USD/JPY rate might be 117.30/117.35, but would be quoted verbally without the first three digits as "30/35."

Quote Convention

Exchange rates in the FOREX market are expressed using the following format:

Base Currency/Quote Currency   Bid/Ask

Examples can be found in Table 5.1.

TABLE 5.1 Examples of Quote Convention	
EUR/USD	1.2604/07
GBP/USD	1.5089/94
CHF/JPY	84.40/45

Normally only the final two digits of the bid price are shown. If the ask price is more than 100 pips above the bid price, then three digits will be displayed to the right of the slash mark (that is, EUR/CZK 32.5420/780). This only occurs when the quote currency is a very weak monetary unit.

Transaction Cost

The critical characteristic of the bid/ask spread is that it is also the transaction cost for a round-turn trade. Round-turn means both a buy (or sell) trade and an offsetting sell (or buy) trade of the same size in the same currency pair. In the case of the EUR/USD rate in Table 5.1, the transaction cost is three pips. The formula for calculating the transaction cost is:

$$\text{Transaction Cost} = \text{Ask Price} - \text{Bid Price}$$

Rollover

Rollover is the process whereby the settlement of an open trade is rolled forward to another value date. The cost of this process is based on the interest rate differential of the two currencies.

The Trader's Nemesis

All traders fear the dreaded margin call. This occurs when the broker notifies the trader that his or her margin deposits have fallen below the required minimum level because an open position has moved against the trader.

Trading on margin can be a profitable investment strategy, but it is important that you take the time to understand the risks. You should make sure you fully understand how your margin account works. Be sure to read the margin agreement between you and your clearing firm. Talk to your account representative if you have any questions.

The positions in your account could be partially or totally liquidated should the available margin in your account fall below a predetermined threshold. You may not receive a margin call before your positions are liquidated.

Margin calls can be effectively avoided by monitoring your account balance on a very regular basis and by utilizing stop-loss orders (discussed later) on every open position to limit risk. For ease of use, most online trading platforms automatically calculate the profit and loss of a trader's open positions.

When you open an online FOREX account, the trading platform will have preset leverage options. These typically run from 10:1 to 200:1. Start low and work your way up as you meet with trading success. You will not be able to enter a trade that exceeds the set leverage value. For more, see Chapter 15, "Money Management Made Simple."

Margin Calls

Nearly all FOREX brokers monitor your account balance continuously. If your balance falls below four percent of the open margin requirement, they will issue the first margin call warning, usually by an online pop-up message on the screen and/or an e-mail notification. If your account balance drops below three percent of the margin requirement for your open positions, they will issue a second margin warning. At two percent, they will liquidate all your open trades and notify you of your current account balance. These percentages may vary from broker to broker. You may not even be able to execute a trade that exceeds certain capital and risk parameters.

Summary

Trading currencies on margin lets you increase your buying power. If you have $2,000 cash in a margin account that allows 100:1 leverage, you could purchase up to $200,000 worth of currency because you only have to post 1 percent of the purchase price as collateral. Another way of saying this is that you have $200,000 in buying power.

With more buying power, you can increase your total return on investment with less cash outlay. To be sure, trading on margin magnifies your profits *and* your losses.

A detailed description on how to calculate profit and loss of leveraged trades occurs in Chapter 6, "The Calculating Trader."

The Calculating Trader

Here is where the rubber meets the road. Take your time with this information, as it is necessary knowledge for all FOREX traders. I recommend that you do not even paper trade until you are completely comfortable with pip values and calculating profit and loss for any pairs or crosses you intend to trade.

Profit and Loss (P&L) for every open position is calculated in real-time on most brokers' trading platforms. The information in this chapter enables traders to track their own P&L tick by tick as the market fluctuates.

It is true your broker's trading platform is capable of making all these calculations. But there will be many times when you will want to make them "on-the-fly" as in the instance of verifying that an anticipated position meets your money management criteria. (See Chapter 15, "Money Management Made Simple.") You simply cannot be an informed and intelligent FOREX trader without knowing these basic calculations. Use the tools on your broker's trading platform as practice for these calculations, not as a substitute for them.

These calculations provide mission-critical information about the relationship between several key factors: pip values, dollar values, leverage, and margin.

TIP: If arithmetic is not your thing, take one of these at a time and learn them over several sessions. Use your broker's demo account to practice. Do the calculation on your own; then do it on the trading platform as a check. If you do not have a demo account, both www.forexcalc.com and www.oanda.com offer online FOREX calculations covering at least some of these equations.

Leverage and Margin Percent

Some brokers describe their gearing in terms of a leverage ratio and others in terms of a margin percentage. The simple relationships between the two terms are:

Leverage = 100 / Margin Percent

Margin Percent = 100 / Leverage

Leverage is conventionally displayed as a ratio, such as 20:1 or 50:1. In the examples that follow which require leverage, I use only the number on the left side of the ratio—that is, 20 or 50—since the number on the right side is always 1.

Pip Values

A pip is the smallest price increment that any currency pair can move in either direction. In the FOREX markets, profits are calculated in terms of pips first, then dollars second. See Table 6.1.

TABLE 6.1 Single Pip Values	
USD = Quote Currency	
EUR/USD	.0001 USD
GBP/USD	.0001 USD
AUD/USD	.0001 USD
USD = Base Currency	
USD/JPY	.01 JPY
USD/CHF	.0001 CHF
USD/CAD	.0001 CAD
Non-USD Cross Rates	
EUR/JPY	.01 JPY
EUR/CHF	.0001 CHF
EUR/GBP	.0001 GBP
GBP/JPY	.01 JPY
GBP/CHF	.0001 CHF
CHF/JPY	.01 JPY

TABLE 6.2 Full Lot Pip Values	
Currencies	1 Pip Value Per Full Lot (100,000 units)
EUR/USD	EUR 100,000 × .0001 = USD 10.00
GBP/USD	GBP 100,000 × .0001 = USD 10.00
AUD/USD	AUD 100,000 × .0001 = USD 10.00
USD/JPY	USD 100,000 × .01 = JPY 1,000 / USDJPY spot (105.50) = USD 9.47
USD/CHF	USD 100,000 × .0001 = CHF 10.00 / USDCHF spot (1.2335) = USD 8.11
USD/CAD	USD 100,000 × .0001 = CAD 10.00 / USDCAD spot (1.3148) = USD 7.61
EUR/JPY	EUR 100,000 × .01 = JPY 1,000 / USDJPY spot (105.50) = USD 9.47
EUR/CHF	EUR 100,000 × .0001 = CHF 10.00 / USDCHF spot (1.2335) = USD 8.11
EUR/GBP	EUR 100,000 × .0001 = CHF 10.00 × GBPUSD spot (1.8890) = USD 5.2
GBP/JPY	GBP 100,000 × .01 = JPY 1,000 / USDJPY spot (105.50) = USD 9.47
GBP/CHF	GBP 100,000 × .0001 = CHF 10.00 / USDCHF spot (1.2335) = USD 8.11
CHF/JPY	CHF 100,000 × .01 = JPY 1,000 / USDJPY spot (105.50) = USD 9.47

Approximate USD values for a one-pip move per contract in the major currency pairs are shown in Table 6.2, per 100,000 units of the base currency.

On a typical day, actively traded currency pairs like EUR/USD and USD/JPY can fluctuate 100 pips or more. The above table is based upon a margin requirement of 100 percent (leverage = 1:1). To calculate actual profit (or loss) in leveraged positions, multiply the pip value per 100k times the leverage ratio (margin percentage divided by 100).

Note that the EUR/GBP cross rate pair in Table 6.2 uses multiplication with the USD spot price instead of division. This is because the USD is the quote (second) currency in the spot conversion pair.

Calculating Profit and Loss

Many FOREX trading platforms offer their clients a variety of online utilities that assist the investor in his or her trading calculations. The utility to compute the profit or loss on each trade should resemble what is shown in Figure 6.1.

Because all profits are expressed in U.S. dollars, a key factor in the calculation of profit and loss is the currency pair and whether the USD is the base currency or the quote currency, or if the currency pair is a non-USD cross rate. Therefore, I will present several examples involving all cases.

Remember that the first currency in a currency pair is called the base currency (determines the number of units traded) and the second is called the quote currency (determines the pip values of each price change).

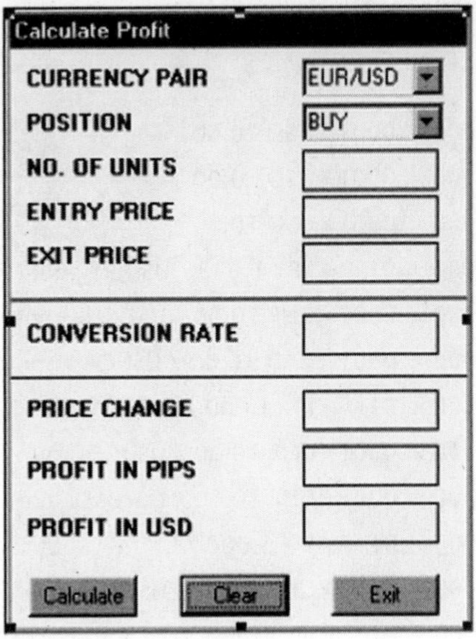

FIGURE 6.1   Online Profit Calculator

Throughout the global spot currency market the term *current price* is normally defined as:

$$\text{Current Price} = \frac{\text{Ask Price} + \text{Bid Price}}{2}$$

TIP: Always make sure that what you mean by any term is the same as what your broker-dealer means by that term. Definitions do vary, usually slightly. But even a small difference can lead to an error.

Scenario 1

USD Is the Quote Currency (Profit)

Currency pair. Select the corresponding currency pair from the dropdown list. The default is the EUR/USD pair.

Position. Choose either "buy" or "sell." The default is "buy."

Number of units. This is the individual number of units and *not* the number of lots or mini-lots. A full lot should be entered as "100000" and a mini-lot as "10000."

Entry price. This is the entry price regardless if the trade was a market order or a limit order. Include the decimal point.

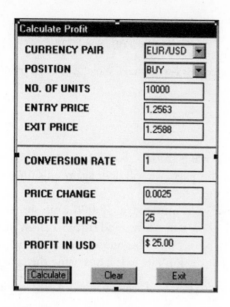

FIGURE 6.2   A 25-Pip Profit in EUR/USD

Exit price. This is the liquidation price regardless if the trade was manually exited or a limit order was triggered.

Conversion rate. This entry is necessary to convert any profit or loss to U.S. Dollars if the quote currency (the second one in the pair) is not USD. In this example, USD is the quote currency. Enter the single digit "1" since we already have conversion parity. Other possibilities are explained later.

Click the "Calculate" button as shown in Figure 6.2.

In this example we bought a mini-lot (10,000 units) of the EUR/USD pair at 1.2563 and sold at 1.2588, netting a clear profit of 25 pips (price change times pip factor, or $0.0025 \times 10,000$). The price change is simply:

$$\text{Price Change} = \text{Exit Price} - \text{Entry Price}$$

The pip factor is the number of pips in the monetary unit of quote currency. There are 10,000 pips in one U.S. Dollar and, conversely, a single pip equals $0.0001. The pip factor is therefore 10,000.

$$\text{Profit in Pips} = \text{Price Change} \times \text{Pip Factor}$$

When the quote currency is the USD, profit or loss is calculated very simply as:

$$\text{Profit in USD} = \text{Price Change} \times \text{Units Traded}$$

In our scenario, this equates to:

$$\$25.00 = 0.0025 \times 10,000$$

Many of you have just exclaimed "Wow! That was painlessly simple. Show me one more!"

Scenario 2

USD Is the Quote Currency (Loss)   For those of you who exclaimed nothing or are staring blankly at this page, we will do it again, this time with the GBP/USD currency pair. See Figure 6.3.

In this instance, we initiated a 30,000-unit short (sell) trade in the GBP/USD pair at 1.8863 and, sadly, it advanced against our hopes. We exited at 1.8883, losing 20 pips. Since the quote currency (the second currency) is USD, we know the conversion rate is 1. Thus using the profit formula

$$\text{Profit in USD} = \text{Price Change} \times \text{Units Traded}$$

we find that our profit is actually a loss:

$$-\$60.00 = -0.0020 \times 30000$$

If the above calculations are still causing some confusion, I recommend that you take a break, then reread Chapter 5, "The FOREX Lexicon." As promised

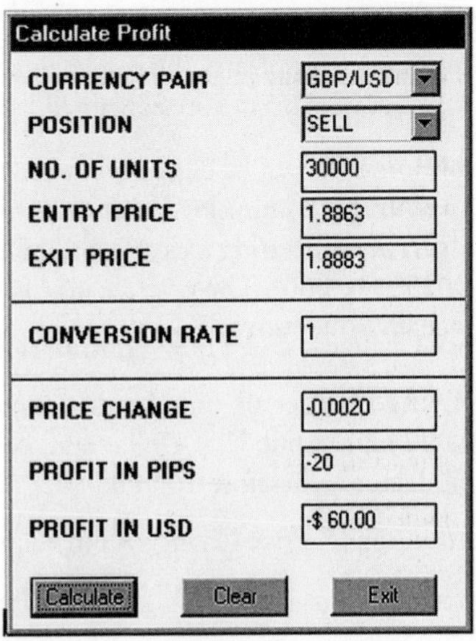

Calculate Profit

CURRENCY PAIR	GBP/USD
POSITION	SELL
NO. OF UNITS	30000
ENTRY PRICE	1.8863
EXIT PRICE	1.8883
CONVERSION RATE	1
PRICE CHANGE	-0.0020
PROFIT IN PIPS	-20
PROFIT IN USD	-$ 60.00

Calculate   Clear   Exit

FIGURE 6.3   A 20-Pip Loss in GBP/USD

before, these calculations only require the four simple arithmetic functions: addition, subtraction, multiplication, and division. No exponents, logs, or trig functions. But this information must be completely clear before proceeding. Keep in mind that it is your money at stake.

Scenario 3

USD Is the Base Currency (Profit) If the quote (second) currency is not the U.S. Dollar, then profit or loss must be converted to U.S. Dollars. For example, a 35-pip profit in the USD/JPY pair means that the 35 pips are expressed in Japanese Yen (see Figure 6.4). Therefore, one extra step is required to convert Yen to Dollars:

Conversion Rate. If USD is the base currency of the currency pair being calculated, then divide the profit or loss by the exit price. This simply converts the pip profit expressed as Yen to a profit expressed as Dollars.

Thus, when calculating currency pairs where the base (first) currency is the U.S. dollar, the profit formula must be adjusted as follows:

$$\text{Profit in USD} = \text{Price Change} \times \text{Units Traded} / \text{Exit Price}$$

or, specifically:

$$\$33.09 = 0.35 \times 10000 / 105.77$$

Obviously, all U.S. brokers perform this simple conversion to U.S. Dollars before adding profits to your margin account.

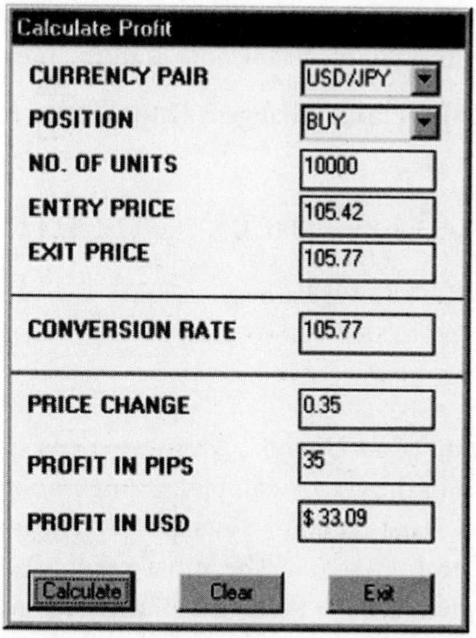

FIGURE 6.4 A 35-Pip Profit in USD/JPY

```
┌─────────────────────────────────────────┐
│ Calculate Profit                         │
│                                          │
│  CURRENCY PAIR        │USD/CAD  ▼│        │
│                                          │
│  POSITION             │BUY      ▼│        │
│                                          │
│  NO. OF UNITS         │5000      │        │
│                                          │
│  ENTRY PRICE          │1.3152    │        │
│                                          │
│  EXIT PRICE           │1.3142    │        │
│                                          │
│  CONVERSION RATE      │1.3142    │        │
│                                          │
│  PRICE CHANGE         │-0.0010   │        │
│                                          │
│  PROFIT IN PIPS       │-10       │        │
│                                          │
│  PROFIT IN USD        │-$ 3.80   │        │
│                                          │
│  │Calculate│   Clear      Exit           │
└─────────────────────────────────────────┘
```

FIGURE 6.5   A 10-Pip Loss in USD/CAD

Scenario 4

USD Is the Base Currency (Loss)   This example is arithmetically identical to the previous example, except that a small loss was incurred. We purchased 5,000 units of the USD/CAD pair at 1.3152 and set a stop-loss limit order at 1.3142, which, unfortunately, was triggered (see Figure 6.5).

Using the same adjusted profit formula as in the previous example,

$$\text{Profit in USD} = \text{Price Change} \times \text{Units Traded} / \text{Exit Price}$$

we find:

$$-\$3.80 = -0.0010 \times 5000 / 1.3142$$

Note: Always keep your losses small.

Scenario 5

Non-USD Cross Rates (USD/Quote)   Most experienced traders can mentally perform the arithmetic in the above examples. It just takes practice. However, we must now tackle cross rates, currency pairs where neither currency is the U.S. Dollar. Obviously the profit in pips will be initially expressed in terms of the quote (second) currency of the cross rate pair. The solution is simple: Look up the current price of the currency pair containing USD and the quote currency of the cross rate pair, as shown in Figure 6.6.

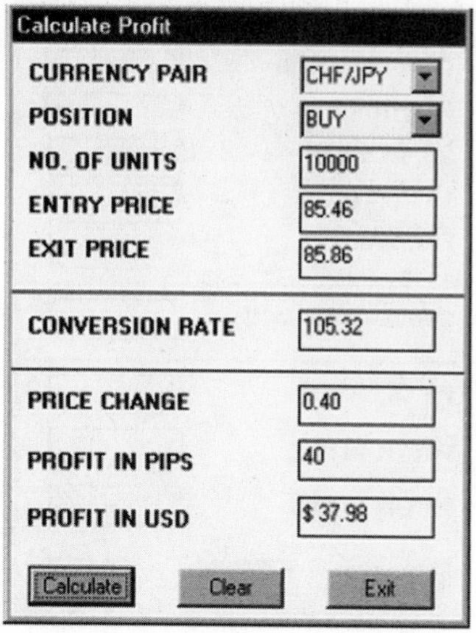

FIGURE 6.6   A 40-Pip Profit in CHF/JPY

The Conversion Rate entry of 105.32 in Figure 6.6 is actually the current price of the USD/JPY pair. The adjusted profit formula for this cross rate trade is:

Profit in USD = Price Change × Units Traded / Conversion Rate

or

$$\$37.98 = 0.40 \times 10000 / 105.32$$

A pattern is developing here ...

Scenario 6

Non-USD Cross Rates (Base/USD)   In the previous example, the USD was the base currency in the conversion pair (USD/JPY). In Figure 6.7 USD is the quote currency of the conversion pair (GBP/USD).

The Conversion Rate entry in Figure 6.7 is the current price of the GBP/USD pair. The reversal of the role of the U.S. Dollar in the conversion pair (GBP/USD) requires another change in the profit formula:

Profit in USD = Price Change × Units Traded × Rate

or

$$\$19.05 = 0.0018 \times 20000 \times 1.8902$$

```
┌─────────────────────────────────────────┐
│ Calculate Profit                         │
│                                          │
│  CURRENCY PAIR      [EUR/GBP  ▼]          │
│  POSITION           [BUY      ▼]          │
│  NO. OF UNITS       [20000     ]          │
│  ENTRY PRICE        [0.6754    ]          │
│  EXIT PRICE         [0.6772    ]          │
│                                          │
│  CONVERSION RATE    [1.8902    ]          │
│                                          │
│  PRICE CHANGE       [0.0018    ]          │
│  PROFIT IN PIPS     [18        ]          │
│  PROFIT IN USD      [$ 19.05   ]          │
│                                          │
│  [Calculate]   [Clear]    [Exit]         │
└─────────────────────────────────────────┘
```

FIGURE 6.7   An 18-Pip Profit in EUR/GBP

Remember that when USD is the quote currency of the conversion pair, you must multiply the rate. If USD is the base currency of the conversion pair, then divide the rate. Give yourself an A+ if you understood the previous examples on the first reading. You are destined for great things.

You may have noticed there was no mention of transaction costs in the six scenarios given. The broker always subtracts the transaction cost at the moment the trade is initiated; therefore transaction costs do not affect the above calculations.

Calculating Units Available

Before initiating a new trade, it is always advantageous to know the maximum number of units that you can safely trade without risking a margin call based upon your current account balance. Most trading platforms provide an online utility that calculates this information, usually resembling what is shown in Figure 6.8.

Enter the following data fields to calculate the maximum number of units to buy or sell:

- **Margin available.** This is the amount in your margin account you want to earmark for the current trade.

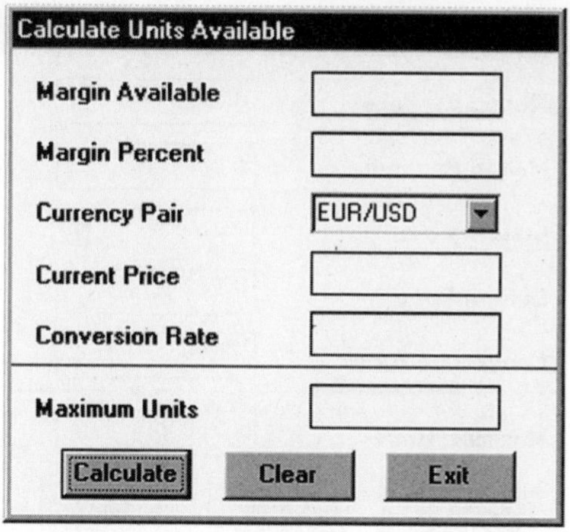

FIGURE 6.8   Units Available Calculator

- **Margin percent.** This is your broker's margin percentage for leveraging trades.
- **Currency pair.** Select the corresponding currency pair. In this example, select EUR/USD.
- **Current price.** Enter the current ask price in the currency pair.
- **Conversion rate.** If the quote currency in the selected currency pair is USD, then enter "1."

Click "Calculate." (See Figure 6.9.)

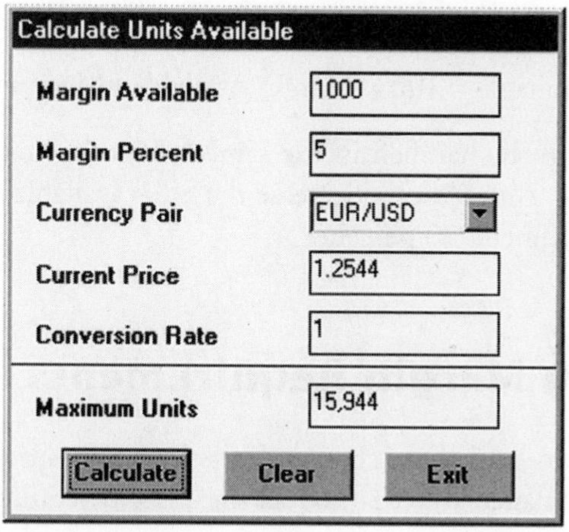

FIGURE 6.9   15,944 Units Available

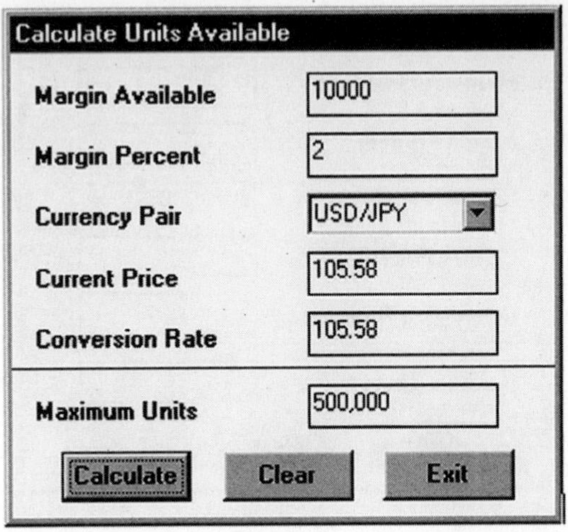

FIGURE 6.10   500,000 Units Available

You can safely trade 15,000 units of EUR/USD in this example. In the next example (Figure 6.10), we calculate the units available for a currency pair in which the base currency is USD. Enter the first four fields as in the previous example. Since USD is the base currency in the USD/JPY pair, we must enter the current price as the conversion rate.

The formula to calculate the maximum units that can be traded is:

$$\text{Units Available} =$$
$$100 \times \text{Margin Available} \times \text{Rate} / (\text{Current Price} \times \text{Margin Percent})$$

If USD is the base currency, then this reduces to:

$$\text{Units Available} = 100 \times \text{Margin Available} / \text{Margin Percent}$$

Cross rates can be handled in the same fashion by simply manipulating the conversion rate. *Note:* Always decrease the units available slightly to avoid a margin call. I recommend 10 percent.

Calculating Margin Requirements

Before executing any trade, you should always have a rough idea of how much of your account balance will be used as the margin requirement. Any trade whose margin requirement exceeds your existing account balance will not be executed. Trades whose margin requirements deplete nearly all the equity in your account are very risky and may incur the dreaded margin call. The formula to calculate the margin requirement for a trade is very simple:

Margin Requirement =
Current Price × Units Traded × Margin Percent / 100

Assume your broker mandates a 5 percent margin percentage. You want to buy a full lot (100,000 units) of the EUR/USD currency pair, which is trading at 1.2538. Thus:

$$\$6,269.00 = 1.2538 \times 100,000 \times 5 \: / \: 100$$

This trade requires $6,269.00 for margin. Proceed accordingly.

Calculating Transaction Cost

Your broker will always calculate the transaction cost because that cost is automatically subtracted from your account balance the instant you initiate a new trade. Nonetheless, it is useful to know just how the broker computes this debit. See Figure 6.11.

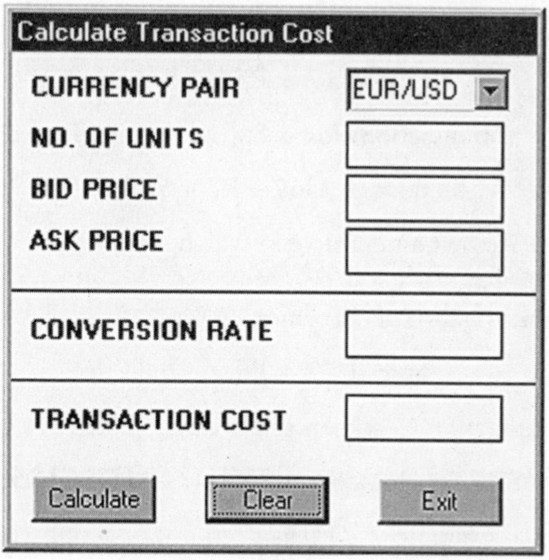

FIGURE 6.11 Calculate Transaction Cost

FIGURE 6.12   A 3-Pip Spread in EUR/USD

Remember that the bid price is used when the trader initiates a new buy (long) trade and the ask price is used when the trader initiates a new sell (short) trade. When the USD is the quote currency in the currency pair, the conversion rate equals 1, as seen in Figure 6.12.

The basic formulas for the transaction cost in this instance are:

$$\text{Spread} = \text{Ask Price} - \text{Bid Price}$$

$$\text{Transaction Cost} = \text{Spread} \times \text{Units Traded}$$

$$\$3.00 = (1.2569 - 1.2566) \times 10{,}000$$

Figure 6.13 shows an example in which we calculate the transaction cost when the base currency is USD.

In this case, the formula becomes:

$$\text{Spread} = \text{Ask Price} - \text{Bid Price}$$

$$\text{Transaction Cost} = \text{Spread} \times \text{Units Traded} / \text{Ask Price}$$

$$\$3.24 = (1.2359 - 1.2355) \times 10{,}000 / 1.2359$$

In our final example, we calculate the transaction cost in U.S. Dollars for a non-USD cross rate. We need to look up the current price of the currency pair containing USD and the quote currency of the cross rate pair (see Figure 6.14).

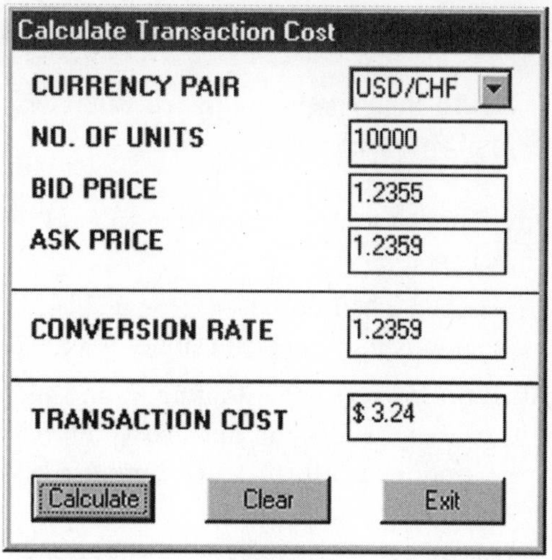

FIGURE 6.13 A 4-Pip Spread in USD/CHF

In this case of non-USD cross rates, the formula becomes:

Transaction Cost = Spread × Units Traded / Conversion Rate

or

$$\$5.69 = (85.52 - 85.46) \times 10000 / 105.43$$

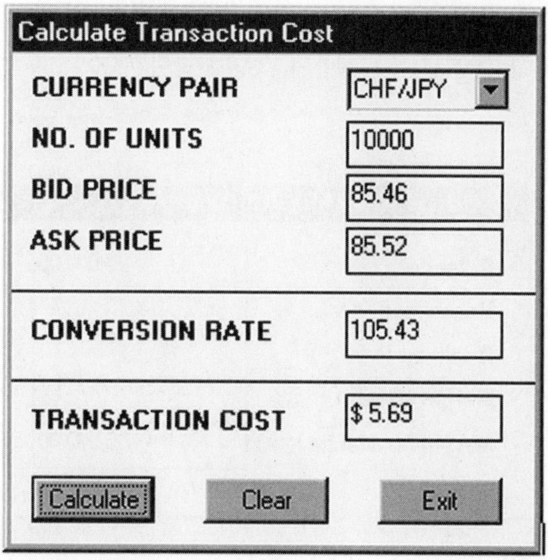

FIGURE 6.14 A 6-Pip Spread in CHF/JPY

Calculating Account Summary Balance

In this section, I make the following assumptions before walking you through the accounting system of your first trade:

- You have read and thoroughly understand the FOREX trading terms described in Chapter 5.

- You have researched a half dozen or so reputable FOREX brokers and selected one that satisfies your financial needs and goals.

- You have used the broker's paper trading feature and/or the demo program that he or she provides and now feel comfortable with the screen layout of the trading platform and its mouse/keyboard navigation system.

- You have opened a new margin account, signed and returned the necessary application forms, and deposited 5,000 USD with the broker.

You are now ready to make your first trade in the FOREX currency markets. The Account Summary section of your broker's trading platform should look similar to what is shown in Figure 6.15.

Let us say that your new broker offers 20:1 leverage, which means that you must "risk" five percent of the total value of any trade that you execute, long or short. Assume that you have analyzed, both technically and fundamentally, several major currency pairs and feel that the USD/JPY pair is overpriced and it will decline in the immediate future. You now execute a very conservative entry order to sell 5,000 units of USD/JPY at a market price of 105.64. The transaction cost (the difference between the bid and the ask price) is three pips for the USD/JPY pair.

ACCOUNT SUMMARY (USD)	
Balance	5,000.00
Unrealized P & L	
Realized P & L	
Margin Used	
Margin Available	5,000.00

FIGURE 6.15   Account Summary before First Trade

ACCOUNT SUMMARY (USD)	
Balance	5,000.00
Unrealized P & L	-1.42
Realized P & L	
Margin Used	250.00
Margin Available	4,750.00

FIGURE 6.16 Account Summary after Market Entry

In Figure 6.16 we see that the Balance and the Realized P&L entries are unchanged. Unrealized P&L show a negative 1.42 USD. This is the round-turn transaction cost, which is subtracted the moment a new trade is executed. Each pip in the USD/JPY trade is worth 0.4733 USD. Therefore:

$$1 \text{ pip} = 1/105.64 \times 50$$
$$1 \text{ pip} = 0.4733 \text{ USD}$$
$$3 \text{ pips} = 1.4199 \text{ USD}$$

The Margin Used entry shows 250.00 USD, calculated as follows:

$$\text{Margin Used} = \text{Total Cost of Trade} \times \text{Margin Percentage}$$

$$250.00 = 5{,}000.00 \times 5\%$$

The Margin Available entry has also changed:

$$\text{Margin Available} = \text{Balance} - \text{Margin Used}$$

$$4{,}750.00 = 5{,}000.00 - 250.00$$

After ten minutes or so, we notice that your "feeling"—that the USD/JPY pair was oversold and would decline—has paid off. The USD/JPY has dropped to 105.51. Not only have you recouped the transaction cost (minus three pips) but you gained a plus 10 pips in profit, as shown in Figure 6.17.

At this point, market activity slows down and the price direction starts moving laterally. You decide that a plus 10 pips on your first trade is satisfactory

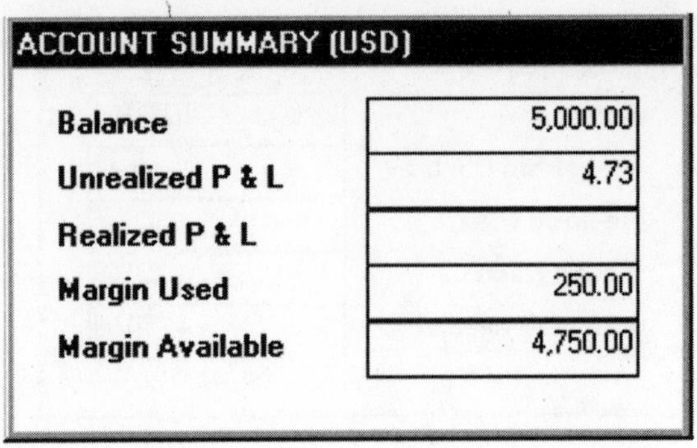

```
ACCOUNT SUMMARY (USD)

  Balance                    5,000.00
  Unrealized P & L               4.73
  Realized P & L
  Margin Used                  250.00
  Margin Available           4,750.00
```

FIGURE 6.17   A 10-Pip Profit

and you close the trade. Essentially, this means purchasing 5,000 units of USD/JPY to offset your previous sale. Once your trade liquidation is logged at the broker's firm, your new Account Summary should resemble what is shown in Figure 6.18.

The example, of course, is merely an illustration. Your first trade may be greater or smaller than the example.

For Futures Traders

Futures traders tend to think in dollars versus a commodity asset (silver, soybeans, pork bellies, etc.). The switch to corelational values—one currency against another—can be a bit trying at first. The trick is to practice calculating profit and loss for fictitious trades. Most broker dealing platforms provide such a calculator.

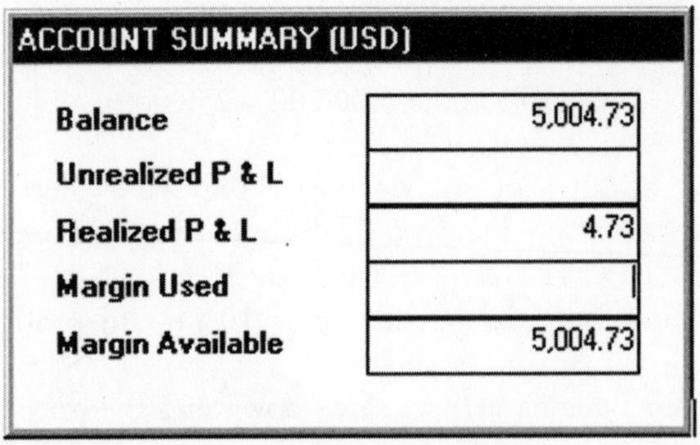

```
ACCOUNT SUMMARY (USD)

  Balance                    5,004.73
  Unrealized P & L
  Realized P & L                 4.73
  Margin Used
  Margin Available           5,004.73
```

FIGURE 6.18   After Liquidating First Trade

Summary

The math in this chapter is not nearly as complex as it may appear at first. In fact I can reduce it all to the following cheat sheet:

$$\text{Price Change} = \text{Exit Price} - \text{Entry Price}$$

$$\text{Leverage} = 100 \,/\, \text{Margin Percent}$$

$$\text{Margin Percent} = 100 \,/\, \text{Leverage}$$

$$\text{Profit in Pips} = \text{Price Change} \times \text{Pip Factor}$$

If the Quote Currency in a trade = USD, then

$$\text{Profit in USD} = \text{Price Change} \times \text{Units Traded}$$

If the Base Currency in a trade = USD, then

$$\text{Profit in USD} = \text{Price Change} \times \text{Units Traded} \,/\, \text{Exit Price}$$

When the profit for non-USD cross rates is being calculated, the following applies:

The conversion rate is the currency pair with the USD and the quote currency of the cross rate pair.

If the base currency of the conversion rate = USD, then

$$\text{Profit in USD} = \text{Price Change} \times \text{Units Traded} \,/\, \text{Conversion Rate}$$

If the quote currency of the conversion rate = USD, then

$$\text{Profit in USD} = \text{Price Change} \times \text{Units Traded} \times \text{Conversion Rate}$$

You can now calculate profit and loss during open positions.

Learning these basic calculations will endue you with confidence, something you will need in substantial measure to succeed as a currency trader.

Practice calculations with the calculator available on most broker web sites (see Chapter 7) or at www.forexcalc.com.

Selecting the Right FOREX Broker for You

A s I wrote in Chapter 4, FOREX is a caveat emptor enterprise. Regulation has increased but is still much less robust than it is in either the securities or commodity futures industries. FOREX has no central clearinghouse making it a substantially different space from commodity futures or listed securities. Prospective traders need to understand the differences and ramifications therein and thereof.

At last count I found over 100 FOREX broker-dealers with online retail platforms. Although some of them are Introducing Brokers (IBs) for other companies, there remain many unique trading platforms from which to choose.

Broker-Dealer Due Diligence

Retail brokers can be divided into *market makers (dealers)* and *ECNs*—Electronic Communications Networks. ECN is the way the true Interbank market operates; each approach has advantages and disadvantages. Most retailers are market makers, but a few are venturing into the ECN world. Both venues have advantages and disadvantages.

The beginner should first determine what tools he or she will need to trade. Of course, the more you study, the more you learn. Your needs may change. Download and do due diligence on *at least* five of these broker-dealers' demo platforms. Use the checklist I have provided to research their services in the categories noted and how they relate to your needs. Keep notes. I've answered some of the questions for you; more can be found on their web sites, in their documents, and on the FOREX Internet review boards and forums.

I like to send an e-mail question or two to sales; to gather information but also to see if and how they respond. Ask to be contacted back by e-mail. Most will ignore your request and call you, a few will e-mail you, many will not contact you at all or simply add you to an automated mailing list. I continue to be amazed by the inability of many broker-dealers to answer an e-mail at all— much less in a timely manner!

Increasing capital requirements for retail broker-dealers may well shake up the industry soon, forcing the smaller players to close or merge. I also expect mergers between major players as competition increases and profit margins fall.

Traders have vastly different experiences with brokers. Listed below are some that I would not fund with five cents but that get overwhelmingly wonderful reviews from others.

Demo Accounts

Always start with a Demo Account! This will allow you to preview most of the broker's platform features and become familiar with how charting, indicators, order placement, and accounting is handled. Do one survey of Demos to decide which brokers to take to the next level with a micro- or mini-account. Typically a micro-account allows for trades of as little as 100 units; a mini-account, for 10,000 units. There may be some difference between the Demo account and a real-time account; make an effort to find out what these are for each broker on which you do due diligence.

Market Maker, ECN, or IB

Market maker or ECN is the single most critical distinction between FOREX broker-dealers. A market maker, or Dealer, is always the counterparty to your trades whereas an ECN requires an actual counter order for execution. Given the liquidity of the FOREX markets a counter order is only a problem in a very fast or very slow market or if you place an enormously large order. An ECN can't play many of the games that market makers do—in large part they don't need to since they have no book to balance. But ECN trading requires a more accurate and delicate trading touch, also an additional skill that the trader must acquire.

Regarding market makers. Some are good, even very good; many are awful. Keep in mind what "counterparty to your trade" means. Then remember they hold all the cards—the data stream, the dealing desk, the trading platform, and all the tools—requoting, pip spreads, trading rules and dealer intervention, accepting or cancelling trades—all for the supposed purpose of maintaining an orderly market.

ECNs have their own issues—the biggest one is their platforms are more difficult to learn and use effectively. They are often bare bones and require integration of third-party charting and technical services. But they have much less leeway since they are functionally trade matchers. In fast or slow markets liquidity may actually be worse with an ECN since they don't have many of the orderly-market tools at their disposal. But on balance, I feel that once you have gotten your feet wet in FOREX—shop for an ECN.

I have been happy with HotspotFX, www.hotspotfx.com, for many years—but conduct your own due diligence, make your own decisions.

The core issue—and the reason the author believes market makers are losing ground to ECNs—is that market makers manipulate the book to maintain order. This involves a number of activities such as requoting, dealer intervention and setting pip spread—as and when they please. Many traders believe market makers trade against their customers (they do) as a profit-making enterprise for the company.

Market makers set or control pip spreads; ECNs generally do not. Some ECNs such as www.hotspotfx.com provide depth of market—the ability to see standing buy and sell orders, the quantities and prices bid and asked.

To complicate matters some firms who are obviously market makers now advertise a *no dealing desk*. The author is unsure how such a hybrid operates; in some instances it appears to be nothing more than semantics in an effort to shake the market maker moniker. Lack of regulation makes knowing how a broker-dealer processes trades difficult if not impossible. The author queried five such brokers and received no response from any of them. FOREX brokers are distancing themselves from the market maker label. But whether the changes advertised are semantic or in how they execute trades remains a question in many instances.

Introducing Brokers

An IB (Introducing Broker) is an independent who routes trades and uses the trading platform and clearing services of a larger FCM (Futures Clearing Merchant) broker-dealer.

The rationale for using an IB is they may offer value-add services you want and cannot get from the broker-dealer. Examples of value-add IBs are

HawaiiFOREX, www.hawaiiFOREX.com, which offers a structured educational program currently based on the work of Joe DiNapoli; www.atcbrokers .com with a variety of platforms; or author Archer's www.fxpraxis.com, which offers the Goodman trading methods (GoodmanWorks).

No two traders are alike, and the landscape is constantly changing. Broker recommendations per se are risky business. That said, the author's opinion is that the new trader should open an account with one of the Big Three or a top rated Popular Broker. A market maker may be the wise choice at the beginning as ECN platforms are a little more difficult to manage. If your FOREX career blossoms—and of course I hope it does—moving on to one of the larger ECN brokers such as www.hotspotfx.com, www.efxgroup.com or www.Dukascopy.com makes some sense. For those who wish to start with an ECN some of them are now offering mini-accounts, such as www. efxgroup.com.

See Appendix A, "How the FOREX Game Is Played," discussing the current issues of importance to traders with respect to broker-dealer structure and practices.

Platform Capabilities

Perhaps the most critical to the trader is a broker-dealer's platform capabilities. Due diligence, vis-à-vis your needs, will take some time and effort on your part. Here is what to look for in several categories. Learn everything possible before making a trade. Demo accounts are ideal for this purpose.

Trading Tools

Traders are fascinated by charts, numbers, and indicators, and most broker-dealers are happy to accommodate them. Downloading a Demo account will give you a good idea of the toolset available. In a few instances the Demo does not offer the entire palette so you will need a mini-account to see and test dive everything. Not sure? Ask the broker.

Most platforms offer integrated charting and technical studies capability. For those that do not you will need to access a third-party vendor. I recommend an integrated platform for the novice.

Most of the popular indicators are available—moving averages, stochastics, relative strength, oscillators, Bollinger bands, and many others. (See Figure 7.1.)

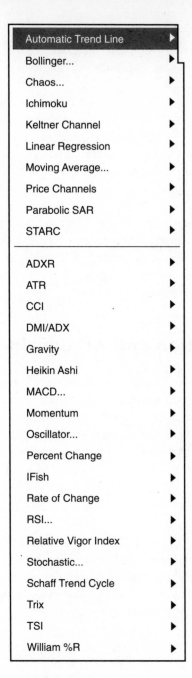

FIGURE 7.1 Technical Indicators
Source: From Intellicharts, Inc. www.FXtrek.com.

Bar charts with a variety of settings for time scales and units are offered. Be sure the dealer has what you need; integrated charting capability is a must, especially for the new trader. Swing charts, candlesticks, and point and figure charts are also available.

Most platforms offer a palette by which you can customize the look and feel of charts. The size, scale, and coloring of charts can make a big difference to your interpretation of them. As an experiment, take a single pair with the same time scale and unit and make a half-dozen or so charts with different parameters. My advice to the beginner is to keep all charts in the same size and color scheme. Trading is an extremely delicate process, and even small differences can tell.

It is best if you have some idea of what you want before beginning your due diligence. Some primary considerations: colors, sizing/scaling, time units, vertical and horizontal scrolling, printing. As an old-time trader the author still likes to print charts for analysis, and some of the trading platform print commands are not particularly easy.

Order Execution and Accounting

How easy is it to place and monitor your orders? View your account information? Most retail dealers do a great job of this but layout and organization vary. Those factors can be important depending on how you trade; especially if you trade frequently. Can that information be easily backed up or saved? Almost all broker-dealers have this process down pat; much of your decision is a matter of personal style. (See Figure 7.2.)

News

Most broker-dealers offer news feeds and news and announcement calendars. There are many third-party providers, but for the average trader what is offered integrated on trader platforms is enough. Don't get mesmerized by the news, but do watch and note how the market reacts to it.

Chat

Some of the larger dealers offer chat rooms or forums. These may or may not be useful. The author believes the many independent forums such as www.global-view.com are a better source of information.

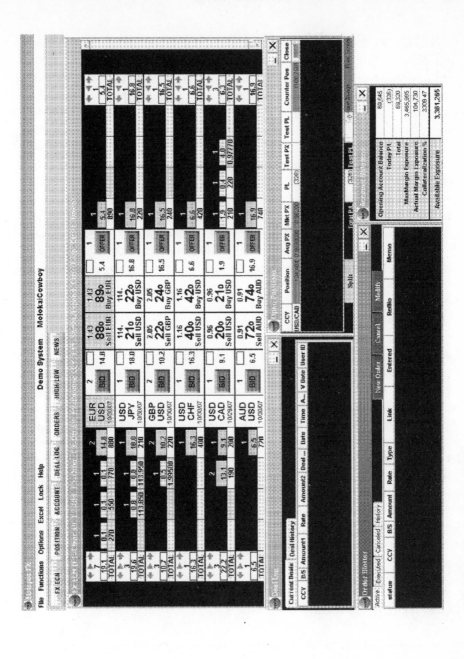

FIGURE 7.2 Trading Platform
Source: HotSpotFX Demo Platform, www.hotspotfx.com.

61

Platform Stability and Backbone

As I have mentioned above, trading platforms are enormously complex software programs. Real-time delivery of information is also a daunting task. Put those factors together and it is a minor miracle they work as well as they do. But . . . things happen. One of the biggest brokers had their trading platform crash for almost 24 hours in February of 2007.

What backbone is a prospective broker-dealer using—Windows, Java, Web-based, or Flash? Windows is the most stable, and Java is cross-platform if you are using a Mac computer. At one time Java platforms had a bad habit of crashing under heavy loads but that seems for the most part to have been remedied. If you use Java *don't* install the latest Sun update without getting the okay from your broker-dealer. Updates are supposed to be downwardly compatible, but there is a lot going on in a real-time trading platform. Having owned a web conferencing business, I have been leery of Java, but it has improved a great deal recently.

Flash platforms are available, but they don't have the years of development behind them that Windows and Java platforms do. They have potential, once developers in FOREX get a handle on the immense Macromedia toolset.

Nor is the Internet perfect. You shouldn't trade online unless you have a high-speed Internet connection. A backup connection from a different vendor is a good idea if you are a serious trader. Cable is more reliable than DSL in most locations. Some brokers offer their platforms on multiple backbones and even recommend specific browsers for their Windows-based venues. Traders should also invest in a reliable battery backup power supply for their computer.

Once you are trading with substantial amounts of money and taking larger positions, consider opening a small secondary account with a different broker-dealer in a different country on a different backbone. Should your primary broker go incommunicado and you need to execute a trade, you have an out. In your due diligence process, after you have sampled four or five mini-accounts and select a primary broker you may consider leaving a mini-account open as a hedge.

Historical Data

If you want to look at charts from months and years gone by, you will need historical data. Some brokers offer it in their trading platform, some as a separate service, and some not at all. For comprehensive historical data, you may wish to consider one of the data vendors in Chapter 8. Historical data is available online, for download or on a CD; www.disktrading.com is a good value.

Historical data is the inexpensive approach for developing and testing trading methods, systems, and theories. See "Market Environments (ME)" in Chapter 16 for methods to effectively test methods and systems.

Data Feed

API (Application Programming Interface) is your broker-dealer's price data stream made available for custom programming. What sources it is composed of is usually difficult if not impossible to ascertain. No two are identical. Market makers use a composite of sources—that may even include its own micro-ECN. But given the enormous liquidity of the market, they don't usually vary a great deal. The exception is when market makers requote.

Most brokers offer their API as a separate service. A trader would use the API to drive third-party software or his or her own software program. On the flipside, third-party vendors offer their services using various dealers' API. It can be confusing. If you use a third-party program for trading or even just for your charts, be sure it has a one-to-one or very close correspondence with your broker-dealer data stream. Rolling your own integration is strictly for experienced programmer gurus. New traders should probably avoid third-party integration, also.

Third-Party Offerings

What third-party services do they support? Are these services integrated with the trading platform or offered as stand-alone? Third-party offerings are detailed in Chapter 8, "Opening a FOREX Account." In the past two years the amount of third-party integration has grown a great deal; there are many options, almost too many! I recommend you only use third-party chart and technical analysis services that integrate with your broker's data feed. At the beginning, stick with the capabilities integrated into your broker's trading platform.

Orders

Traders use a wide variety of different orders for entry, stop protection, and exit (price objectives). Our advice: Keep it simple. Thoroughly understand what an order does and how it works before using it. Many exotic order types add a level of complexity to the trading process beginners normally don't need. Some orders also offer an extra license to the broker-dealer to manage their book; ergo, they generally love them and encourage them. Functionality of orders may differ slightly from market makers to ECNs.

I offer more detail on orders in Chapter 9, "Pulling the Trigger."

Margin Requirements

Because a trader can open an account from $1 to $1,000,000 and trade any size lot, margins and leverage are something of a misnomer in FOREX.

Broker-dealers allow you to set your own fixed maximum leverage—typically from 10:1 to 100:1. Dealers are mostly concerned that you do not hold open positions in excess of your account balance. If you do—or even come close—you will get a margin call, and you will be expected to meet it immediately.

The lower the margin requirement, the higher the leverage factor. Profits and loses are magnified as the leverage is increased.

In reality today margin calls in FOREX are rare. Brokers are able to electronically monitor all parameters based on your account size, trading activity, and experience. If you attempt to enter an order outside of those parameters it won't execute.

Simple money management rules—that you implement—are the key to avoiding margin calls and overtrading. In Chapter 15, "Money Management Made Simple," I offer the Campaign Trade Method for novices.

I recommend these basic ideas to new traders: (1) never commit more than one-half of your account balance to open positions, (2) never trade more than two market pairs concurrently, (3) never commit more than 25 percent of your capital to a single position, and (4) never trade over 50:1 leverage. Begin your trading career at 20:1 and work up in increments of 10:1 as you are successful. Experienced traders often modulate these parameters according to how confident they are of a trade. But that requires experience to make it an effective tool. New traders should keep the number of money management parameters simple and to a bare minimum.

Order Backup

Does your broker offer the capability to phone an order if their trader platform goes down or your Internet drops? Be sure telephone order backup is available, although lines will be swamped if it is a system-wide outage and not your own Internet connection. If you open a mini- or micro-account, ask your broker to let you test a telephone order so that you know it exists and have the process down pat for when and if you need it. Keep in mind that brokers do not expect their platforms to go down, and when they do, their backup systems tend to be overwhelmed.

Account Minimums

Micro-accounts now start at $1! Micro accounts begin at $300, mini accounts (10k lots) at $1,000, and standard accounts (100k lots) at $2,500. ECNs tend to have higher minimums. This is a far cry from the days in the commodity futures markets where $5,000 was considered a mini-account and $25,000 was the standard. In FOREX the ability to set your own lot sizes and leverage make smaller accounts justifiable. Account size, leverage, and lot size should all work in harmony and be consistent; your broker-dealer monitors such parameters carefully in an effort to protect both parties.

Pairs, Crosses, and Exotics

A *pair* is a tradable set of currencies including the USD. A *cross* is a set without the USD. An *exotic* is a set with the USD but with an exotic currency such as the Hungarian Forint, Indonesian Rupiah, or Thai Baht. There are 25 or so exotics offered currently. Today's exotic may be tomorrow's pair; the Polish Zloty is considered an exotic, but its rising popularity may move it to a standard pair sometime in the not too distant future. The big banana remains the EUR/USD major pair.

Deposits and Withdrawals

Typically accomplished by check or wire. eGold—www.efundsfinance.com— and PayPal—www.paypal.com—are also used by some broker-dealers for account deposits. These latter two options may disappear as the NFA implements and enforces a Know Your Client regulation for broker-dealers. An attempt to deposit funds for a small account to Oanda via PayPal was difficult and time-consuming. Needless to say, keep complete hardcopy, cross-referenced records of all monetary transactions with your broker. A date log of all transactions and communications is also advised. Beware of brokers who make withdrawals difficult or take an inordinate amount of time to make them.

Transaction Costs

There are no commissions in FOREX in the form they exist for securities or commodity futures traders. Similar to the NASDAQ market, FOREX operates on a bid-ask spread. The minimum fluctuation of a currency pair is a *pip* and spreads (and just about everything else) are quoted in pips.

The more liquid a market, either with respect to time-of-day (TOD) or pair, the lower will be the pip spread to trade. Temporal conditions of a market maker may also affect spreads. Remember, you pay the spread both going in and going out. The EUR/USD is far and away the most liquid pair. Some

ECNs offer it at 1 pip, most retail market makers are now at 1.5 to 3 pips with 2 pips the standard. Again, when markets are illiquid for a market maker or generally because of prevailing fast conditions, pip spreads balloon—sometimes enormously. By following a pair for a few weeks you can *usually* get a very good idea of when and under what circumstances this will occur. See Appendix A, "How the FOREX Game Is Played" for more.

Two pips does not sound like much, but for active short-term or high-frequency traders, costs add up quickly. Two pips reduces a 10 pip trade by 20 percent, but a 50 pip trade by only 4 percent. There are now ultra high-frequency traders—we called it churning an account in days gone by—but don't think I could mouse-click that fast.

ECNs may also or alternately charge a small lot fee commission. Calculate the lot fee across the lot size to get the full, correct spread. Lot fees on less than 10,000 size can be expensive; one reason ECNs are most likely to have higher account minimums.

Trading Hours

FOREX is more or less a round-the-clock activity. The day begins with the Asian session, dovetails to the European session, and ends with the North American session. (See Appendix F.)

The North American session is the most active—and volatile. I have found relatively quieter opportunities, good for beginners, in the other two sessions. But be aware of potentially larger pip spreads, as markets may be thin. All currencies trade in all sessions although they tend to be most active in the session to which the country belongs. I prefer trading the EUR/USD from 8:00 P.M. to 12:00 P.M. Eastern time. This may be a function of the markets being less volatile—or the children being asleep!

Executions of market orders at odd hours can take your breath away! Early in a session, late in the week, and so forth. The market may be very thin even though the chart looks fine. I recently made the mistake of entering a market order in the EUR/GBP for a small 25,000 lot with a market maker and was filled 10 pips off in a quietly—too quietly—trading market.

Customer Service

As every Boomer knows, the quality of customer service (at least in the United States) has fallen dramatically in the past 30 years. Practices that would have put a company out of business in 1977 are SOP today. Retail FOREX is no different and in my humble opinion is worse than many other industries. If you are old enough to have done business with a retail brokerage firm in the 1960s or 1970s, you are in for a shock.

The actual quality of service varies enormously from broker-dealer to broker-dealer, but the general level in the industry is appalling. My pet peeve: brokers with great trading platforms, good pip spreads, and horrific customer service. Nothing can derail a trader from his trading process faster than poor customer service. The reviews are an essential guide to what people have experienced with sales, customer service, and technical support. Most noncritical support is handled via e-mail. Critical issues warrant a telephone call or an IM-style chat if it is available. Please don't burden your dealer's customer service people with telephone calls for noncritical issues.

One would think at least sales support would be stellar; if not as a customer after they have signed you up to an account. Not so. I have found sales support at many firms to be perfectly dreadful. Inability to answer e-mail in a timely manner or at all, failure to intelligently address basic questions, and abysmal understanding of what they are selling are typical trader issues.

Retail FOREX is relatively new, and it is still growing rapidly. The number of qualified sales and customer support personnel in relationship to inquiries and customers is currently grossly inadequate. I have found a large number of sales and CS representatives who could only be described as clueless. Better training is one solution to the problem; actually reading an e-mail from a prospect or client before responding is another. Answering e-mail in a timely fashion would be a nice touch, also. The industry as a whole needs customer service help and desperately. Technical support is generally stronger but still fraught with difficulties. Many tech support representatives feel the customer is always wrong or are simply unqualified for the job.

To do a proper due diligence will require that you open several demo accounts and at least three or four micro- or mini-accounts. The good news is this will give you some idea of a broker-dealer's customer service. The bad news is it will unleash their salespeople on you. I attempted to unsubscribe to one broker's mailing lists on four occasions—twice using their automatic unsubscribe, which promises you will not hear from them again. A simple e-mail inquiry took 17 days to be answered.

It behooves the trader to learn everything possible about a broker-dealer's customer service practices and policies before making a single trade. Ditto for their trading platforms, technical support, and other services such as withdrawing funds. Retail FOREX is not a perfect world; if you can't stand the heat, stay out of the kitchen.

Documentation

Most brokers have excellent documentation to protect both them and you. Lawyers are expensive, but there are a lot of them! You may wish to have your accountant or lawyer review the firm's documentation if you don't understand something. But don't expect to get the broker-dealer to make any changes in it for you. Keep hard copies of all documentation and especially those requiring your signature.

Don't spare the ink or paper—print all of your brokers documentation and study it in depth.

Similar to securities and futures, you may open an individual account, joint account, partnership account, or corporate account. Beyond the individual account additional paperwork is required. If you have someone manage your money, there is a separate form for that purpose.

Requoting

This can get ugly. Only market makers requote. It is the soft underbelly and Achilles' heel of FOREX. If anything brings in the regulators to control the industry it will be requoting. In requoting, market makers fill your order with prices not seen on their standard online price feed. Fortunately requoting is not nearly the problem it was two or three years ago, but it is out there, and if you are a small trader, you will probably experience it. Broker-dealers are learning that traders run so quickly and complain so loudly about requoting, they are encouraged to refrain from the practice. Requoting is sometimes equated with dealer intervention and is most typical of market makers.

Financials

The CFTC (Commodity Futures Trading Commission) is beginning to set minimum net worth for broker-dealers, requiring certain thresholds for offering at different levels. An overextended broker with a high net worth is not better than a small net-worth broker with a strong balance sheet as Refco traders learned in 2005. Unfortunately the NFA is not likely to think in that fashion, resulting in the closing or merger of solid small capitalized firms and allowing relatively anemic big fish to continue to swim. Financial disclosure requirements remain minimal in FOREX but the authors believe that will change over the next two or three years. If you dig deep on some of the forums and on the NFA web site, www.nfa.org, you can find financial information that is difficult to pry from the broker-dealers themselves. At least in theory an ECN should require less capital than a moneymaker. Because an ECN matches trades for execution, finding themselves on a potentially dangerous large unbalanced position is less likely for them than for a market maker. The CFTC tallies this information: http://www.cftc.gov/files/tm/fcm/tmfcmdata0705.xls.

Rollovers and Interest

Rollover charges are determined by the difference between U.S. interest rates and the interest rates of the corresponding pair country. The greater the interest rate differential between the two countries in the currency pair or cross, the greater will be the rollover charge. For example, if the British Pound (GBP) has the greater differential with the U.S. Dollar (USD), then the rollover charge for holding the GBP positions would be the most expensive. Conversely if the Swiss Franc (CHF) were to have the smallest interest rate differential to the U.S. Dollar, then the session carryover ("overnight") charges for the USD/CHF would be the least expensive of the currency pairs.

Rollovers are a complex issue, fortunately of limited importance to the small trader, and are discussed in Chapter 16, "Tactics and Strategy." If you trade intersession a substantial amount of the time, ask for specific broker-dealer policies on rollovers; they do vary, and some are much better than others.

Some dealers offer interest on your unused account balance. Again, policies within those companies differ. If you have a large amount of unused account monies, it can make a real difference. Larger traders tend to get better deals to keep them from shuffling money in and out of their accounts to maximize interest.

You may download this form at www.fxpraxis.com in the Currency Codex section. The online version is updated from time to time as services expand and evolve.

FOREX Broker-Dealers

You can please some of the traders some of the time, but you can't please all of the traders all of the time. As you peruse broker-dealer reviews, you will see many that have both one-star and five-star reviews. Some of these are just plain sour grapes, and some are shills. Look for similar issues mentioned over long periods of time and on different review boards. Focus on the reviews in the context of what you as a trader require. As in anything else, a larger sample is a better indicator than a small sample.

The inclusion of a broker-dealer herein does not constitute a recommendation; exclusion likewise does not imply disapproval. Your experience may differ from mine.

Popular Broker-Dealers

I have done substantial due diligence on the companies listed below, including downloading and reviewing their platforms, making e-mail contact, and asking a few questions. I've sampled micro- and mini-accounts with a dozen or more brokers. I believe those below are among the best retail broker-dealers in the FOREX industry. But, one person's fine wine is another's poison. None are perfect by any stretch of the imagination.

Expectations vary. The more knowledgeable you become, the lower will be your expectations if only because you understand how the game is played. Many of the review board complaints are from traders with limited knowledge and unrealistic expectations—but not all of them. Pip spreads are going to balloon occasionally, prices will be requoted to you, customer service will frustrate you, platforms and the Internet will go down. Make an attempt to build the occasional minor disaster into your trading and into your expectations.

My hot button remains the pitiful sales and customer service in the retail FOREX industry.

You will notice references to "news trading" on the review boards. This refers to the practice of attempting to trade on news or announcements. It is a dangerous practice; prices may jump or fall quickly ("spikes"), and pip spreads will expand enormously. It can be very profitable—or deadly—and is not for the new trader in my humble opinion. Market makers are on the lookout for news traders. I believe many of the negative news trading reviews are sour grapes although market makers do seem to use the occasion to trade against their clients. On the other hand it is ridiculous for market makers to advertise "2 pip spreads" when they regularly balloon to 25 or 30 pips on any pending news. If you must trade the news, do it with an ECN, and don't use market orders. For news trading, an execution tool such as www.secretnewsweapon.com is de rigueur.

FOREX is the most laissez-faire of all markets, and that cuts both ways. No one wants to be cheated, but if you can't take the knocks, don't play the game. The profit opportunities are enormous, and that attracts all kinds. Opportunists and strongly driven business people are in plentiful supply in the FOREX market.

Hotspot FX

On Hotspot FX's ECN (www.hotspotfx.com), clients trade directly on prices streamed by large FX banks or can enter their own bids and offers. In contrast to dealer or market maker platforms, Hotspot FX claims to not make prices or take positions against client orders. Further, because traders are anonymous, pricing on the ECN is neutral; that is, prices reflect market conditions only, not a perception of the client's trading direction based on their trading strategies, tactics, or current market positions. This is a very professionally run operation, well respected in the industry, and they know the business. The firm is a subsidiary of Knight Capital Group, Inc. (Nasdaq: NITE). Trading platform is basic but efficient; it caters to larger traders who have their own charting and indicator services. The order palette is limited but adequate. Hotspot FX now offers a $3,500, 10k lot minimum account size. Hotspot FX's web site provides all the basic information you need with no showy buy-me glitz, which I appreciated. Customer service is well above average. It has some negative reviews from news traders who probably used market orders at midnight.

Oanda

Oanda (www.oanda.com) started with quite a poor reputation in the late 1990s but it now is considered one of the best retail houses. There are lots of educational tools on the web site for beginners. Customer service telephone support is iffy, but e-mail is quick and efficient. The technical tool set is very good and adequate to most traders. Box options are a unique feature. Their API for developers is excellent.

Oanda claims to have no dealing desk (NDD), which would make it an ECN, if that is the case. The line of demarcation between market maker and ECN is beginning to blur as brokers attempt to distance themselves from the market maker moniker, and NDD may refer to any of a number of different setups.

EFX Group—MB Trading

This company (www.efxgroup.com) is an ECN and www.mbtrading.com, EFX also offers mini-accounts; low minimums usually only found with market makers. They offer excellent webinars to teach their ECN platform and how to use it effectively. EFX has come on strong in the last year based on these efforts and excellent reviews. They are one of the few brokers who seem to follow the review boards and respond to negative reviews with their side of the story. EFX is also very strong on following regulations and recommended practices set by the NFA. Customer service is superior. They offer a free API, which can be a big advantage if you intend to develop your own trading software program.

Reviews of their Navigator trading platform have been mixed with regard to both stability and usability. Much of this may be because ECN platforms are different from market-maker platforms. EFX is extremely helpful in getting traders familiar with their platform.

Avail Trading Corporation

ATC (www.atcbrokers.com). Excellent reviews and customer care. Services in both futures and FOREX for retail and professional traders.

Ikon GM Royal Division

Ikon GM Royal Division (www.ikon-royal.com) is another established market-maker. It uses the MetaTrader4 platform. Their platform download and set up is very smooth; someone has obviously made an extra effort to get this often frustrating process right. The author found initial communication iffy, but a telephone representative answered all of his questions quickly and efficiently—and even followed up several days later to make certain everything I needed had been addressed. Wow! Reviews are generally very good.

Let the mergers begin! As of this writing, Royal has announced a merger with Ikon Global Markets and is now www.ikon-royal.com.

FOREX Capital Trading

This is a newer, apparently relatively small company. But reviews have been good and customer service is above average. New traders seem to be having a positive experience with FOREXct, www.FOREXct.com. Based in Melbourne, Australia.

DukasCopy

Dukascopy offers a unique "centralized-decentralized" clearing system. An interesting article on this new approach is on www.e-FOREX.net in the January 2007 edition. It has enormous potential to revolutionize retail FOREX. They provide a wide variety of FOREX services and products under one roof as well as substantial market depth. They offer emergency "back-up" with other, smaller ECNs. The web site was recently redesigned, vastly improving navigation which had been an issue. Users may select either a Java or a web-based trading platform. The recommended browser for the web-based platform is Firefox. If you like Dukascopy's clearing services and trading platform a great deal of customization is possible with either their FIX API or jFOREX. Not for small traders, the minimum account is $50,000. Commission is $40 per one-million lot and spreads seem generally very tight. Email inquiries regarding services were answered promptly by a real person.

MF Global

A major player with high account minimums for individual traders but excellent Interbank services in FOREX and members of numerous futures and equity exchanges. www.mfglobal.com.

TradeStation

If the TradeStation (tradestation.com) software, tool set, and programming script is to your liking, you can trade FOREX with it also. They clear their trades through Gain Capital at the present time. A number of dealers are integrating TradeStation at some level, including Oanda in association with Snap-Dragon, www.snapdragon.co.uk.

Deutsches Bank

Now you can trade with the huge Deutsches Bank (www.dbfx.com), a major player in the Interbank market. Initial reviews have not been encouraging but may relate to roll-out pains as retail FOREX is new to them—worth watching. Account minimum has just been lowered to $5,000 as of this writing.

The Big Three

These three companies seem to account for perhaps 50% of the retail FOREX business. When you are big, you get noticed. These folks are all either loved or hated. They all appear to have strong financial positions. All three are primarily market makers at the time of this writing but appear to be migrating at various levels to ECN or at least to No Dealing Desk.

Gain Capital

Gain's trading station (www.gaincapital.com) has an excellent accounting and order tracking interface. Their charts are not as robust as some others, but they do offer third-party integration with other venders such as the excellent NinjaTrader, www.ninjatrader.com. Gain has recently raised their account minimum to $25,000. You can still trade with them on www.FOREX.com a wholly-owned subsidiary for smaller cap traders. FOREX.com shares data feed and most platform features with Gain. As do all the Big Three, they have their share of detractors. Platform seems very stable, and customer service is well above average.

GFT

GFT (www.gftFOREX.com) has a large palette of products and services for the trader. Their DealBook is a terrific platform although it is complex. GFT allows you to integrate several third-party services. Many IBs use GFT as their backbone.

FOREX Capital Markets

FOREX Capital Markets (www.fxcm.com) is the classic love/hate broker-dealer. Everyone goes after the 800-pound gorilla on the street in any business.

For the Professional

These services are currently not available to the retail trader at this time. However you may find their platforms in use by other broker-dealers, such as PropFx, listed previously.

- www.currenex.com
- www.fxall.com
- www.aarontrading.com

Fxall and Currenex white label their platforms for other broker-dealers. You need to trade with one of them or be an institutional client to fully access their services. As I write there is a rumor that Currenex may open to the retail trade soon. EBS (www.icap.com) is one of the Interbank network system providers.

Fraud, Scams, and Off-Exchange

Even though there is no Exchange (central clearinghouse) for currency trading, broker-dealers who operate from telephone boiler rooms are still referred to as off-exchange. Beware of these practitioners and avoid them like the plague. Most of them have no web site or a few shoddy pages built in straight HTML and operate primarily via telephone solicitations. They typically sell FOREX options. (See Chapter 19 for information on legitimate FOREX options trading.) They are almost never registered with the CFTC, NFA, or any recognized regulatory body.

You can spread-bet on FOREX through legitimate, licensed bookmakers. We offer some web site links in Chapter 13. The new online gambling laws may affect the ability of U.S. citizens from participating in spread-betting.

Broker-Dealer Due Diligence Form

You may wish to use the Broker-Dealer Due Diligence Checklist in your research. (See Figure 7.1.) Feel free to customize it to fit your specific needs and wants. For example, adding specific platform features, indicators, currencies or orders you require. An expanded spreadsheet of this may be downloaded at www.fxpraxis.com.

Table 7.1　Broker-Dealer Due Diligence Checklist

Name					
Web Site					
Contact					
Demo Account	Yes	No			
Mini Account	Yes	No			
Minimum					
Full Account					
Minimum					
Type	ECN	Market Maker	No Dealing Desk	IB	
Backbone	Java	Windows	Flash	Other	
Recommended Browser					
Charts					
	Bar	Line	P&F	Candlestick	Swing	Specialty
Indicators					
	Moving Averages		Oscillators	Others	
Chart Tools					
	Scaling	Scrolling	Time Increments	Printing	
Platform Customization					
Third-Party Integration					
Historical Data					
Orders	Limit	Stop	Market	Combination	Specialty
Order Backup Procedure					
Trading Hours					

(continued on next page)

Table 7.1 *(Continued)*		
Spreads		
Margins		
Leverage		
Currencies Traded		
Exotics	Yes	No
Options	Yes	No
Rollover Policy		
Financials		
Reviews		
Documentation		
Customer Service		
Likes/Dislikes		
Summary		

Summary

It is critical the prospective trader, especially the beginner, perform due diligence on a broker-dealer thoroughly before depositing money and making a trade.

The recommended process is:

Due Diligence → Demo Account → Mini-Account → Full Account

Don't leave questions unanswered and hope for the best. On the other hand, don't e-mail a flurry of questions the answers to which are found on the web site or by spending an evening with their demo account and documentation. If your experience is similar to mine, they won't be answered anyway.

Once you begin trading you will want to devote 100 percent of your effort to that activity; not readjusting your processes because you found out something about your broker-dealer you should have known at the outset. No broker is perfect, don't expect to find one.

Chapter

Opening a FOREX Account

I n the Fall of 1974 I accompanied a friend to the local Denver office of E.F. Hutton to open a new commodity futures account. The broker handed my friend the account form—an $8\frac{1}{2} \times 5\frac{1}{2}$ card. On the front side one was to enter Name, Address, Telephone, Social Security Number, Employer, Position, and Estimated Net Worth. On the reverse, a two-paragraph disclosure requiring a signature and the date. After filling out the form my friend handed it back to the broker, opened his briefcase and counted out $30,000 in one hundred dollar bills. The broker calmly recounted the money, handed it to the cashier along with the account card. The cashier issued my friend an account number, wished him good trading, and we were done.

Times have changed. Opening an online retail FOREX account is easy business, but the information required is much more extensive than it was in the halcyon days of 1974.

Don't open an account until you have completed a thorough due-diligence of the broker-dealer and worked several hours with their Demo trading platform. Sadly, you will need to follow this entire process even if you are opening a $100 micro-account. Fortunately you will not need to redo the process if you decide to open your full trading account with the broker-dealer in question.

Account Types

As in other investments, the FOREX trader may open a wide variety of accounts: for self-directed trading: Individual Accounts, Joint Accounts (with different flavors), Partnership Accounts, Corporate Accounts, and Retirement/Investment Accounts (also with multiple flavors). The easiest to open is, of course, an individual account or a joint account. All the others require extra documentation: Retirement/Investment accounts the most; and you must confirm the account is eligible for FOREX trading—many are not.

Should you desire to have your account managed by a third party, such as a professional money manager, that also requires additional forms. The due diligence required to select capable money managers is a book in and of itself; beyond the charter of this tome, which assumes you want to make your own trading decisions. Professional accounts may be managed by individual managers or placed in a FOREX trading fund. Many hedge funds now trade currencies, either with other investment vehicles or FOREX-only. Please see Chapter 13, The FOREX Marketplace, for FOREX management resources.

Be sure you are opening a FOREX spot account and not a FOREX forwards or futures account—unless of course one of the latter is your choice. Almost all FOREX dealing is in the spot market, both at the institutional and retail level.

The forms for each dealer do vary, in number and in specific content—if only slightly. It goes without saying: read carefully any document before signing. If you have questions, ask the broker for clarification. If in doubt, ask your attorney or your accountant. Like all legal forms today, they are wordy and complex. FOREX can be a dangerous game, and the broker wants to protect your interest and, especially, theirs. As the regulatory environment firms, you can expect forms to get wordier and longer to incorporate the requirements of new laws, rules, and regulations.

Opening the Account: Steps

Attorneys are not cheap, but they are plentiful. You can be assured your broker-dealer's account forms generated substantial fees or hours for their legal team.

Account forms are online and may be printed out in hard copy. The broker may request two sets, one of which is returned to you, or should be. If they only request a single set of account documents, verify you will receive a copy. Print an extra clean copy for your records in case the online forms change or are modified.

Forms are usually in Adobe Acrobat PDF format. If so, the broker-dealer's Open an Account page will have the link to the PDF reader if it is not already installed on your computer.

TIP: Grab a screenshot of each page you view on your broker's web site for the account registration process. Do this by holding down the ALT+ Print Screen keys. You may then copy it to a Word document with CTRL+V.

You will generally encounter four steps to opening an account although they may go by different names or phrases:

1. **Select an Account Type:** As stated, you must first select the account type. Because most forms are online, the selection of an account type tells the automated registration module what to dish up next.

2. **Personal Information:** This is the bread-and-butter name, address, telephone, fax, e-mail, employer, position, social security number. Forms beyond Individual and Joint will require more kinds of personal and account information.

3. **Financial Information:** This step is getting more and more involved. The broker wants to make sure you are qualified to trade currencies— even if it is a $100 mini-account. I am even seeing broker-dealers requiring what could be called mini financial statements from prospective customers. If you want to play the game, there is no way out, at least legally. A tax form is usually included in this step, also.

4. **Review:** You will be asked to review the documents carefully before submitting. Again—ask the broker any questions you might still have or query your attorney, accountant and/or financial planner.

Review your documents twice. If the broker finds something wrong at Step 5 you will have wasted a great deal of time.

Two threads run through these documents. The desire of the broker to protect both parties and the NFA's Know Thy Customer Rules, which are getting stricter.

TIP: Start a folder and keep copies of everything! I like to keep a time log of all communications with the broker including correspondence, telephone conversations, and e-mail.

I have not seen electronic signatures appear in the industry. Given the NFA's Know Thy Customer emphasis of late, I doubt they will appear at all.

You will be asked to mail or scan-and-mail the forms with appropriate information and signatures to the broker. You will need to include a scan of your Driver's License or other picture ID. I don't like this either, but it is the way things work with electronic registration; there is a downside to everything.

1. **Acceptance:** Once your documents are accepted, you will be notified that your account is ready to fund and trade. Typically acceptance takes only one or two days unless there is a problem.

2. **Funding:** Now you are ready to fund your account and begin trading. Funding is either by cashier's check or bank wire. Personal checks may be accepted by some brokers, but they take a long time to clear, and they add a step to the process. Better to take the 30 minutes for a trip to your bank for a cashier's check or a wire transfer.

Some brokers have been accepting PayPal and eGold. Yes, they deduct the fee from your opening balance. Again, the KTC rule is probably going to send these methods to the sidelines. (See Figure 8.1.)

Depositing Funds

Wire Instructions:

US Dollars only.

Credit**:	Deutsche Bank AG, New York
Swift:	DEUTUS33
ABA:	026003780
Beneficiary:	Hotspot FXR
Beneficiary account #:	106105190008

REFERENCE: For further Credit to Clients Name and User ID

Note: Hotspot FXR does not guarantee exchange rates for clients who attempt to wire non-USD deposits. Clients are urged to speak with their bank to obtain their US Dollars conversion rate.

**A branch address is not necessary for a transaction that is destined for an account that is maintained with Deutsche Bank New York. If the sender advises that a branch address is required, Deutsche Banks New York office address is provided:
Deutsche Bank, New York
60 Wall Street...
NY, NY 10005-2858
Checks and correspondence should not be sent to the above address.

Checks:

US Dollars only

Make checks payable in United States Dollars to:
Hotspot FXR

Mail checks to:
Hotspot FXR/Knight Capital Group
Second Floor
Attn: Hotspot FXR Accounts
545 Washington Blvd.
Jersey City, NJ, USA 07310

Note: Upon notification of check remittance clearing value date, Hotspot FXR will wait an additional 3 (three) business days before applying the funds to your Hotspot FXR account.

FIGURE 8.1   Account Deposits
Source: HotspotFX, www.hotspotfx.com.

Before actually trading, spend one last hour with the Demo account. Keep at the ready a small notebook with the following information at your side; it may either be handwritten or copied from the broker web site:

- The broker's hours of operation
- The bid-ask pip spread for the currencies you intend to trade
- The amount of margin and leverage ratio you are using
- The minimum trading unit size

All other primary concerns—requoting practices, pip ballooning, platform features, and stability should have been completed long before you decided to open an account.

Summary

Just one more chapter before you are ready to at least get your feet wet with a mini- or micro-account. You need to understand thoroughly how the various basic FOREX calculations are made. You will want to know them so that they are second nature. The time you spend at the computer should be directed 100% to trading decisions, not trying to figure out how many pips equals $100 or what your leverage factor will be on a trade.

Your goal here is to open a mini- or micro-account and get your feet wet. Since you do not have a trading method developed as yet, think in terms of "finger exercises"—getting familiar with basic FOREX calculations, order types and entry, all the platform features—all with a small quantity of real money on the line.

Figure 8.2 shows the basic functionalities you will want to learn. They must become second nature to you. It is also important to understand how to manipulate the platform, create charts and indicators, and adjust time scales, colors and other features.

Demo and Mini Account—Things to Learn

Basic FX Calculations
Basic FX Conversions and Ratios
Reading and Understanding Transaction Reports
Entering a Trade
Exiting a Trade
Cancelling a Trade
Entering a Stop
Failsafe Procedures

FIGURE 8.2 Learning FOREX—Process

Before trading a full account you should finish reading this book. It will assist you to develop at least a barebones approach to trading. After you finish Chapter 9, you will be ready to trade a Demo account and thereafter a mini-account with small amounts of real money in play.

Chapter

9

Pulling the Trigger

With the completion of this chapter, you will be ready to open a few Demo accounts and see for yourself why the FOREX markets are so exciting and popular.

Orders

An order is an instruction with defined parameters to your broker to take a specific action in the market, either now or in the future.

The number and types of currency trading orders that can be used with broker-dealers has expanded substantially in the past few years. Customer demand for more flexibility and trade execution options and competition have been the main driving forces. Broker-dealers, especially market makers, are happy to oblige, since a large palette of orders helps them manage their book.

Orders may be broken down into three primary categories of functionality—market, limit, and stop (see Table 9.1). All broker-dealers offer the basic three, and some brokers have unique in-house specialty orders. Because orders can be classified according to different criteria, they are cross-category. Some orders are not mutually exclusive and can be combined.

The trader's guiding rule should be to keep it simple. Don't use an order simply because it looks fun or interesting. Your trading method should be your primary guide to selecting an order arsenal. Complex orders distract from the

TABLE 9.1 Common Broker-Dealer FOREX Orders

FOREX Order Types	Combined
Market	No
Limit	Yes, with Stop
Stop	Yes, with Limit
Combination	Varies from Broker to Broker
Specialty	Varies from Broker to Broker

primary job of watching and analyzing the markets, are difficult to execute, and increase the chances for error.

Most broker-dealers delineate the various orders they accept in their trading platform documentation; please look there before e-mailing them. Order functionality is typically integrated into the trading platform but some of them can still be difficult to execute. You can Google "FOREX orders" and variations thereof to find some listings of broker-dealer web sites, FOREX portals, and learning web sites.

The exact definitions of many orders may vary slightly from broker to broker. Be sure you know your broker's terms before making any order.

Market Orders

A market order is an order to buy or sell at the market price. The buy may be to initiate a new position or liquidate a previous sell position. The sell may be to initiate a new position or liquidate a previous buy position. A market order may not be at the current price since like a river, prices are always flowing. Most market makers show you the price you will receive before you execute the order. In requoting, you do not get that price. Large orders, slow, fast, and illiquid ("thin") markets affect the price you will receive on a market order.

A buy adds to aggregate demand and pushes prices up, if only slightly; a sell adds to aggregate supply and has the opposite effect. The bid-ask spread in FOREX reflects this, as well as protecting your broker and helping him maintain an orderly book—and make a fair profit by serving you.

Limit Orders

A limit order specifies a specific price to execute your order. It may also specify duration; how long you wish to keep the order active. If the price is touched within the specified duration, your order becomes a market order.

There is also a stop-limit order. You specify a price and also a maximum range beyond that price for which the order can be executed. The advantage of a stop-limit order is that you will get the price you want if that price is reached. The disadvantage is that if prices do not trade in your specified range, your order remains unexecuted. In a fast market a stop-limit order may be a complete waste of effort; it simply will not be executed.

Suggested Rules of Thumb:

- Use market orders in normal markets; use limit orders for large orders and in fast, slow, and thin markets. A market order in a fast market, such as after the release of a news item, can be a disaster.

- A Good Till Cancelled (GTC) order remains active until the trader cancels it.

- A Good For The Day (GTD) order remains in the market for the duration of the trading day. Insofar as FOREX is a continuous market, the end of the day must be for a set hour.

- Be sure to keep track of all open orders you have in every market. It is your responsibility to cancel them, not the broker's.

Stop Orders

A "stop order" is the terminology used for a limit order that liquidates or offsets an open position.

An automatic trailing stop is offered by several broker-dealers. This raises or lowers your stop by a fixed value as the market goes in your position, thus protecting some of your profits. You can, of course, mechanically apply trailing stops. They are great in theory, not quite so great in practice. They work better with some trading methods than with others.

A major debate has raged for years as to whether traders should use stop-loss orders in the market or simply keep them to themselves—mental stops—and wait for the market to reach that price and then use a market order. Many traders believe brokers use stops entered in the market to balance their book. Brokers are occasionally accused of running or harvesting stops—moving their data feed specifically to execute the stop order. This does happen; how often is very difficult to say.

Beginners should use stops. Once you have some experience in the market—and if and only if you have good discipline—then keep mental stops. It is very easy to ignore a mental stop and hope the market will turn back in your favor—and it usually does not. Yes, by using stops the broker can see your order; and, yes, stops may be harvested; and, yes, stop fills—especially without limits—may be poor. But we still recommend that the new trader use them.

Never leave an open position unattended without a stop. I still remember an incident from when I was a young commodities trader and watched the markets from the local Peavey office. Soybeans were limit up with a profit of $1,000. I left to get a cup of coffee from the cantina, returning in less than five minutes to see the market was limit down—a $1,000 loss.

Combination Orders

Many orders are not mutually exclusive and can, if the broker permits it, be combined. A common one is a One Cancels The Other (OCO) order. The execution of one order automatically cancels the other. You might enter both a buy and sell order in a market awaiting a breakout from a narrow trading range. If either is executed, it cancels the other.

Specialty Orders

There are perhaps a dozen or more specialty orders; the beginner is advised to stay away from them. A few brokers offer orders unique to their trading platform. Time triggers specify a time when an order should become active and for how long. A Box-Top is a market order that automatically changes to a limit order if it is not. executed at the market price right away. Limit On Close (LOC) and Limit On Open (LOO) are executed at the closing price or the limit price if that price is equal to or better than a specified limit price.

The FOREX forums are a good place to find out how traders use specialty stops as well as the pros and cons.

Order Placement Walk-Through

This will vary from broker to broker, depending on how their trading platform is organized. As of 2008 placing an order is a simple and pleasant experience. Your trading platform really does all the calculation for you. Traders can typically see the various parameters of their orders before executing—leverage, margins, pips-to-dollars (if the dollar is your account-denominated currency), and other pertinent information.

Practice with a broker's order placement system first on a Demo account. When you open a mini or micro account, practice again with very small amounts of real money. I suggest lots of a maximum of 500 units initially.

Order Execution

Traders using an online trading platform click on the "Buy" or "Sell" button after having specified the underlying currency pair, the desired number of units

> **FX Order Classification**
>
> Market Orders
> Limit Orders
> Stop Orders
> Combination Orders
> Specialty Orders

FIGURE 9.1 HotspotFX Online Order Screen
Source: HotspotFX, www.hotspotfx.com.

to trade, the price, and the order type. The execution of the order is almost always instantaneous. This means that the price seen at the exact time of the click will be given to the customer. See Figure 9.1.

It is possible to place an order by phone in an emergency situation, but almost unheard of today.

Order Confirmation

Online traders receive a screen message indicating confirmation of an order within seconds after the trade has been accepted and executed, as shown in Figure 9.2. The trade will also show up on the platform's Open Positions page.

Traders can also cancel any limit order that has not been executed at any time. Most brokers respond with a message similar to the one seen in Figure 9.3.

Transaction Exposure

Your broker's trading platform will also inform you of your transaction exposure: how much of your capital and margin you have used for the trade (see Figure 9.3).

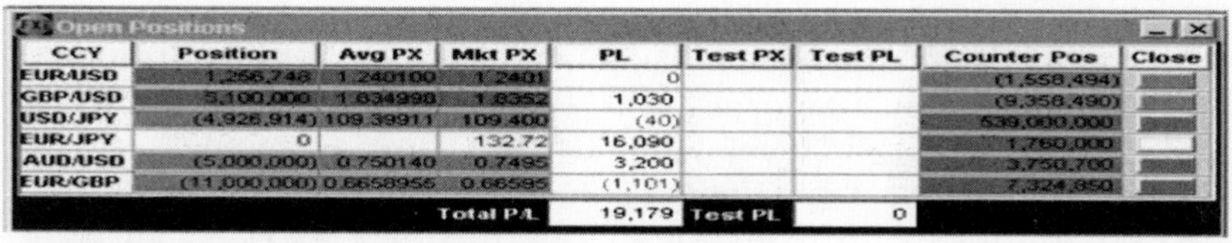

CCY	Position	Avg PX	Mkt PX	PL	Test PX	Test PL	Counter Pos	Close
EUR/USD	1,256,748	1.240100	1.2401	0			(1,558,494)	
GBP/USD	5,100,000	1.834990	1.8352	1,030			(9,358,490)	
USD/JPY	(4,928,914)	109.39911	109.400	(40)			539,000,000	
EUR/JPY	0		132.72	16,090			1,780,000	
AUD/USD	(5,000,000)	0.750140	0.7495	3,200			3,750,700	
EUR/GBP	(11,000,000)	0.6658956	0.66595	(1,101)			7,324,850	
			Total P/L	19,179	Test PL	0		

FIGURE 9.2 HotspotFX Open Positions Screen
Source: HotspotFX, www.hotspotfx.com.

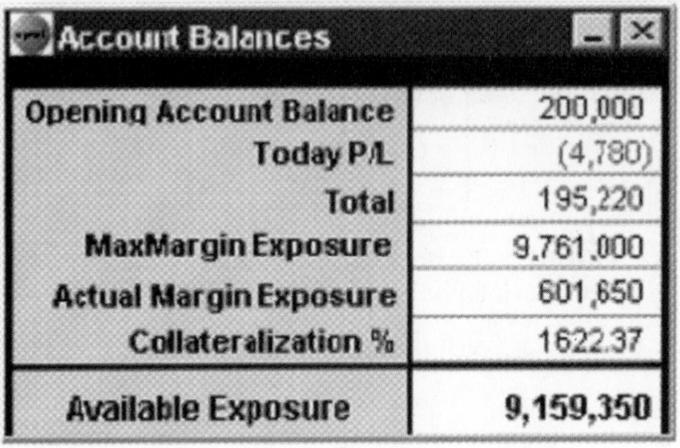

Account Balances	
Opening Account Balance	200,000
Today P/L	(4,780)
Total	195,220
MaxMargin Exposure	9,761,000
Actual Margin Exposure	601,650
Collateralization %	1622.37
Available Exposure	9,159,350

FIGURE 9.3 HotspotFX Transaction Exposure Screen
Source: HotspotFX, www.hotspotfx.com.

Once your trade is executed, it will show on your broker's Open Trades page. When the trade is closed and complete, a summary will show on the Account Summary page. As far as the order and accounting information you require is concerned, almost all brokers have this down pat on their platforms. One of the purposes of the Demo account is allowing you to become second-nature comfortable with how it all works and ties together.

Tip: Before executing an order, close your eyes for a few seconds, take a deep breath. Review all aspects of the order one last time before clicking "Submit." The two most common order entry errors are selecting "Buy" instead of "Sell" (especially to offset an order) and entering the incorrect number of units. Note what values are preset (if any) on your broker's trading platform.

Remember, to offset an order it must be for the identical currency pair and number of units. A Buy is offset with a Sell and a Sell is offset with a Buy. If you initially buy 10,000 units and then sell 15,000 units, you will have a new open position selling 5,000 units.

Summary

A book could be written about FOREX orders, especially stop orders; how and when to execute them, the pros and cons. The vast majority of traders can fully work their trading method with market, limit, and stop orders. *Commodity Trading with Stops* by Joseph Maxwell (Speer Books, 1977) is an excellent overview of the subject. It is out of print but typically available on eBay.com and Amazon.com.

Know which type of orders you need, and know how they work. Make sure you and your broker are on the same page with respect to what they mean. Test your orders thoroughly in a Demo account. A few trading systems require substantial order manipulation, but your time is generally better spent studying the markets than worrying about how to execute complicated order strategies and techniques.

"Well, doggies," as Jed Clampett would say, you are ready to trade. At this stage in the game only execute very small unit lots on a micro- or mini-account to get a feel for how things work. You need to develop a trading method and money management parameters before trading larger amounts on a mini-account or moving on to a full account.

Part

The Tools of the Trade

10

Fundamental Analysis

I t is commonly accepted that there are two major schools when formulating a trading strategy for any market, be it securities, futures, or currencies. These two disciplines are called fundamental analysis and technical analysis. The former is based on economic factors while the latter is concerned with price actions. Of course, the trader may opt to include elements of both disciplines while honing his or her personal trading strategy. Typically, fundamentals are about the long term; technicals are about the short term. Keep in mind what Lord Keynes once wrote: "In the long run we are all dead."

Supply and Demand

Fundamental analysis is a study of the economy and is based on the assumption that the supply and demand for currencies is a result of economic processes that can be observed in practice and that can be predicted. Fundamental analysis studies the relationship between the evolution of exchange rates and economic indicators, a relationship which it verifies and uses to make predictions.

For currencies, a fundamental trading strategy consists of strategic assessments in which a certain currency is traded based on virtually any criteria excluding the price action. These criteria include, but are not limited to, the economic condition of the country that the currency represents, monetary policy, and other elements that are fundamental to economies.

The focus of fundamental analysis lies in the economic, social, and political forces that drive supply and demand. There is no single set of beliefs that guides fundamental analysis, yet most fundamental analysts look at various macro-economic indicators, such as economic growth rates, interest rates, inflation, and unemployment. Several theories prevail as to how currencies should be valued.

Done alone, fundamental analysis can be stressful for traders who deal with commodities, currencies, and other "margined" products. The reason for this is that fundamental analysis often does not provide specific entry and exit points, and therefore it can be difficult for traders to control risk when utilizing leverage techniques.

Currency prices are a reflection of the balance between supply and demand for currencies. Interest rates and the overall strength of the economy are the two primary factors that affect supply and demand. Economic indicators (for example, gross domestic product, foreign investment, and the trade balance) reflect the overall health of an economy. Therefore, they are responsible for the underlying changes in supply and demand for a particular currency. A tremendous amount of data relating to these indicators is released at regular intervals, and some of this data is significant. Data that is related to interest rates and international trade is analyzed very closely.

Interest Rates

If there is an uncertainty in the market in terms of interest rates, then any developments regarding interest rates can have a direct effect on the currency markets. Generally, when a country raises its interest rates, the country's currency strengthens in relation to other currencies as assets are shifted away from it to gain a higher return elsewhere. Interest rate hikes, however, are usually not good news for stock markets. This is due to the fact that many investors withdraw money from a country's stock market when there is an increase in interest rates, causing the country's currency to weaken. See Figure 10.1.

Knowing which effect prevails can be tricky, but usually there is an agreement among practitioners in the field as to what the interest rate move will do. The producer price index, the consumer price index, and the gross domestic product have proven to be the indicators with the biggest impact. The timing of interest rate moves is usually known in advance. It is generally known that these moves take place after regular meetings of the BOE (Bank of England), FED (U.S. Federal Reserve), ECB (European Central Bank), BOJ (Bank of Japan), and other central banks.

Balance of Trade

The trade balance portrays the net difference (over a period of time) between the imports and exports of a nation. When the value of imports becomes more than that of exports, the trade balance shows a deficit (this is, for the most part,

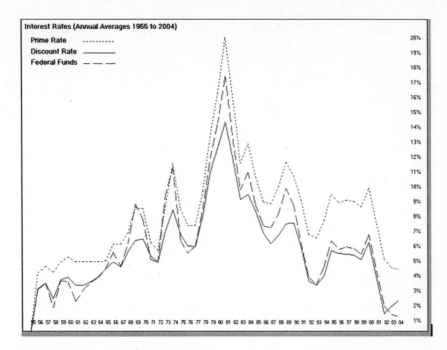

FIGURE 10.1 U.S. Interest Rates

considered unfavorable). For example, if Euros are sold for other domestic national currencies, such as U.S. dollars, to pay for imports, the value of the currency will depreciate due to the flow of dollars outside the country. By contrast, if trade figures show an increase in exports, money will flow into the country and increase the value of the currency. In some ways, however, a deficit is not necessarily a bad thing. A deficit is only negative if the deficit is greater than market expectations and therefore will trigger a negative price movement. See Table 10.1.

TABLE 10.1 U.S. Balance of Trade, 2003 (in thousands of U.S. dollars)			
Country	Exports	Imports	Balance
China	28,418.5	152,379.1	−123,960.6
Japan	52,063.7	118,029.0	−65,965.3
Canada	169,768.8	224,165.3	−54,396.5
Mexico	97,457.3	138,073.5	−40,616.2
Germany	28,847.9	68,047.1	−39,199.2
Italy	10,569.9	25,436.6	−14,866.7
Taiwan	17,487.9	31,599.9	−14,112.0

(continued on next page)

TABLE 10.1 *(continued)*			
Country	Exports	Imports	Balance
Saudi Arabia	4,595.9	18,069.1	−13,473.2
South Korea	24,098.6	36,963.3	−12,864.7
France	17,068.2	29,221.2	−12,153.0
Thailand	5,841.8	15,180.8	−9,339.0
United Kingdom	33,895.7	42,666.9	−8,771.2
India	4,986.4	13,052.7	−8,066.3
Sweden	3,225.5	11,124.7	−7,899.2
Indonesia	2,520.1	9,520.0	−6,999.9
Russia	2,450.0	8,598.4	−6,148.4
Israel	6,878.4	12,770.3	−5,891.9
Norway	1,467.5	5,212.2	−3,744.7
Austria	1,792.6	4,489.3	−2,696.7
Denmark	1,548.3	3,718.5	−2,170.2
Philippines	7,992.1	10,061.0	−2,068.9
Switzerland	8,660.0	10,667.8	−2,007.8
Finland	1,713.8	3,597.9	−1,884.1
South Africa	2,821.3	4,637.6	−1,816.3
Hungary	934.1	2,699.2	−1,765.1
Portugal	863.0	1,967.3	−1,104.3
Turkey	2,904.3	3,788.0	−883.7
Kuwait	1,509.0	2,276.8	−767.8
Spain	5,935.3	6,708.1	−772.8
Czech Republic	672.3	1,394.4	−722.1
Poland	758.7	1,325.8	−567.1
Lichtenstein	15.9	261.9	−246.0
Iceland	242.2	283.0	−40.8
Albania	9.8	4.4	5.4
North Korea	7.9	0.1	7.8
Luxembourg	279.0	265.0	14.0
Greece	1,191.3	616.2	575.1
Singapore	16,575.8	15,158.0	1,417.8
Hong Kong	13,542.1	8,850.2	4,691.9
Belgium	15,217.9	10,140.6	5,077.3
Australia	13,103.8	6,413.9	6,689.9
Netherlands	20,703.0	10,971.8	9,731.2

Source: FTDWebMaster, Foreign Trade Division, U.S. Census Bureau, Washington, D.C.

Purchasing Power Parity

Purchasing power parity (PPP) is a theory that states that exchange rates between currencies are in equilibrium when their purchasing power is the same in each of the two countries. This means that the exchange rate between two countries should equal the ratio of the two countries' price level of a fixed basket of goods and services. When a country's domestic price level is increasing (i.e., a country experiences inflation), that country's exchange rate must depreciate in order to return to PPP.

The basis for PPP is the "law of one price." In the absence of transportation and other transaction costs, competitive markets will equalize the price of an identical good in two countries when the prices are expressed in the same currency. For example, a particular TV set that sells for 500 U.S. Dollars (USD) in Seattle should cost 750 Canadian Dollars (CAD) in Vancouver when the exchange rate between Canada and the United States is 1.50 USD/CAD. If the price of the TV in Vancouver cost only 700 CAD, however, consumers in Seattle would prefer buying the TV set in Vancouver. If this process (called arbitrage) is carried out on a large scale, the American consumers buying Canadian goods will bid up the value of the Canadian Dollar, thus making Canadian goods more costly to them. This process continues until the goods again have the same price. There are three caveats with this law of one price: (1) As mentioned above, transportation costs, barriers to trade, and other transaction costs can be significant. (2) There must be competitive markets for the goods and services in both countries. (3) The law of one price only applies to tradable goods; immobile goods such as houses and many services that are local are, of course, not traded between countries.

Economists use two versions of purchasing power parity: absolute PPP and relative PPP. Absolute PPP was described in the previous paragraph; it refers to the equalization of price levels across countries. Put formally, the exchange rate between Canada and the United States ECAD/USD is equal to the price level in Canada PCAN divided by the price level in the United States PUSA. Assume that the price level ratio PCAD/PUSD implies a PPP exchange rate of 1.3 CAD per 1 USD. If today's exchange rate ECAD/USD is 1.5 CAD per 1 USD, PPP theory implies that the CAD will appreciate (get stronger) against the USD, and the USD will in turn depreciate (get weaker) against the CAD.

Relative PPP refers to rates of changes of price levels, that is, inflation rates. This proposition states that the rate of appreciation of a currency is equal to the difference in inflation rates between the foreign and the home country. For example, if Canada has an inflation rate of one percent and the United States has an inflation rate of three percent, the U.S. Dollar will depreciate against the Canadian Dollar by two percent per year. This proposition holds well empirically, especially when the inflation differences are large.

Symbol	Currency	PPP
CHF	Swiss Franc	+54
DKK	Danish Krone	+42
JPY	Japanese Yen	+36
SEK	Swedish Krona	+35
NOK	Norwegian Krone	+30
GBP	British Pound	+22
EUR	Euro Currency	+16
AUD	Australian Dollar	+5
NZD	New Zealand Dollar	-1
CAD	Canadian Dollar	-10
KRW	Korean Won	-38
MXN	Mexican Peso	-40
HUF	Hungarian Forint	-43
CZK	Czech Koruna	-45
PLN	Polish Zloty	-51

FIGURE 10.2   Purchasing Power Parity

Source: Office for Economic Cooperation and Development.

The simplest way to calculate purchasing power parity between two countries is to compare the price of a "standard" good that is, in fact, identical across countries. Every year *The Economist* magazine publishes a lighthearted version of PPP: Its "Hamburger Index" lists the price of a McDonald's hamburger in various countries around the world. More sophisticated versions of PPP look at a large number of goods and services. One of the key problems in computing a comprehensive PPP is that people in different countries consume very different sets of goods and services, making it difficult to compare the purchasing power between countries. See Figure 10.2.

Gross Domestic Product

The gross domestic product (GDP) is the total market value of all goods and services produced either by domestic or foreign companies within a country's borders. GDP indicates the pace at which a country's economy is growing (or shrinking) and is considered the broadest indicator of economic output and growth.

GDPs of different countries may be compared (see Table 10.2) by converting their value in national currency according to either (a) exchange rates prevailing on international currency markets, or (b) the purchasing power parity (PPP) of each currency relative to a selected standard (usually the U.S. dollar).

The relative ranking of countries may differ dramatically depending upon which approach is used: Using official exchange rates can routinely understate the relative effective domestic purchasing power of the average producer or consumer within a less-developed economy by 50 to 60 percent, owing to the weakness of local currencies on world markets.

TABLE 10.2	Gross Domestic Product, PPP Basis		
Rank Entity	PPP Total USD (billions)	PPP/Capita USD	Population 2003 est.
1. European Union	10,840	28,600	379,000,000
2. USA	10,400	37,600	290,343,000
3. China	5,700	4,400	1,287,000,000
4. Japan	3,550	28,000	127,215,000
5. India	2,660	2,540	1,049,701,000
6. Germany	2,180	26,600	82,399,000
7. France	1,540	25,700	60,181,000
8. United Kingdom	1,520	25,300	60,095,000
9. Italy	1,440	25,000	57,998,000
10. Russia	1,350	9,300	144,526,000
11. Brazil	1,340	7,600	182,032,000
12. South Korea	931	19,400	48,249,000
13. Canada	923	29,400	32,207,000
14. Mexico	900	9,000	104,908,000
15. Spain	828	20,700	40,218,000
16. Indonesia	663	3,100	234,894,000
17. Australia	528	27,000	19,732,000
18. Turkey	468	7,000	68,110,000
19. Iran	456	7,000	68,279,000
20. Netherlands	434	26,900	16,151,000
21. South Africa	432	10,000	42,769,000
22. Thailand	429	6,900	70,000,000
23. Taiwan	406	18,000	22,116,000
24. Argentina	391	10,200	38,000,000
25. Poland	368	9,500	38,000,000

Source: CIA World Factbook: PPP, PPP/Capita, Population.

However, comparison based on official exchange rates can offer a better indication of a country's purchasing power on the international market for goods and services.

Intervention

Another important fundamental influence on FOREX currency prices is called intervention. This occurs when an official regulatory agency or a financial institution with one government directly coerces the exchange rate of its currency, usually by reevaluation, devaluation, or by the manipulation of imports and exports in some way.

Such actions may cause broad and erratic changes in the exchange rate with foreign currencies. However, it is from such anomalies that the FOREX trader may profit, if the proper stop-loss safeguards are in place.

Other Economic Indicators

Industrial Production

Industrial production (IP) is a chain-weighted measure of the change in the production of the nation's factories, mines, and utilities, as well as a measure of their industrial capacity and how many available resources among factories, utilities, and mines are being used (commonly known as capacity utilization). The manufacturing sector accounts for one-quarter of the economy. The capacity utilization rate provides an estimate of how much factory capacity is in use.

Purchasing Managers Index

The National Association of Purchasing Managers (NAPM), now called the Institute for Supply Management, releases a monthly composite index of national manufacturing conditions, constructed from data on new orders, production, supplier delivery times, backlogs, inventories, prices, employment, export orders, and import orders. It is divided into manufacturing and non-manufacturing subindices.

Producer Price Index

The producer price index (PPI) is a measure of price changes in the manufacturing sector. It measures average changes in selling prices received by domestic producers in the manufacturing, mining, agriculture, and electric utility industries for their output. The PPIs most often used for economic analysis are those for finished goods, intermediate goods, and crude goods.

Consumer Price Index

The consumer price index (CPI) is a measure of the average price level paid by urban consumers (80 percent of the population) for a fixed basket of goods and services. It reports price changes in over 200 categories. The CPI also includes various user fees and taxes directly associated with the prices of specific goods and services.

Durable Goods

The durable goods orders indicator measures new orders placed with domestic manufacturers for immediate and future delivery of factory hard goods. A durable good is defined as a good that lasts an extended period of time (over three years) during which its services are extended.

Employment Cost Index

Payroll employment is a measure of the number of jobs in more than 500 industries in all 50 states and 255 metropolitan areas. The employment estimates are based on a survey of larger businesses and count the number of paid employees working part-time or full-time in the nation's business and government establishments.

Retail Sales

The retail sales report is a measure of the total receipts of retail stores from samples representing all sizes and kinds of business in retail trade throughout the nation. It is the timeliest indicator of broad consumer spending patterns and is adjusted for normal seasonal variation, holidays, and trading-day differences. Retail sales include durable and nondurable merchandise sold, and services and excise taxes incidental to the sale of merchandise. Excluded are sales taxes collected directly from the customer.

Housing Starts

The housing starts report measures the number of residential units on which construction is begun each month. A start in construction is defined as the beginning of excavation of the foundation for the building and is comprised primarily of residential housing. Housing is very interest rate–sensitive and is one of the first sectors to react to changes in interest rates. Significant reaction of starts/permits to changing interest rates signals that interest rates are nearing a trough or a peak. To analyze the data, focus on the percentage change in levels from the previous month. The report is released around the middle of the following month.

Forecasting

Fundamental analysis refers to the study of the core underlying elements that influence the economy of a particular entity. It is a method of study that attempts to predict price action and market trends by analyzing economic indicators, government policy, and societal factors (to name just a few elements) within a business cycle framework. If you think of the financial markets as a big clock, the fundamentals are the gears and springs that move the hands around the face. Anyone walking down the street can look at this clock and tell you what time it is now, but the fundamentalist can tell you how it came to be this time and more importantly, what time (or more precisely, what price) it will be in the future.

There is a tendency to pigeonhole traders into two distinct schools of market analysis—fundamental and technical. Indeed, the first question posed to you after you tell someone that you are a trader is generally "Are you a technician or a fundamentalist?" The reality is that it has become increasingly difficult to be a purist of either persuasion. Fundamentalists need to keep an eye on the various signals derived from the price action on charts, while few technicians can afford to completely ignore impending economic data, critical political decisions, or the myriad of societal issues that influence prices.

Bearing in mind that the financial underpinnings of any country, trading bloc, or multinational industry take into account many factors, including social, political, and economic influences, staying on top of an extremely fluid fundamental picture can be challenging. At the same time, you'll find that your knowledge and understanding of a dynamic global market will increase immeasurably as you delve further and further into the complexities and subtleties of the fundamentals of the markets.

Fundamental analysis is a very effective way to forecast economic conditions, but not necessarily exact market prices. For example, when analyzing an economist's forecast of the upcoming GDP or employment report, you begin to get a fairly clear picture of the general health of the economy and the forces at work behind it. However, you'll need to come up with a precise method as to how best to translate this information into entry and exit points for a particular trading strategy.

A trader who studies the markets using fundamental analysis generally creates models to formulate a trading strategy. These models typically utilize a host of empirical data and attempt to forecast market behavior and estimate future values or prices by using past values of core economic indicators. These forecasts are then used to derive specific trades that best exploit this information.

Forecasting models are as numerous and varied as the traders and market buffs that create them. Two people can look at the same data and come up with two completely different conclusions about how the market will be influenced by it. Therefore it is important that before casting yourself into a particular mold regarding any aspect of market analysis, you study the fundamentals and see how they best fit your trading style and expectations.

Do not succumb to "paralysis by analysis." Given the multitude of factors that fall under the heading of "The Fundamentals," there is a distinct danger of information overload. Sometimes traders fall into this trap and are unable to pull the trigger on a trade. This is one of the reasons why many traders turn to technical analysis. To some, technical analysis is seen as a way to transform all of the fundamental factors that influence the markets into one simple tool: prices. However, trading a particular market without knowing a great deal about the exact nature of its underlying elements is like fishing without bait. You might get lucky and snare a few on occasion, but it's not the best approach over the long haul.

For FOREX traders, the fundamentals are everything that makes a country tick. From interest rates and central bank policy to natural disasters, the fundamentals are a dynamic mix of distinct plans, erratic behaviors, and unforeseen events. Therefore, it is easier to get a handle on the most influential contributors to this diverse mix than it is to formulate a comprehensive list of all the fundamentals.

Economic indicators are snippets of financial and economic data published by various agencies of the government or private sector. These statistics, which are made public on a regularly scheduled basis, help market observers monitor the pulse of the economy. Therefore, they are religiously followed by almost everyone in the financial markets. With so many people poised to react to the same information, economic indicators in general have tremendous potential to generate volume and to move prices in the markets. While on the surface it might seem that an advanced degree in economics would come in handy to analyze and then trade on the glut of information contained in these economic indicators, a few simple guidelines are all that is necessary to track, organize, and make trading decisions based on the data.

Know exactly when each economic indicator is due to be released. Keep a calendar on your desk or trading station that contains the date and time when each statistic will be made public. You can find these calendars on the N.Y. Federal Reserve Bank web site using this link: http://www.ny.frb.org/. Then search for "economic indicators." The same information is also available from many other sources on the Web or from the company you use to execute your trades.

Keeping track of the calendar of economic indicators will also help you make sense out of otherwise unanticipated price action in the market. Consider this scenario: It's Monday morning and the U.S. Dollar has been in a tailspin for three weeks. As such, it is safe to assume that many traders are holding large short USD positions. However, the employment data for the United States is due to be released on Friday. It is very likely that with this key piece of economic information soon to be made public, the USD could experience a short-term rally leading up to the data on Friday as traders pare down their short positions.

The point here is that economic indicators can affect prices directly (following their release to the public) or indirectly (as traders massage their positions in anticipation of the data).

Understand which particular aspect of the economy is being revealed in the data. For example, you should know which indicators measure the growth of the economy (GDP) versus those that measure inflation (PPI, CPI) or employment (nonfarm payrolls). After you follow the data for a while, you will become very familiar with the nuances of each economic indicator and which part of the economy it measures.

Not all economic indicators are created equal. Well, they might have been created with equal importance but along the way, some have acquired much greater potential to move the markets than others. Market participants will place higher regard on one statistic versus another depending on the state of the economy.

Know which indicators the markets are keying on. For example, if prices (inflation) are not a crucial issue for a particular country, the markets will probably not as keenly anticipate or react to inflation data. However, if economic growth is a vexing problem, changes in employment data or GDP will be eagerly anticipated and could precipitate tremendous volatility following its release.

The data itself is not as important as whether or not it falls within market expectations. Besides knowing when all the data will hit the wires, it is vitally important that you know what economists and other market pundits are forecasting for each indicator. For example, knowing the economic consequences of an unexpected monthly rise of 0.3 percent in the producer price index (PPI) is not nearly as vital to your short-term trading decisions as it is to know that this month the market was looking for PPI to fall by 0.1 percent. As mentioned, you should know that PPI measures prices and that an unexpected rise could be a sign of inflation. But analyzing the longer-term ramifications of this unexpected monthly rise in prices can wait until after you have taken advantage of the trading opportunities presented by the data. Once again, market expectations for all economic releases are published on various sources on the Web and you should post these expectations on your calendar along with the release date of the indicator.

Do not get caught up in the headlines, however. Part of getting a handle on what the market is forecasting for various economic indicators is knowing the key aspects of each indicator. While your macroeconomics professor might have drilled the significance of the unemployment rate into your head, even junior traders can tell you that the headline figure is for amateurs and that the most closely watched detail in the payroll data is the nonfarm payrolls figure. Other economic indicators are similar in that the headline figure is not nearly as closely watched as the finer points of the data. PPI, for example, measures changes in producer prices. But the statistic most closely watched by the markets is PPI, minus food and energy price changes. Traders know that the food and energy component of the data is much too volatile and subject to revisions on a month-to-month basis to provide an accurate reading on the changes in producer prices.

Speaking of revisions, do not be too quick to pull that trigger should a particular economic indicator fall outside of market expectations. Contained in each new economic indicator released to the public are revisions to previously released data. For example, if durable goods should rise by 0.5 percent in the current month, while the market is anticipating them to fall, the unexpected rise could be the result of a downward revision to the prior month. Look at revisions to older data because in this case, the previous month's durable goods figure might have been originally reported as a rise of 0.5 percent but now, along with the new figures, it is being revised to indicate a rise of only 0.1 percent. Therefore, the unexpected rise in the current month is likely the result of a downward revision to the previous month's data.

Do not forget that there are two sides to a trade in the foreign exchange market. So, while you might have a handle on the complete package of economic indicators published in the United States or Europe, most other countries also publish similar economic data. The important thing to remember here is that not all countries are as efficient as the G8 in releasing this information. Once again, if you are going to trade the currency of a particular country, you need to find out the particulars about that country's economic indicators. As mentioned earlier, not all of these indicators carry the same weight in the markets and not all of them are as accurate as others. Do your homework so you won't be caught off guard.

When it comes to focusing exclusively on the impact that economic indicators have on price action in a particular market, the foreign exchange markets are the most challenging. Therefore, they have the greatest potential for profits of any market. Obviously, factors other than economic indicators move prices and as such make other markets more or less potentially profitable. But since a currency is a proxy for the country it represents, the economic health of that country is priced into the currency. One very important way to measure the health of an economy is through economic indicators. The challenge comes in diligently keeping track of the nuts and bolts of each country's particular economic information package. Here are a few general comments about economic indicators and some of the more closely watched data.

Most economic indicators can be divided into leading and lagging indicators. Leading indicators are economic factors that change before the economy starts to follow a particular pattern or trend. Leading indicators are used to predict changes in the economy. Lagging indicators are economic factors that change after the economy has already begun to follow a particular pattern or trend.

The problem with fundamental analysis is that it is difficult to convert the "qualitative" information into a specific price prediction. With FOREX leverage being what it is, it is seldom enough to know that a report is "bullish" for a currency without being able to attach specific values.

Econometric analysis attempts to quantify the often qualitative fundamental factors into a mathematical model. These models can become enormously complex. The problems with econometric analysis are twofold: It is difficult to objectively quantify qualitative information such as a news announcement. The interactions and specific weights of each factor are constantly in flux and the relationships between them are almost certainly nonlinear. Relationships that hold today are invalid tomorrow.

Even if you opt for a technical analysis trading approach, as most traders do, *do not* completely ignore the fundamentals. Use a new service to do a daily take on what's happening. Remember: Be aware of pending reports, statistical releases, and so on, as they often will cause a violent market reaction one way or the other. I offer more on using the news in Chapter 16, Tactics and Strategy.

I consulted numerous sources while compiling the current chapter. I wish to acknowledge specifically http://www.sbfx.net/fundamental_analysis.aspx for their informative web site. Fundamental analysis is a very deep well. It is important to understand the basic fundamentals that drive currency prices, even though most traders use technical analysis to make specific day-to-day trading decisions.

Chapter 11

Technical Analysis

Overview

Probably the most popular and successful method of making decisions and analyzing FOREX markets is technical analysis. The difference between technical and fundamental analyses is that technical analysis ignores fundamental factors and is applied only to the price action of the market. While fundamental data can often provide only a long-term forecast of exchange rate movements, technical analysis has become the primary tool to successfully analyze and trade shorter-term price movements, as well as to set profit targets and stop-loss safeguards because of its ability to generate price-specific information and forecasts.

Historically, technical analysis in the futures markets has focused on the six price fields available during any given period of time: open, high, low, close, volume, and open interest. Since the FOREX market has no central exchange, it is very difficult to estimate the latter two fields, volume and open interest. In this chapter, we therefore limit our analysis to the first four price fields.

Technical analysis consists primarily of a variety of technical studies, each of which can be interpreted to predict market direction or to generate buy and sell signals. Many technical studies share one common important tool: a price-time chart that emphasizes selected characteristics in the price motion of the underlying security. One great advantage of technical analysis is its "visualness."

Bar Charts

Bar charts are the most widely used type of chart in security market technical analysis and date back to the last decade of the nineteenth century. They are popular because they are easy to construct and understand. These charts are constructed by representing intraday, daily, weekly, or monthly activity as a vertical bar. Opening and closing prices are represented by horizontal marks to the left and right of the vertical bar respectively. Spotting both patterns and the trend of a market, two of the essentials of chart reading, is often easiest using bar charts. Bar charts present the data individually, without linking prices to neighboring prices. Each set of price fields is a single "island."

Each vertical bar has the components shown in Figure 11.1.

Figure 11.2 shows a daily bar chart for the EUR/USD currency pair for the month of June 2003. The vertical scale on the right represents the cost of one Euro in terms of U.S. Dollars. The horizontal legend at the bottom of the chart represents the day of week.

A common method of classifying the vertical bars is to show the relationships between the opening and closing prices within a single time interval, as seen in Figure 11.3.

Graphically, an open/high/low/close (OHLC) bar chart is defined using the following algorithm:

OHLC Bar Chart Algorithm

- Step 1—One vertical rectangle whose upper boundary represents the high for the day and whose lower boundary represents the low for the given time period.

- Step 2—One horizontal rectangle to the left of the high-low rectangle whose central value represents the opening price for the given period.

- Step 3—One horizontal rectangle to the right of the high-low rectangle whose central value represents the closing price for the given period.

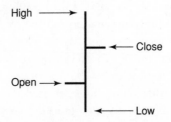

FIGURE 11.1   Anatomy of Single Vertical Bar

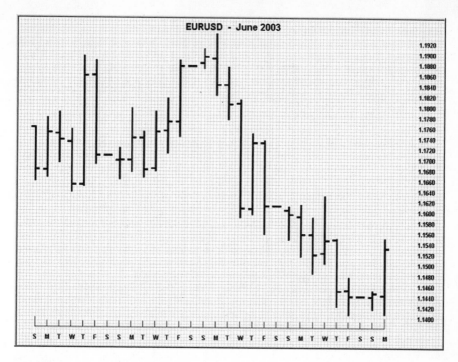

FIGURE 11.2 Vertical Bar Chart

One interesting variation to the standard OHLC bar chart was developed by author/trader Burton Pugh is the 1930s. His model involved connecting the previous set of quotes to the current set of quotes, which generates a continuous line representation of price movements. There are four basic formations between two adjacent vertical bars in Burton's system. (See Figure 11.4.)

Bar chart interpretation is one of the most fascinating and well-studied topics in the realm of technical analysis. Recurring bar chart formations have been labeled, categorized, and analyzed in detail. Common formations like tops, bottoms, head-and-shoulders, inverted head-and-shoulders, lines of support and resistance, reversals, and so forth, are examined in the following sections.

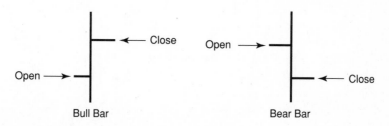

FIGURE 11.3 Anatomy of Bull and Bear Bars

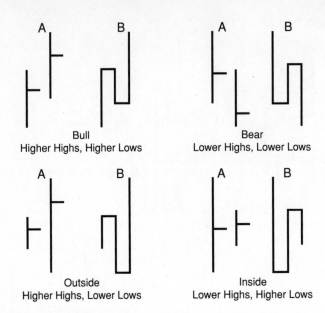

Bull
Higher Highs, Higher Lows

Bear
Lower Highs, Lower Lows

Outside
Higher Highs, Lower Lows

Inside
Lower Highs, Higher Lows

FIGURE 11.4   Continuous Line Bar Chart

Trend Lines

A trend can be up, down, or lateral and is represented by drawing a straight line above the daily highs in a downward trend and a straight line below the daily lows in an upward trend. See Figure 11.5.

A common trading technique involves the intersection of the trend line with the most recent prices. If the trend line for a downward trend crosses

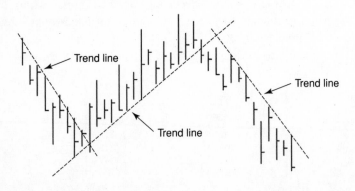

FIGURE 11.5   Bar Chart with Trend Lines

through the most recent prices, a buy signal is generated. Conversely, if the trend line for an upward trend passes through the most recent prices, then a sell signal is generated.

Support and Resistance

Support levels indicate the price at which most traders feel that prices will move higher. There is sufficient demand for a security to cause a halt in a downward trend and turn the trend up. You can spot support levels on the bar charts by looking for a sequence of daily lows that fluctuate only slightly along a horizontal line. When a support level is penetrated (the price drops below the support level) it often becomes a resistance level; this is because traders want to limit their losses and will sell later, when prices approach the former level.

Like support levels, resistance levels are horizontal lines on the bar chart. They mark the upper level for trading, or a price at which sellers typically outnumber buyers. When resistance levels are broken, the price moves above the resistance level, and often does so decisively. See Figure 11.6.

Many traders find lines of support and resistance useful in determining the placement of stop-loss and take-profit limit orders.

Recognizing Chart Patterns

Proper identification of an ongoing trend can be a tremendous asset to the trader. However, the trader must also learn to recognize recurring chart patterns that disrupt the continuity of trend lines. Broadly speaking, these chart patterns can be categorized as reversal patterns and continuation patterns.

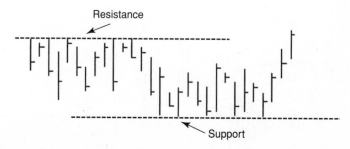

FIGURE 11.6 Bar Chart with Support and Resistance Lines

Reversal Patterns

Reversal patterns are important because they inform the trader that a market entry point is unfolding or that it may be time to liquidate an open position. Figures 11.7 through 11.10 illustrate the most common reversal patterns.

FIGURE 11.7   Double Top

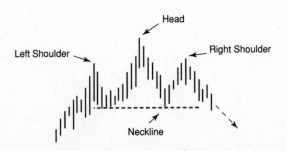

FIGURE 11.8   Double Bottom

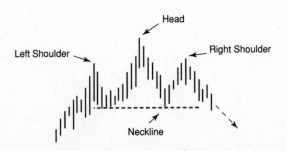

FIGURE 11.9   Head-and-Shoulders Top

FIGURE 11.10   Head-and-Shoulders Bottom

Continuation Patterns

A continuation pattern implies that while a visible trend was in progress, it was temporarily interrupted, and then continued in the direction of the original trend. The most common continuation patterns are shown in Figures 11.11 through 11.15.

The proper identification of a continuation pattern may prevent the trader from prematurely liquidating an open position that still has profit potential.

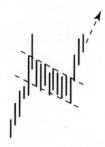

FIGURE 11.11   Flag or Pennant

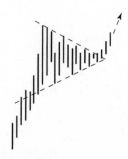

FIGURE 11.12   Symmetrical Triangle

FIGURE 11.13   Ascending Triangle

FIGURE 11.14   Descending Triangle

FIGURE 11.15   Rectangle

Candlestick Charts

Candlestick charting is usually credited to the Japanese rice trader Munehisa Homma in the early eighteenth century, though many references indicate that this method of technical analysis probably existed as early as the 1600s. Steven Nison of Merrill Lynch is credited with popularizing candlestick charting in Western markets and has become recognized as the leading expert on their interpretation. See Figure 11.16.

The candlestick is the graphic representation of the price bar: the open, high, low, and closing price of the period. The algorithm to construct a candlestick chart follows (see page 116).

The elements of a candlestick bar are shown in Figure 11.17.

The nomenclature used to identify individual or consecutive combinations of candlesticks is rich in imagery: Hammer, hanging man, dark cloud cover, morning star, three black crows, three mountains, three advanced white soldiers, and spinning tops are only a few of the candlestick patterns that have been categorized and used in technical analysis.

FIGURE 11.16 Candlestick Chart

Candlestick Chart Algorithm

- Step 1—The candlestick is made up of a body and two shadows.
- Step 2—The body is depicted as a vertical column bounded by the opening price and the closing price.
- Step 3—The shadows are just vertical lines—a line above the body to the high of the day (the upper shadow) and a line below the body to the low of the day (the lower shadow).
- Step 4—It is customary for the body to be empty if the close was higher than the open (a bull day) and filled if the close was lower than the open (a bear day).

A thorough description of how to interpret candlestick charts is given in Steven Nison's books: *Japanese Candlestick Charting Techniques*, Hall, 1991, and *Beyond Candlesticks: More Japanese Charting Techniques Revealed*, Wiley, 1994. A summary of the different candlestick patterns can also be found at www.hotcandle.com/candle.htm.

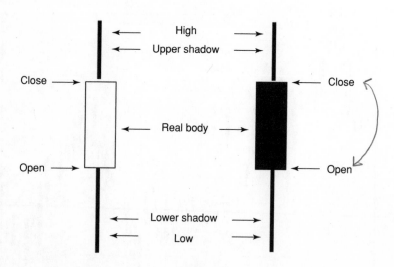

FIGURE 11.17 Anatomy of Candlestick Bar

Point and Figure Charts

The modern point and figure (P&F) chart was created in the late nineteenth century and is roughly 15 years older than the standard OHLC bar chart. This technique, also called the three-box reversal method, is probably the oldest Western method of charting prices still around today.

Its roots date back into trading lore, as it has been intimated that this method was successfully used by the legendary trader James R. Keene during the merger of U.S. Steel in 1901. Mr. Keene was employed by Andrew Carnegie to distribute the company shares, as Carnegie refused to take stock as payment for his equity interest in the company. Keene, using point and figure charting and tape readings, managed to promote the stock and get rid of Carnegie's sizeable stake without causing the price to crash. This simple method of charting has stood the test of time and requires less time to construct and maintain than the traditional bar chart. See Figure 11.18.

The point and figure method derives its name from the fact that price is recorded using figures (*X*s and *O*s) to represent a point, hence the name "Point and Figure." Charles Dow, the original founder of the *Wall Street Journal* and the inventor of stock indexes, was rumored to be a point and figure user. Indeed, the practice of point and figure charting is alive and well today on the floor of all futures exchanges. The method's simplicity in identifying price trends and support and resistance levels, as well as its ease of upkeep, has allowed it to endure the test of time, even in the age of Web pages, personal computers, and the information explosion.

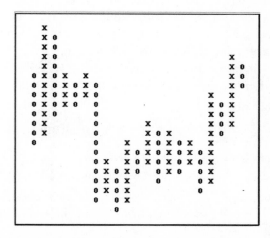

FIGURE 11.18 Point and Figure Chart

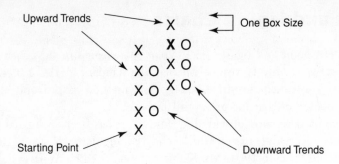

FIGURE 11.19   Anatomy of Point and Figure Columns

The elements of the point and figure anatomy are shown on Figure 11.19.

Two user-defined variables are required to plot a point and figure chart, the first of which is called the box size. This is the minimum grid increment that the price must move in order to satisfy the plotting of a new X and O. The selection of the box size variable is usually based upon a multiple of the minimum tick size determined by the commodity exchange. If the box size is too small, then the point and figure chart will not filter out white noise, while too large a filter will not present enough detail in the chart to make it useful. I recommend initializing the box size for a FOREX P&F chart with the value of one or two pips in the underlying currency pair.

The second user-defined parameter necessary to plot a point and figure chart is called the reversal amount. If the price moves in the same direction as the existing trend, then only one box size is required to plot the continuation of the trend. However, in order to filter out small fluctuations in price movements (or lateral congestion), a reversal in trend cannot be plotted until it satisfies the reversal amount constraint. Typically, this value is set at three box sizes, though any value between one and seven is a plausible candidate. The daily limit imposed by most commodity exchanges can also influence the trader's selection of the reversal amount variable.

The algorithm to construct a point and figure chart follows:

Point and Figure Algorithm

- Upward trends are represented as a vertical column of Xs, while downward trends are displayed as an adjacent column of Os.

- New figures (Xs or Os) cannot be added to the current column unless the increase (or decrease) in price satisfies the minimum box size requirement.

- A reversal cannot be plotted in the subsequent column until the price has changed by the reversal amount times the box size.

Point and figure charts display the underlying supply and demand of prices. A column of *X*s shows that demand is exceeding supply (a rally); a column of *O*s shows that supply is exceeding demand (a decline); and a series of short columns shows that supply and demand are relatively equal. There are several advantages to using P&F charts instead of the more traditional bar or candlestick charts.

P&F charts automatically:

Advantages of P&F Charts

- Eliminate the insignificant price movements that often make bar charts appear "noisy."
- Remove the often misleading effects of time from the analysis process (whipsawing).
- Make trend line recognition a "no-brainer."
- Make recognizing support/resistance levels much easier.

  Nearly all of the pattern formations discussed above have analogous patterns that appear when using a standard OHLC bar chart. Adjusting the two variables, box size and reversal amount, may cause these patterns to become more recognizable. P&F charts also:

- Are a viable online analytical tool in real time. They require only a sheet of paper and pencil.
- Help you stay focused on the important long-term price developments.

For a more detailed examination of this charting technique, we recommend *Point & Figure Charting* by Thomas J. Dorsey (John Wiley & Sons, 2001).

Charting Caveat—Prediction versus Description

Chart patterns always look impressive and convincing after the fact. The question is: Can they be predicted or are they simply descriptive? One simple method for studying this idea is to take an old chart with an already well formed chart pattern. Cover it with a sheet of blank, opaque paper. Move the paper slowly to simulate real-time trading. Would you be able to predict the chart pattern in advance?

Indicators and Oscillators

Beyond charting are various market indicators—calculations using the primary information of open, high, low, or close. Indicators may also be charted or graphed. Buy and sell signals and complete systems may be generated from a battery of indicators. The most popular indicators are: relative strength, moving averages, oscillators or momentum analysis (actually a superset of relative strength), and Bollinger bands.

Relative Strength Indicator

The relative strength indicator (RSI) shows whether a currency is overbought or oversold. Overbought indicates an upward market trend, since the financial operators are buying a currency in the hope of further rate increases. Sooner or later saturation will occur because the financial operators have already created a long position. They show restraint in making additional purchases and try to make a profit. The profits made can very quickly lead to a change in the trend or at least a consolidation.

Oversold indicates that the market is showing downward trend conditions, since the operators are selling a currency in the hope of further rate falls. Over time saturation will occur because the financial operators have created short positions. They then limit their sales and try to compensate for the short positions with profits. This can rapidly lead to a change in the trend.

You cannot determine directly whether the market is overbought or oversold. This would suppose that you knew all of the foreign exchange positions of all the financial operators. However, experience shows that only speculative buying, which leads to an overbought situation, makes very rapid rate rallies possible.

The RSI is a numerical indication of price fluctuations over a given period; it is expressed as a percentage.

$$RSI = \text{sum of price rises} / \text{sum of all price fluctuations}$$

To illustrate this, we have selected the daily closes (multiplied by 10,000) for the EUR/USD currency pair when it first appeared on the FOREX market in January of 2002. The running time frame in this example is nine days. See Table 11.1.

An RSI between 30 and 70 percent is considered neutral. Below 25 percent indicates an oversold market, over 75 percent indicates an overbought market. The RSI should never be considered alone but in conjunction with other indicators and charts. Moreover, its interpretation depends largely on the period studied. The example in Table 11.1 is nine days. An RSI over 25 days would show,

TABLE 11.1 Calculating RSI						
Date	Close	Daily Chg	Ups	Downs	Total	Percent
1/01/02	8894					
1/02/02	9037	+43				
1/03/02	8985	−51				
1/04/02	8944	−41				
1/07/02	8935	−9				
1/08/02	8935	0				
1/09/02	8914	−21				
1/10/02	8914	0				
1/11/02	8925	+11	54	122	176	30.7
1/14/02	8943	+18	72	122	194	37.1
1/15/02	8828	−15	29	137	166	17.5
1/16/02	8821	−7	29	93	122	23.8
1/17/02	8814	−7	29	59	88	33.0
1/18/02	8846	+32	61	50	111	55.0
1/21/02	8836	−10	61	60	121	50.4
1/22/02	8860	+24	85	39	124	68.5
1/23/02	8783	+23	108	39	147	73.5
1/24/02	8782	−1	97	40	137	70.8
1/25/02	8650	−132	79	171	250	31.6
1/28/02	8623	−27	79	183	262	30.2
1/29/02	8656	+33	112	176	288	39.0
1/30/02	8610	−46	112	215	327	34.3
1/31/02	8584	−26	80	232	312	25.6

given a steady evolution of rates, fewer fluctuations. The advantage of obtaining more rapid signals for selling and buying (by using a smaller number of days) is counterbalanced by a greater risk of receiving the unconfirmed signals.

Momentum Analysis

Like the RSI, momentum measures the rate of change in trends over a given period. Unlike the RSI, which measures all the rate changes and fluctuations within a given period, momentum allows you to analyze only the rate variations between the start and end of the period studied.

The larger n is, the more the daily fluctuations tend to disappear. When momentum is above zero or its curve is rising, it indicates an uptrend. A signal to buy is given as soon as the momentum exceeds zero, and when it drops below zero, triggers the signal to sell.

$$\text{Momentum} = \text{price on day } (X) - \text{price on day } (X - n)$$

where n = number of days in the period studied.

The following example in Table 11.2 of momentum analysis uses the EUR/USD currency pair as the underlying security.

TABLE 11.2 Calculating Momentum

Date	Close	9-Day Momentum
1/01/02	8894	
1/02/02	9037	
1/03/02	8985	
1/04/02	8944	
1/07/02	8935	
1/08/02	8935	
1/09/02	8914	
1/10/02	8914	
1/11/02	8925	
1/14/02	8943	+49
1/15/02	8828	−209
1/16/02	8821	−164
1/17/02	8814	−130
1/18/02	8846	−99
1/21/02	8836	−99
1/22/02	8860	−54
1/23/02	8783	−131
1/24/02	8782	−143
1/25/02	8650	−293
1/28/02	8623	−205
1/29/02	8656	−165
1/30/02	8610	−204
1/31/02	8584	−262

Examination of the nine-day momentum shows a clear downward trend. Momentum analysis should not be used as the sole criterion for market entry and exit timing, but in conjunction with other indicators and chart signals.

Moving Averages

The moving average (MA) is another instrument used to study trends and generate market entry and exit signals. It is the arithmetic average of closing prices over a given period. The longer the period studied, the weaker the magnitude of the moving average curve. The number of closes in the given period is called the moving average index.

Market signals are generated by calculating the residual value:

$$Residual = Price(X) - MA(X)$$

When the residual crosses into the positive area, a buy signal is generated. When the residual drops below zero, a sell signal is generated.

A significant refinement to this residual method (also called moving average convergence divergence, or MACD for short) is the use of two moving averages. When the MA with the shorter MA index (called the oscillating MA index) crosses above the MA with the longer MA index (called the basis MA index), a sell signal is generated.

$$Residual = Basis\ MA(X) - Oscillating\ MA(X)$$

Again we use the EUR/USD currency pair to illustrate the moving average method (see Table 11.3).

The reliability of the moving average residual method depends heavily on the MA indices chosen. Depending on market conditions, it is the shorter periods or longer periods that give the best results. When an ideal combination of moving averages is used, the results are comparatively good. The disadvantage is that the signals to buy and sell are indicated relatively late, after the maximum and minimum rates have been reached.

The residual method can be optimized by simple experimentation or by a software program. Keep in mind that when a large sample of daily closes is used, the indices will need to be adjusted as market conditions change.

Bollinger Bands

This indicator was developed by John Bollinger and is explained in detail in his opus called *Bollinger on Bollinger Bands*. The technique involves overlaying three

TABLE 11.3 Calculating Moving Average Residuals				
Date	Close	3-Day MA	5-Day MA	Residual
1/01/02	8894			
1/02/02	9037			
1/03/02	8985	8972		
1/04/02	8944	8989		
1/07/02	8935	8955	8959	4
1/08/02	8935	8938	8967	29
1/09/02	8914	8928	8943	15
1/10/02	8914	8921	8928	7
1/11/02	8925	8918	8925	7
1/14/02	8943	8927	8926	−1
1/15/02	8828	8899	8905	6
1/16/02	8821	8864	8886	22
1/17/02	8814	8821	8866	45
1/18/02	8846	8827	8850	23
1/21/02	8836	8832	8829	−3
1/22/02	8860	8847	8835	−12
1/23/02	8783	8826	8828	2
1/24/02	8782	8808	8821	13
1/25/02	8650	8738	8782	44
1/28/02	8623	8685	8740	55
1/29/02	8656	8643	8699	56
1/30/02	8610	8630	8664	34
1/31/02	8584	8617	8625	8

bands (lines) on top of an OHLC bar chart (or a candlestick chart) of the underlying security.

The central band is a simple arithmetic moving average of the daily closes using a trader-selected moving average index. The upper and lower bands are the running standard deviation above and below the central moving average. Since the standard deviation is a measure of volatility, the bands are self-adjusting, widening during volatile markets and contracting during calmer periods. Bollinger recommends 10 days for short-term trading, 20 days for intermediate-term trading, and 50 days for longer-term trading. These values

FIGURE 11.20   Bollinger Bands

typically apply to stocks and bonds, thus shorter time periods will be preferred by commodity traders. See Figure 11.20.

Bollinger bands require two trader-selected input variables: the number of days in the moving average index and the number of standard deviations to plot above and below the moving average. Over 95 percent of all the daily closes fall within three standard deviations from the mean of the time series. Typical values for the second parameter range from 1.5 to 2.5 standard deviations.

As with moving average envelopes, the basic interpretation of Bollinger bands is that prices tend to stay within the upper and lower band. The distinctive characteristic of Bollinger bands is that the spacing between the bands varies based on the volatility of the prices. During periods of extreme price changes (that is, high volatility), the bands widen to become more forgiving. During periods of stagnant pricing (that is, low volatility), the bands narrow to contain prices.

Bollinger notes the following characteristics of Bollinger bands:

- Sharp price changes tend to occur after the bands tighten, as volatility lessens.
- When prices move outside the bands, a continuation of the current trend is implied.
- Bottoms and tops made outside the bands followed by bottoms and tops made inside the bands call for reversals in the trend.

- A move that originates at one band tends to go all the way to the other band. This observation is useful when projecting price targets.

Bollinger bands do not generate buy and sell signals alone. They should be used with another indicator, usually the relative strength index. This is because when price touches one of the bands, it could indicate one of two things: a continuation of the trend or it could indicate a reaction the other way. So Bollinger bands used by themselves do not provide all of what technicians need to know, which is when to buy and sell. MACD can be used in conjunction with Bollinger bands and RSI.

Indicator Caveat—Curve-Fit Data

Most indicators curve-fit data. You must define one or more price or time variables to calculate the indicator. In a moving average you must select how many time units to average. The indicator is said to be "curve-fit" to that data. The pre-Socratic philosopher Heraclitus said it best: "You cannot step twice into the same river"; and so it is with the FOREX markets. An instance variable that worked perfectly in one trading session may fail miserably in the next as the market environment changes. Opinions vary widely on this caveat. Indicators are immensely popular in FOREX. Co-author of the first edition Jim Bickford was a champion of them, whereas I believe they have limited value. At the very least an indicator should be constructed in such a fashion that the instance variables are adjusted for the changes in market environment. Indicators that work well in "trending markets" (high directional movement and low volatility) fail in "trading" markets (low directional movement and high volatility) and vice versa.

Swing Analysis

Swing analysis is one of those nebulous terms that means different things to different people. It is often associated with swing trading, which also harbors a variety of connotations (the swing trader usually keeps a trade open longer than the typical session or day trader).

Within the framework of this book, I will define swing analysis as the study of the distance between local peaks and troughs in the closing prices for the purpose of identifying recurring patterns and correlations. The swing chart, like its older sibling the point and figure chart, requires the use of a massaging algorithm that filters out lateral congestion (whipsawing) during periods of low volatility. For this purpose, a minimum box size must be selected. Within

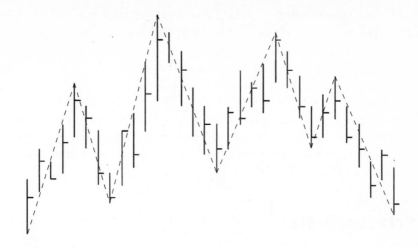

FIGURE 11.21   Bar Chart with Swing Analysis Overlay

currency trading, this is almost always a single pip in the quote (second) currency of the currency pair. Additionally, a minimum reversal quantity must be
selected. This is simply the number of pips (box sizes) required before a retracement can be drawn in the opposite direction (the continuation of an existing
trend requires only one box size to plot the next point).

Unlike the P&F chart, the swing chart does not distort the time element.
That is, swing charts are frequently overlaid directly on top of a vertical bar
chart since both use the same numerical scaling for the x- and the y-axis. See
Figure 11.21.

In Figure 11.21, it is clear that a swing chart is a sequence of alternating
straight lines, called waves, which connect each peak with its succeeding trough
and vice versa.

The swing analyst is particularly interested in retracement percentages.
Market behavior is such that when a major trend does break out, there is a
sequence of impulse waves in the direction of the trend with interceding retracement waves (also called corrective waves). The ratio of the corrective wave
divided by the preceding impulse wave is referred to as the percentage of retracement. Famous analysts such as William D. Gann and Ralph N. Elliott have ded-
icated their lives to interpreting these ratios and estimating the length of the
next wave in the time series.

Gann believed that market waves moved in patterns based upon, among
other things, the Fibonacci number series, which emphasizes the use of so-called
magic numbers such as 38.2 percent, 50 percent, and 61.8 percent. Actually,
there is no magic involved at all; they are simply proportions derived from the
Golden Mean or Divine Ratio. This is a complete study unto itself and has

many fascinating possibilities. Visit http://www-groups.dcs.st-and.ac.uk/~history/ Mathematicians/Fibonacci.html for more details on Fibonacci and his work.

In his analysis of stocks in the 1920s and 1930s, Elliott was able to identify and categorize nine levels of cycles (that is, a sequence of successive waves) over the same time period for a single bar chart. This entailed increasing the minimum reversal threshold in the filtering algorithm, which creates fewer but longer waves with each new iteration. He believed each major impulse wave was composed of five smaller waves while major corrective waves were composed of only three smaller waves. I refer interested readers to the web site www.elliottwave.com for more details on Elliott and his theories.

Cycle Analysis

Every market is composed of traders at different levels slugging it out. Scalpers, day traders, and position traders are all attempting to profit from price changes. Each group has a different time focus or horizon. Cycle theory believes these groups behave in cyclical fashion and that some composite of their behavior would parallel the market. Once that composite were identified, the cyclical parameters could be run past today's price into tomorrow's, resulting in a forecast. I experimented with a cycle tool, the Expert Cycle System, not to predict the market but to examine the ways to find such a composite. (See Figure 11.22.)

Advanced Studies

This chapter serves as a road map into the realm of technical analysis. It is a wondrous realm indeed, but it is very easy to get lost there. Time series analysis is a complex and ever-changing discipline. Advanced studies include deviation analysis, retracement studies, statistical regressions, Fibonacci progressions, Fourier transforms, and the Box-Jenkins method, to name just a few. A separate realm is the attempt to transfer methods from other disciplines to market analysis.

FOREX traders may also wish to consider the technical analysis of Charles B. Goodman, including the Goodman Swing Count System (see Chapter 12) and the Goodman Cycle Count System. Joe DiNapoli's DiNapoli Levels are popular and the basis of the educational course of Derek Ching's HawaiiForex (www.HawaiiForex.com). Charles Drummond's Point & Line Method has many ardent followers.

As previously mentioned, there are also those using techniques from other disciplines to analyze the markets. Michael Duane Archer has deeply explored the use of Cellular Automata and other complexity theory models to forecast FOREX prices. See Chapter 20, "The Final Frontiers."

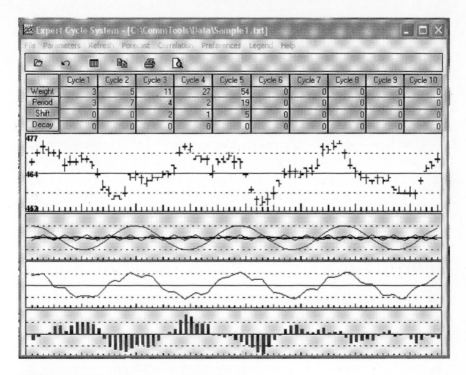

FIGURE 11.22 The Expert Cycle System.

The Technician's Creed

All market fundamentals are depicted in the actual market data. So the actual market fundamentals need not be studied in detail.

History repeats itself, and therefore markets move in fairly predictable, or at least quantifiable, patterns. These patterns, generated by price movement, are called signals. The goal in technical analysis is to uncover the signals exhibited in a current market by examining past market signals.

Prices move in trends. Technicians typically do not believe that price fluctuations are tandom and unpredictable. Prices can move in one of three directions: up, down, or sideways. Once a trend in any of these directions is established, it usually will continue for some period. Trends occur at all price levels: tick, 5-minute, 1-hour, 1-day, weekly. What is a trend at the 1-minute level is obviously just a small blip on the radar on a weekly chart. Curiously, the various price levels are interconnected.

Never make a trading decision based solely on a single indicator. The electric approach of comparing several indicators and charts at the same time is the best strategy.

As in all other aspects of trading, be very disciplined when using technical analysis. Too often, a trader fails to sell or buy into a market even after it has reached a price that his technical studies have identified as an entry or exit point. This is money management and psychology, not technical analysis, and both are *very* important.

Do you understand the differences between fundamental analysis and technical analysis?

The basic types of technical analysis tools are charts, moving averages, oscillators, and momentum analysis. Chapter 12, The Toolbox Approach, will put forth a suggested program for developing your own technical analysis arsenal. Your analysis of the markets is only one of three components to successful trading—money management and psychology are the others.

Summary

Keep your technical analysis aresenal to a minimum. Remember that the most popular methods, such as bar chart formations and support and resistance, are used by many traders. Most traders do not succeed—draw your own conclusions.

Your analysis of the markets is only *one* component of your trading system. In fact, two other components are more important, in the opinion of the authors: money management and psychology (discussed in detail in later chapters). Most traders who fail (and most traders do fail) tend to spend all their energies on developing a trading system at the expense of money management and trading psychology. *Don't be like them!*

12

The Toolbox Approach

While fundamentals almost certainly drive the long-term trends of currencies, trading is a very short-term affair. Most traders do not even hold a position from one eight-hour session to another. "If U.S. interest rates go up, then the USD will rise"—this is true in some cases, false in others. (There are so many other factors determining currency prices that a very accurate observation one time may even be incorrect the next.) But even if one knew a statement to be correct, how does that help a trader in the short term? Leverage is the name of the game, and no one wants a $10,000 loss while waiting for a fundamental factor to kick in.

Ergo, I strongly recommend the new trader develop a simple technical analysis toolbox to trade currencies. You may add to the toolbox later or make adjustments. But start your FOREX career by keeping it simple.

For a look at the *Codex* approach to trade program development see, *Getting Started in Forex Trading Strategies* (John Wiley & Sons, 2008) by Michael D. Archer.

General Principles

As you select technical analysis tools keep in mind:

1. Many traders use similar tools, and I know in fact the majority almost always loses.

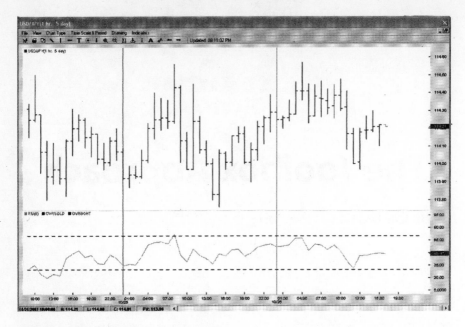

FIGURE 12.1 Charts or Indicators?
Source: Intellicharts, Inc., www.FXtrek.com.

2. Be certain you know what a technical tool is doing, what it is measuring, before adding it to your toolbox.

3. Seek synergy. Does your tool add to and or complement your other selections?

4. Avoid overkill. Keep it simple!

Consider Figure 12.1. This shows prices depicted as a bar chart on the top and a relative strength indicator (see Chapter 11) on the bottom. Functionally Relative Strength measures the slope of a line (trend). Does the Relative Strength indicator below add anything that you cannot see on the bar chart?

It is quite often possible to eliminate indicators because you can more easily see the same information on a chart. This is the thesis of Charles Goodman's Market Environment (ME) charting technique. See Chapter 16 for more on ME.

A KIS Toolbox

This toolbox is only an example of how to select a few basic tools for trading. Survey the field—it is huge—and pick wisely.

I recommend a toolbox consisting of:

1. A chart interpretation technique
2. At the most three Indicators
3. A noncomplementary check tool (one that is substantially different from your primary trading tools; i.e., if you use indicators to trade, a simple bar chart would be a noncomplementary tool)
4. A heuristic for analyzing a market with your tools

The Goodman Swing Count System

The Goodman Swing Count System (GSCS) was developed by commodity trader Charles B. Goodman and used by him until his death in 1984. Michael D. Archer, whom he mentored, further developed the system. GSCS is a method for interpreting charts. You may use bar, swing, or point and figure; bar charts are the easiest and most common.

Like all chart interpretation techniques, it is not applicable to all charts all the time. Not every chart forms a pennant or a head and shoulders, and not every chart forms a Goodman Wave. But the variety in FOREX is rich enough that you will find many trading opportunities.

I can only introduce GSCS here. For a deeper look please consult the companion volume, *Getting Started in Forex Trading Strategies* (John Wiley & Sons, 2007), by Michael D. Archer and www.fxpraxis.com.

GSCS Rules

The 50 Percent Rule

This rule is almost as old as the market itself. It states simply that at the 50 percent retracement of a trend, prices find at least a temporary equilibrium.

The logic is that in the aggregate all the traders who participated in the initial trend are at a break-even point. More specifically: half the buyers have losses, half have profits; half the sellers have losses, half have profits.

As seen in Figure 12.2, the price value of trend or swing B is 50 percent of A.

The Measure Move Rule

This could be considered a corollary of the 50 Percent Rule. Should prices start to trend in the direction of the initial trend from the 50 percent price point, the buyers will hold on to their positions, and the sellers will be forced to liquidate.

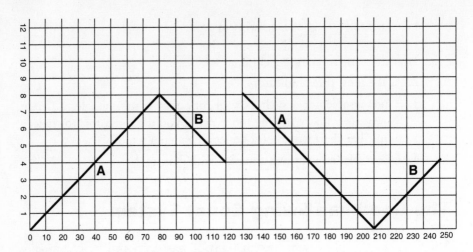

FIGURE 12.2 The 50 Percent Trade Rule

The end result is that a second trend will form of equal value to the initial trend.

Charles Goodman called this A-B-C formation a "matrix" and considered it the primary market formation. It is a subset of the Pugh Bull or Bear formations, discussed below.

As seen in Figure 12.3, The price value of trend or swing C is the same as A and twice B.

The Wave Propagation Rule

One of Goodman's most useful discoveries was that prices often form or build as a series of propagating matrices or measured moves. Each matrix becomes a trend in the propagation of successively larger matrices.

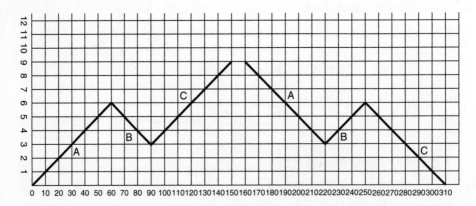

FIGURE 12.3 Basic Trade Wave or Matrix

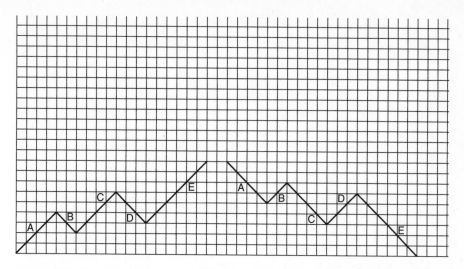

FIGURE 12.4 The Return or Propagation Wave

This is a distinct difference and, in my opinion, improvement over Elliott Wave Theory.

As seen in Figure 12.4, the price value of D is 50 percent of A-B-C. The matrix A-B-C is now considered itself as a single trend in GSCS theory.

Trend E is anticipated to be of the net price value of A-B-C. The complete formation of A-B-C-D-E is a Goodman Wave. Though it may look similar to an Elliott Wave, the Return Trend and how it is calculated makes an enormous difference. Compare to the Flat-Complex, Figure 12.8 for the same concept from a different viewpoint.

The 3C Rule

This was the most astonishing discovery Mr. Goodman made about the markets. It says that if the 50 percent objective is not perfectly met, the over or under of the measurement will be made on the measured move.

In Figure 12.5 the 50 percent measurement missed by one price unit (the value of B is three instead of four units) and is made up by the full measured move measurement in the third trend.

The 3C Rule states that whatever price value is missed on the 50 percent move will be made up on the measured move. Calculations are done in this way: (1) Calculate the value missed (either over or under the 50 percent move); (2) begin counting from the 50 percent price point in the direction of trend A; (3) calculate the final price point as if the 50 percent move had been in effect; and (4) add or subtract the value in Step 1 to find the anticipated adjusted price points for trend C.

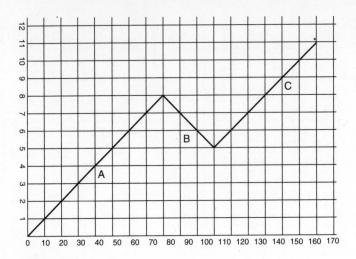

FIGURE 12.5 The GSCS 3-C Rule

"3C" Stands for Carryover, Compensation, and Cancellation

There are a number of other GSCS rules and principles but these three will suffice for getting started.

The three most useful Goodman formations are the Double Intersection Trade, Trading the Return D Swing, and the Flat/Complex Trade.

The Double Intersection

This is the most useful chart formation I have ever used. It occurs when the 50 Percent Rule intersects or cancels at two price points. If one 50 percent move represents equilibrium, two represents even stronger equilibrium. Prices very often react sharply from these double intersections.

Although this is not factually correct, it is useful to think of traders at different price levels or matrices. Like irrational numbers, they may not in truth exist, but they are useful for analysis.

In the Double Intersection in Figure 12.6, the traders in matrix A-B-C have the same equilibrium point as the traders in B1-B2-B3. The 50 percent move of A-B (1,2,3) meets the measured move of B1-B2-B3.

There are several Double Intersection templates using the various combinations of the 50 Percent Rule and Measured Move Rule at different points of a matrix.

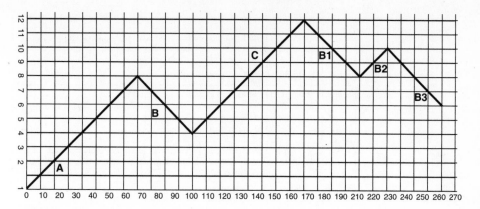

FIGURE 12.6 The Double Intersection Formation

The Return Trend or Swing

Refer again to the Wave Propagation in Figure 12.4.

When most traders see the D trend or swing on a chart they think in terms of Elliott Wave Theory where D is simply related to C. In GSCS D is in fact the Return or Propagation Wave, representing a 50 percent return of the entire A-B-C matrix. It almost always has a longer price duration than A, B, or C, and price reversals may be powerful. Such behavior is very tradable. (See Figure 12.7.)

TIP: Watch for charts where trend D digs into the marked spot intersecting B and C. This spot often offers strong support and resistance, and can be a good point to watch to enter for a trend E in the direction of A and C.

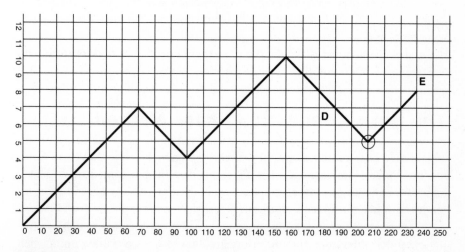

FIGURE 12.7 Trading the Return Swing

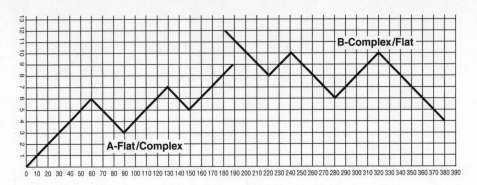

FIGURE 12.8   The Flat-Complex GSCS Rule

The Flat/Complex Trade

A flat trend is one consisting of no other components. A complex trend is itself an A-B-C matrix.

This is a trading technique because it allows you to sometimes anticipate price behavior. It states that if the first primary trend or swing (A) of a matrix is flat, the second primary trend (C) will be complex.

In Figure 12.8, the A wave is a flat followed by a complex. The B wave is a complex followed by a flat.

If you spot a flat trend A that makes a 50 percent return swing, you can anticipate—and visually map on your chart—a complex swing C.

TIP: Given a flat swing A and a 50 percent measured move B, the swing C will stop momentarily just above the highest price of A to conform with the Flat/Complex Rule. You will find many examples of this trade on FOREX charts!

GSCS is a price-based system. Mr. Goodman also developed a time-based counting system, the Goodman Cycle Count System. For information, go to www.fxpraxis.com in the Currency Codex section.

I have concluded that GSCS complements two other trading ideas very well: Nofri's Congestion Phase and Pugh Formations.

The Nofri Congestion Phase Method

This simple but useful idea was presented by Eugene Nofri in *Success in Commodities* (Success Publishing, 1975). It is out of print but sometimes available on www.eBay.com or www.abebooks.com. Nofri was a floor trader in the corn market, but like most technical trading ideas this one is applicable to FOREX.

There are 32 total formations, but the simplest one is to watch for two trading units when price goes up or down followed by two trading units when prices go down or up but remain inside the range formed by the first two units.

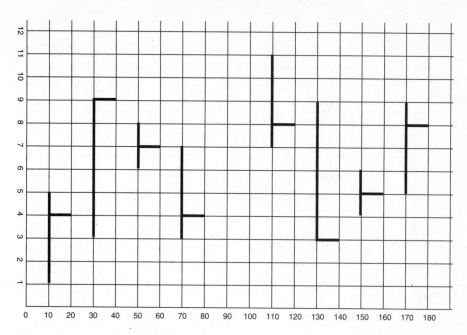

FIGURE 12.9　Basic Nofri Formation

The prediction is that the fifth price unit will be in the direction of the first two units (see Figure 12.9).

Pugh Swing Chart Formations

This is a simple but effective method. The basic formations were identified by Burton Pugh, a famous grain trader of the 1930s and 1940s. There are only four basic chart formations: Bull, Bear, Inside, and Outside. Highs and lows are always referenced to the previous data unit. (See Figure 12.10.)

A Pugh formation is always in reference to the preceding formation's high and low.

A. Bull Formation

Higher high and higher low from preceding formation

B. Bear Formation

Lower low and lower high from preceding formation

C. Outside Formation

Higher high and lower low from preceding formation

D. Inside Formation

Lower high and higher low from preceding formation

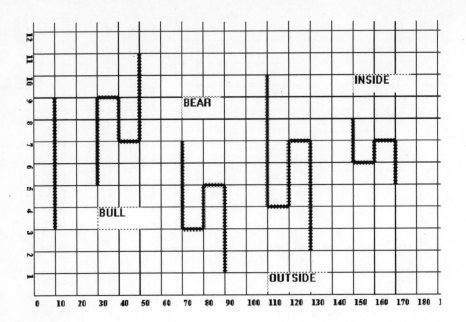

FIGURE 12.10   Pugh Chart Formations

Trends tend to be series of Bull Formations (up trend) and Bear Formations (down trend). Consolidations tend to be combinations of Inside and Outside formations.

The famous Head and Shoulders Top and Bottom is actually two sequential Bull (or Bear) Formations followed by a Bear (or Bull) Formation.

In fact all conventional bar chart formations shown in Chapter 11 can be reduced to a Pugh series.

I keep a running notation of Pugh Formations and look for patterns in the series.

You may use 1, 2, 3, 4 for the four formations. I use "1" for a Bull, "0" for a Bear, "11" for an Outside, and "00" for an Inside. A vertical line "|" is used to separate them. You might also use brackets "[ ]."

A notation might look like this:

1|10|10|00|11|1|01|10

A Moving Average and Oscillator Battery

This would be a good noncomplementary tool. Almost all trading platforms offer moving averages and oscillators.

A moving average typically works when a market is trending in one direction or another. An oscillator is most effective when a market is moving sideways.

Look for points where either:

1. A market is above the Moving Average line but the oscillator is falling sharply or below the zero line. This may indicate that a market is still in an up trend but in a buying range because it has lost some downward velocity, at least temporarily.
2. A market is below the Moving Average line but the oscillator is rising sharply or above the zero line. This may indicate that a market is still in a down trend but in a selling range because it has lost some of the downward velocity, at least temporarily. (See Figure 12.11.)

TIP: Remember, trends and trading ranges are relative to the price scale you are using. A trend on an hourly chart is probably made up of a number of 5-minute minitrends and trading areas. Use scales for your moving averages and oscillators in harmony with the scale of the price chart you are watching. Don't use a 10-day moving average on a 10-minute chart; you will see essentially nothing but a straight line.

Table 12.1 shows some recommended moving average and oscillator scales. You can use them for other indicators, as well. Some trading platforms do the work for you: Indicators are pre-scaled in definable units based on the price scale.

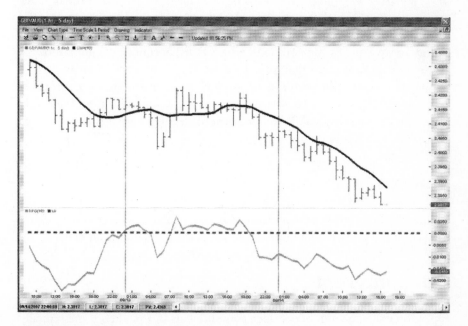

FIGURE 12.11 A Simple Indicator Battery
Source: Intellicharts, Inc., www.FXtrek.com.

TABLE 12.1 Recommended Indicator Scales			
Indicator Scaling			
Guerilla	5–Second	1–Minute	5–Minute
Scalper	5–Minute	15–Minute	1–Hour
Day Trader	5–Minute	1–Hour	3–Hour
Position Trader	1–Hour	3–Hour	1–Day

Contrary Opinion

At the old Peavey commodity office, around 1975, I befriended a trader who successfully traded using nothing but a Moving Average-Oscillator tool in conjunction with contrary opinion. Contrary opinion states that if a large majority of traders think a market will rise, it will fall. If a large majority think it will fall, it will rise. The reasoning is that if everyone thinks a market will go up, they have already bought, and there is no more buying power to maintain the trend.

R. Earl Hadady wrote a book on Contrary Opinion. Again, it was for the futures markets, but it would be a good read for any FOREX trader. Take a look at *Contrary Opinion* (Hadady Publications, 1983).

If everyone believes a market will go up, it will go down. If everyone believes a market will go up—it will go down. This is the basic premise of Contrary Opinion theory. While well developed and quantified in futures, it is less so in FOREX. Jay Meisler's www.global-view.com does a weekly trader poll. Archer's www.fxpraxis.com will soon offer a FOREX contrary opinion tool.

More on Contrary Opinion in Chapter 16, "Tactics and Strategy."

Two exceptionally useful tools—volume and open interest—are not currently available to the FOREX trader, although commodity futures traders do have them at their disposal. Without a central clearinghouse it is impossible to collect this information.

Volume

Volume is the number of transactions, both to enter a market and to exit a market, over a given period of time. In futures the standard unit is daily.

Open Interest

Open interest is the number of open commitments in a market. It is essentially a cumulative number of all open trades—trades that have not been offset.

I am currently working on methods for creating synthetic FOREX volume and open interest; stay tuned.

Heuristics

Every chess player worth his salt uses a heuristic with every turn to move. A heuristic is typically a set of ordered questions that must be answered before making a move. A heuristic can be very simple or extremely complex. The FOREX trader would be advised to develop a simple heuristic for every contemplated trade.

The more involved your trading method, the longer will be your heuristic. I recommend simplicity and clarity in all aspects of trading.

Your final heuristic should include both money management and psychology parameters.

For the previously mentioned KIS trading program a bare-bones heuristic might look like this:

- Is there a GSCS formation worth considering?
- If "yes," which one?
- What are the Pugh formations and series?
- Is there a Nofri formation?

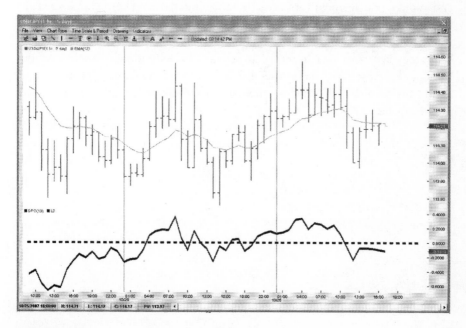

FIGURE 12.12 A Simple Trading Heuristic

- Do all of these occur in the same tie and price zone?
- Does the Moving Average-Oscillator battery confirm the trade or anticipated price direction?

Begin with your primary tool and work through the others. Optimally each will identify a trade or potential trade at the same price and time level. (See Figure 12.12.)

Summary

As the late Jim Bickford liked to say, "You can torture the numbers, but you can't make them talk!" No matter how involved your trading method is, remember the markets can only go up, down, or sideways. And sideways doesn't count unless you are trading options.

For a more comprehensive discussion of developing both a toolbox and a trading program see the sequel to this volume, *Getting Started in Forex Trading Strategies* (John Wiley & Sons, 2007) by Michael D. Archer.

There are many books on technical analysis. Appendix H lists some that I have found of value, beyond those mentioned in this chapter.

As I have said before, your trading method is only one of the three components to marshalling a successful FOREX campaign. The others, psychology and money management, are actually more important. These are covered in Chapter 14, "Psychology of Trading" and Chapter 15, "Money Management Made Simple." Sadly, trading techniques get the most publicity; perhaps because they are easier to communicate. Traders have hundred of tools to trade from, and almost every trader uses a different set of tools. But almost all successful traders share the same psychological attributes and basic money management rules.

The FOREX
Marketplace

*You can't always get what you want, and if you try sometime you find
you get what you need.*

Rolling Stones

The growing popularity of FOREX trading has spawned a very large online marketplace of products and services. Sorting through this vast plethora of information is a daunting task; services come and go rapidly, changes and upgrades are frequent, and the sheer volume is constantly increasing. Most of the material may be divided into these categories:

- Portals, forums, and reviews
- Charting and technical services
- FOREX education
- Trading signals and software
- News and announcement boards and calendars
- Live data streams
- Historical data
- System development tools
- Management services
- Odds and ends

Broker-dealers often partner with third-party vendors. For example, a broker-dealer may offer a charting service that will integrate into its trading platform and vice versa.

The selection and reviews in this chapter are intended as a sampler of what is available. The inclusion of a web site should not be considered a recommendation of it, and the exclusion of another should not be considered disapproval. Space is limited. My editor works on a one-martini-lunch budget, and I am reminded of it constantly. Reviews of all the services now offered would require a complete book—a very large one. I have generally omitted categories not pertinent to beginners, such as robots and automated order-entry tools. My emphasis is on web sites with content for traders who intend to do their own thing, although I have included a section on money management for those who wish to explore the option of having a professional trade FOREX for them.

I have endeavored to exclude web sites with annoying pop-ups, but always beware; a reliable pop-up blocker is recommended when cruising the Internet. Almost all of these web sites have advertisements; many of them are quite obtrusive and distractive. Welcome to Capitalism 101.

Organizing Your Bookmarks

There are several good programs for organizing your web site links.

Bookmark Buddy, www.urlorg.com: Most FOREX web sites offer content on more than one of the subjects listed above. I've found Bookmark Buddy to be very good for organizing this information with its Category/Sub-Category/Bookmark arrangement. The purchase mechanism is convoluted and time-consuming, but it is a good product.

LinkStash, www.rosecitysoftware.com: A new flavor, the social bookmark, assumes someone else can surf the Web better than you can or that a thousand surfers are better than one, www.del-icio-us.com.

The Onfolio, www.onfolio.com: A bookmark organizer—perhaps the best ever offered—was purchased by Microsoft and is now integrated into the Microsoft Live Toolbar. You must download the toolbar before you can download and install Onfolio. Unfortunately, some of the features were stripped away, including the wonderful Publisher tool. Go slowly when installing anything from Microsoft. If you do not deselect options you will be accepting all sorts of MS services, not the least of which is changing your default web site!

Cross-Category Services

To make things even more interesting, many services fall within two or more categories. A single service may offer trading, charts, technical services, data, and development tools such as www.strategybuilder.com, www.tradestation.com, and www.dukascopy.com.

Portals, Forums, Reviews

These sites offer link lists (directories) as well as reviews of FOREX services, products, and broker-dealers. Forums allow traders to communicate on a variety of issues and have become enormously popular.

As anyone who has surfed the Internet realizes, there is enormous cross-pollination of links. If you find one or two good directories or link lists on a subject, they will lead you to many others. The key is keeping everything organized so you aren't constantly backtracking or cruising down dead-end cyber roads.

Regarding Broker-Dealer Reviews

Traders are more likely to complain than compliment. A small sample of reviews may not be meaningful. The same information from different web sites is generally most reliable. In doing a broker-dealer due diligence (Chapter 7), it may be a good idea to throw out the top one or two reviews and the bottom one or two reviews to make the sample more reliable. Look for issues occurring multiple times on more than a single review board over a significant period of time. Focus on broker-dealers who meet your initial requirements as a trader. As you zero in on two or three prospects, don't be afraid to e-mail them and inquire about issues on the reviews of concern. How they respond—or even if they do—may tell you as much as what they actually say.

Forum Dos and Don'ts

Do carefully read the forum rules before subscribing. Read your posting over once or twice before submitting. Don't say something on a forum you would not say in person. Before posting, check your facts, and be sure you can substantiate the information.

Do not waste your time engaging in polemics with professional forum trawlers who have nothing better to do. Forums can be very useful, but don't get hooked on them; they are addictive. I take one hour each week to scan the forums.

> **www.global-view.com:** This is the granddaddy of FOREX portals and forums, and is loaded with excellent content; a recent web site

redo makes navigation easier. If you are new to FOREX this web site is a one-stop-shop. Jay Meisler's site also offers excellent links, educational, and resource and advisory tools. Unlike most others where new traders reign, many of the industry's movers and shakers frequent the GVI forms. Jay, like many forum operators, is a stickler about his rules and etiquette. (See Figure 13.1).

www.goFOREX.net: Operated by Steve Moxham from New Zealand, this is a fine resource, with a new design; slick and well organized. The Articles repository is superior and the Links directory is representative. It is becoming somewhat commercialized, but that is the name of the game in portals. I was booted from the Ask-an-Expert e-column for my nonmainstream ideas but it is still a must-see beginner's reference.

www.foxnews.com: A little bit of everything.

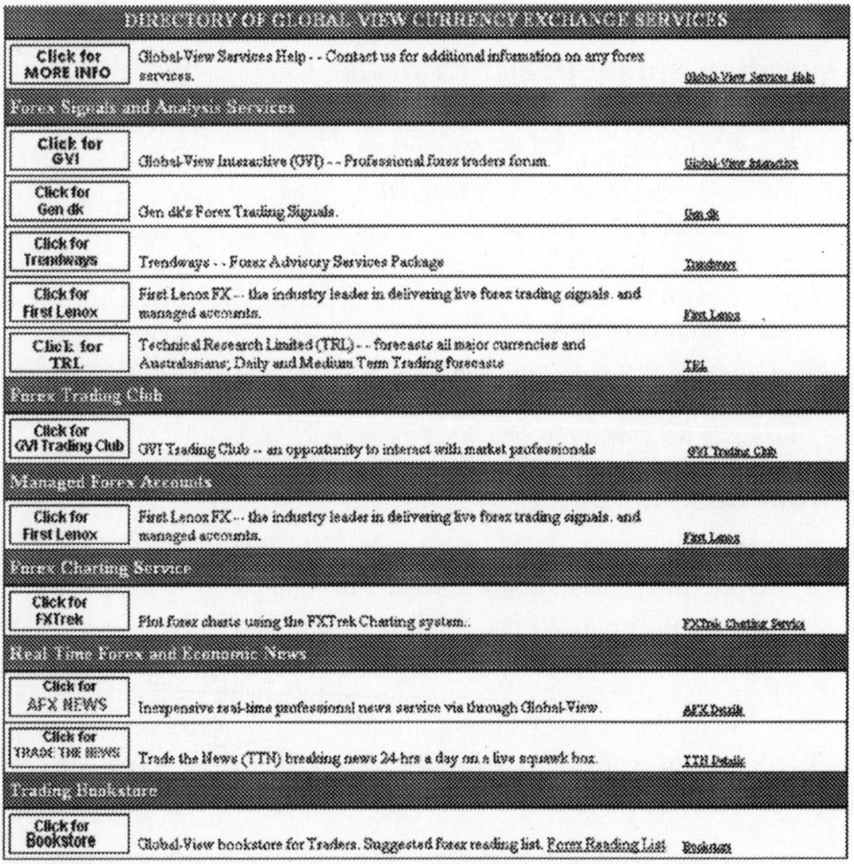

FIGURE 13.1 The Global View Web Site
Source: Global Viewpoint, Inc., www.global-view.com.

www.fxvibes.com: Friendly, chatty forums.

www.fxfisherman.com: Relatively new. Not very well developed but active forums with an emphasis on MetaTrader.

www.moneytec.com: Perhaps the most popular of the forum web sites. It also is a portal. Some people love it, some don't. (See Figure 13.2.)

www.FOREXpeacearmy.com: Formerly www.forexbastards.com. Felix Homogratus' web site. Recently redesigned and solid content. The most active review board around today—brokers, signals, and education topics. Felix promotes his own services—they are excellent—but makes that clear to avoid conflict-of-interest issues.

www.currencysecrets.com: Great coverage on specific topics but lacks breadth.

www.FOREXreviews.org: "Read reviews on FOREX brokers, trading signal providers, courses, eBooks and managed FOREX accounts." Limited content but clean format.

www.piptrader.com: Strength is reviews but an informative portal, also.

www.FOREXfactory.com: Excellent and very active forums.

www.fxstreet.com: Excellent content and a longstanding member of the FOREX online community.

www.trade2win.com: Lots going on here but very commercial.

www.FOREX-ratings.com: Relatively new. Not much action but shows promise; especially reviews.

www.dailyFOREX.com: Strength is reviews. Brokers rated by a number of useful categories.

www.FOREXmagazine.com: This site started strong but appeared in stasis at the time of this writing. Leland Liu had a good concept; I hope FOREXMagazine is able to get rebooted.

MOST POPULAR FOREX FORUMS AND PORTALS

Global-View
www.Global-View.com

GoFOREX
www.GoFOREX.net

FX Street
www.FXstreet.com

MoneyTec
www.MoneyTec.com

FIGURE 13.2 Popular FOREX Forums and Portals

Charting and Technical Services

These services generally are combined into a single entity especially if they are live, but not always. They can be expensive and are difficult to justify if you are, for example, trading a mini-account with $500.

A significant issue is how your charts will integrate into your trading platform. If you are using a live chart service, the data stream may be different from the data stream on which you enter orders with your broker-dealer. It is best if you can integrate your charting service into your trading platform or at least your broker-dealer's data stream. In Chapter 7 I noted the broker-dealers who offer integrated third-party charts and technical tools.

For many traders, the charting and technical tools offered with the broker-dealers trading platform are sufficient. Next best is a third-party vendor whose service is integrated into the broker's platform or at least reads the broker's data feed. Don't be overwhelmed. As a new trader Keep It Simple is your touchstone to success.

Chart services are either (1) live, (2) daily (End-of-Day), or (3) historical. Some services offer a combination of chart types. Most live services and daily services offer historical charts. Daily data is not of much use to the FOREX trader. I suggest the new trader try to be happy with his or her broker-dealer's charts, at least initially.

> **www.Intellichart.com:** Superior charting service with a strong set of tools and parameter settings. The service is named FXtrek and integrates with several broker-dealer platforms. Customer service— a weak area in FOREX—is lightning fast at IntelliChart. (See Figure 13.3.) A simple scripting language for testing new trading tools is in development. I would not be without it.

> **www.esignal.com:** This service has been around for many years. Its early life was difficult but it is a reliable service today. It caters to stock and commodity traders but offers a wealth of charts and technical tools; a FOREX data stream is available. Their Formula Script 2 (EFS2) for development of technical indicators and methods is weaker than TradeStation's EasyLanguage. The web site is difficult to follow, and I found sales support poor.

> **www.4xcharts.com:** A division of Trading Intl, www.tradingintl.com. Popular charts for currency traders.

> **www.tradestation.com:** Like eSignal, a difficult early life but solid now. Strength is to stocks and commodities, but they offer both trading and a FOREX data feed (through Gain Capital). For system developers, their EasyLanguage script is well developed and documented. Support is excellent.

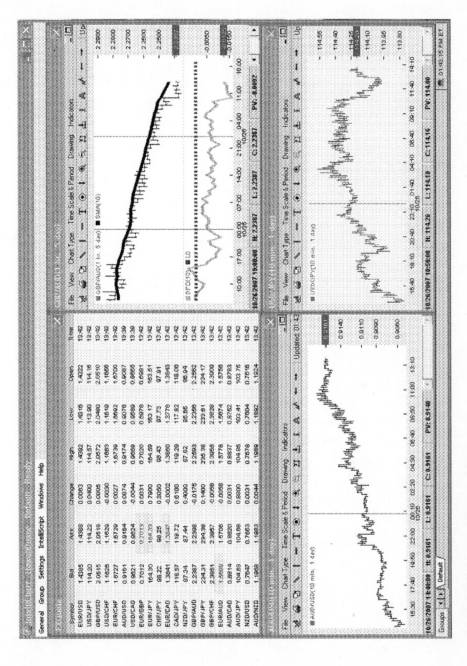

FIGURE 13.3   The FXTrek Web Site

Source: Intellicharts, Inc., www.FXtrek.com.

151

www.metastock.com: Now owned by Reuters. MetaStock integrates with several retail broker-dealer trading platforms. Live or EOD. A popular question on forums is "Who is a good MetaStock broker?" indicating the charting service is worth sticking with even if the broker is a disaster.

www.dailyfx.com: Online charts in a Java environment.

www.barchart.com: Offers stock, commodity, and FOREX charts. EOD and historical. Web site is confusing, but the charting services are very good, and customer support is decent.

FOREX Education

Most of the larger retail broker-dealers offer some level of educational experience for beginners. Supplement any training or mentoring you do with at least mini-account trading. Experience is the ultimate teacher.

www.FOREXlearner.com: FOREX portal for beginners. Very well organized content.

www.hawaiiFOREX.com: This Introducing Broker offers an integrated educational tract along with their FOREX trading services through GFTFOREX. Derek Ching works hard to find the best instructional programs and does very substantial due diligence before offering a new service. His current program is based on the technical analysis work of Joe DiNapoli. Perhaps your accountant will approve expenses for a trip to Hawaii for one of his excellent seminars. Aloha!

http://www.FOREXinterbank.com/: This is a very comprehensive training and mentoring program with some good reviews.

http://www.theFOREXtrader.net/: Basic tutorials and beginner articles.

http://www.FOREXtradingandeducation.com/: Tutorials, coaching, and mentoring.

www.FOREXforay.com: This web site has a page of FOREX calculation links. Good practice to get your feet wet making and understanding basic FOREX calculations; www.FOREXcalc.com has a good instructional video with their calculator. You may also use the Demo trading platforms of most broker-dealers for practice.

http://www.babypips.com/: A truly excellent beginner's resource. Well maintained and organized. (See Figure 13.4.)

http://www.FOREXtrainingworks.com/: Sid Wyemann's FOREX training courses.

Pre-school	FOREX Basics
ELEMENTARY SCHOOL	
Kindergarten	Types of charts
1st Grade	Japanese Candlesticks
2nd Grade	Support and Resistance, Trend Lines, and Channels
3rd Grade	Fibonacci
4th Grade	Moving Averages
5th Grade	Common Chart Indicators
	Bollinger Bands, MACD, Stochastics, RSI, and Parabolic SAR
MIDDLE SCHOOL	
6th Grade	Oscillators and Momentum Indicators
7th Grade	Important Chart Patterns
8th Grade	FOREX Pivot Points
HIGH SCHOOL	
9th Grade	Multiple Timeframes
10th Grade	Elliott Wave Theory
11th Grade	Create Your Own Trading System
12th Grade	Market Hours - Know When to Trade
13th Grade	Money Management
14th Grade	Plan Your Trade and Trade You Plan
COLLEGE	
	Multiple Trading Personality Disorder
	Trading News
	Market Sentiment
	U.S. Dollar Index
	Carry Trade
	The Lazy FOREX Trader's Way to Riches
	Be a FOREX Trader's Not a FOREX Sucker
	The Number One Cause of Death for FOREX Traders

FIGURE 13.4 The Babypips Web Site
Source: Babypips.com LLC, www.babypips.com.

Trading Signals and Software

This is a huge market today. It speaks to some degree to people's desire to make money without effort. I recommend beginners roll their own with a KIS system of charts and a few indicators. With these products the question is: "If it's so good, why are you selling it for $99.00?" These may be subdivided into either manual or automated tools. I am not convinced of the appropriateness of automated systems for beginners. I have been trading since 1973 and still don't trust automated execution programs.

Services—Internet-Based

www.FOREXdiamonds.com

www.secretFOREXsociety.com

www.secretnewsweapon.com

Three services are offered by Felix Homogratus who also operates www.FOREXpeacearmy.com, an excellent general resource for signal and software. If you trade the news, you should definitely consider www.secretnewsweapon.com as an execution-timing tool.

Technical Analysis-Based Service

I offer these as a sampling of what is available. Request as much documentation as possible along with referrals. Try to determine how the services do in a wide range of markets. A reasonable possibility is to use a service as a check on your own trading method.

www.kingFOREXsignals.com

www.cashmonster.com

www.fxtrendtrader.com

www.gfsignals.com

Software—Desktop-Based

Because retail FOREX is an online experience, there are more vendors of signals than of software.

www.stealthFOREX.com

www.leveragefx.com

News, Announcement Services, and Calendars

Most broker-dealers offer a news and announcement service, and it is enough for most traders. My take on the news is this: Don't try to trade it, but watch how the market reacts to it for trend indications. Remember the initial price impact of news is often dramatic, but it may take several hours to be fully absorbed. It is not uncommon for prices to react sharply in one direction initially, then gradually trend in the opposite direction for much of the trading session. This phenomenon is called Price Trace Dispersement (PTD). It is quantifiable and useful to traders. See Chapter 14. (See also Figure 13.5.)

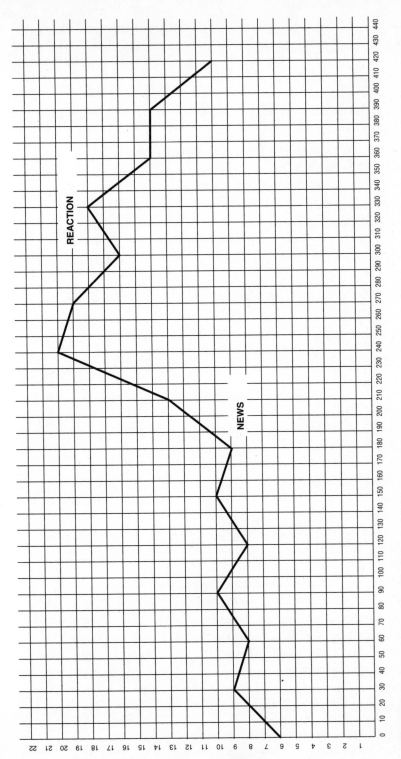

FIGURE 13.5 A News Shockwave and PTD

Your daily trade plan should always note relevant news and announcements for the pairs you trade. If you must trade the news, use one of the news trading tools available. Perhaps the best is Felix Homogratus' www.secretnewsweapon.com.

www.global-view.com: Offers an e-mail calendar to subscribers (see Figure 13.6).

www.econoday.com: The best subscription service for serious traders. They offer a few basic services at http://basic.econoday.com. If you trade on fundamentals, here is the depth of information you require.

www.tradethenews.com: Offers a News Squawk (audio) service through your computer speakers. Close your eyes, and it's 1970, again—squawk boxes were a feature of old-time retail brokerage houses!

www.FOREXeconomiccalendar.com: Well organized and useful news web site.

www.afxnews.com: Out of London. Very comprehensive news source.

2/29/2008 18:14

Calendar				Quicklinks-Sources			
Local Date	GMT			Mon Mar 3, 2008	cons	prev	**actual**
Mon Mar 3, 2008	08:30	CH	Feb	Mfg PMI	n/a	61.6	
Mon Mar 3, 2008	09:00	EZ	Jan	Mfg PMI?	52.3	51.7	
Mon Mar 3, 2008	09:30	UK	Jan	Mfg PMI	51.0	50.6	
Mon Mar 3, 2008	10:00?	EZ	Feb	HICP (flash) y/y	+3.2%	+3.2%	
Mon Mar 3, 2008	13:30	CA	Dec	GDP m/m	−0.1%	+0.1%	
Mon Mar 3, 2008	15:00	US	Feb	ISM mfg PMI	52.1	52.5	
Mon Mar 3, 2008	15:00	US	Jan	Cons Spending	−1.0%	−1.1%	

Calendar				Quicklinks-Sources			
Local Date	GMT			Tue Mar 4, 2008	cons	prev	**actual**
Tue Mar 4, 2008	00:30	AU	Jan	Retail Sales		+0.5%	
Tue Mar 4, 2008	00:30	AU	4Q	Current Acct (A$ bn)		−15.59	
Tue Mar 4, 2008	03:30	AU	Mar	RBA (7.00%)	+25	+25	
Tue Mar 4, 2008	06:45	CH	4Q	GDP (y/y)	n/a	+2.9%	
Tue Mar 4, 2008	10:00	EZ	4Q	rev GDP (y/y)	+2.3%	2.7%	
Tue Mar 4, 2008	14:00	CA	Mar	BOC (4.00%)	−25	−25	

FIGURE 13.6 The Global View News Calendar
Source: Global Viewpoint, Inc., www.global-view.com.

Live Data Streams

Live data streams typically come bundled with some other service such as live charting. If you receive the data stream or feed by itself it is called an API. Most broker-dealers offer an API service, but it is not inexpensive or is only offered to clients with large accounts. API data streams are used if you plan on developing your own trading system(s).

APIs also drive web-based tools, or applets.

Similar to a charting service, your API should closely match the feed from your broker-dealer, otherwise your trading signals will not match the prices offered to you on your trading platform. The best solution is to get the API from your broker-dealer for system development. Don't mess with this unless you are an experienced programmer. Integrating data I/Os and caching algorithms are not for the squeamish.

If you plan on purchasing an API for system development, be sure you can receive thorough documentation and support; each has their own little quirks. You will also want a good communications channel with the vendor's technical people.

The primer development tool, NinjaTrader, www.ninjatrader.com, offers live data from Gain Capital but can interface with many others.

www.oanda.com: An excellent API from a broker-dealer but pricey.

www.hotspotfx.com: Their API is available to traders who generate significant daily trading volume on a monthly look-back basis.

www.netdania.com: Excellent and expensive.

www.olsendata.com: Also good. Also expensive.

www.cqg.com: One of the oldest data vendors and very reliable.

www.tenfore.com: Very expensive, but most are in this category.

www.efxgroup.com: Their API is free for proprietary applications.

Historical Data

If you are developing a trading system, begin with historical data available by CD or download. It is much less expensive than an API. You also at least postpone the programming headaches of an API. Most charting and testing platforms also offer historical data. A strong correlation with your broker's data feed is not as important for systems testing—if you use a sample including a wide range of market environments.

www.disktrading.com: Not the cleanest data available, but the price is right, and customer service is very good.

www.dukascopy.com: Dukascopy offers many FOREX services. It is somewhat difficult to decipher all their web site offerings and how they are related and priced, and I found support to be unsatisfactory to my needs.

www.csidata.com: A seasoned and reliable vendor. Clean data but currently only EOD.

www.cqg.com: Also offers historical data.

www.snapdragon.co.uk: Exceptionally clean historical data but not cheap. Offers other excellent services to the FOREX trader and developer. Founder Adam Hartley is very knowledgeable and helpful. A new product offering integrates TradeStation with Oanda. (See Figure 13.7.)

"Date",	"Time",	"Close"
10408	17 4	1.2355
10408	17 4	1.2356
10408	17 7	1.2355
10408	17 7	1.2356
10408	17 7	1.2355
10408	17 7	1.2356
10408	17 7	1.2355
10408	17 8	1.2356
10408	17 9	1.2355
10408	17 9	1.2356
10408	17 10	1.2355
10408	17 10	1.2356
10408	17 11	1.2355
10408	17 11	1.2356
10408	17 11	1.2355
10408	17 12	1.2356
10408	17 15	1.2355
10408	17 19	1.2356
10408	17 20	1.2358
10408	17 20	1.2357
10408	17 20	1.2358
10408	17 20	1.2357
10408	17 21	1.2358
10408	17 26	1.2357
10408	17 27	1.2358
10408	17 30	1.2356
10408	17 30	1.2355
10408	17 31	1.2357
10408	17 32	1.2355
10408	17 33	1.2356
10408	17 34	1.2355
10408	17 34	1.2355
10408	17 35	1.2354
10408	17 35	1.2355

FIGURE 13.7   SnapDragon Historical Data
Source: SnapDragon Systems, LTD, www.snapdragonsystems.com.

System Development Tools

Somewhere over the rainbow is the perfect trading system; I hope you find it! When testing any trading system—yours or someone else's—be sure to test it over a wide range of market environments. The article "Backtesting and Market Environments" is available from www.fxpraxis.com in the Currency Codex area. Most back tests fail in real time because the test data is not representative of a wide range of market environments.

> **www.ninjatrader.com:** NinjaTrader is a free application for advanced charting, market analytics, automated strategy development, and trade simulation. Many traders already consider it to be the Cadillac of system development tools, because it does everything and does it all well. Traders can use live data from Gain Capital, TradeStation, eSignal as well as many other broker-dealers and data vendors. It includes a very nice strategy wizard for basic strategy development and uses NinjaScript™, a C#-based scripting language for advanced work. Support is awesome. (See Figure 13.8.)

FIGURE 13.8 NinjaTrader
Source: Ninjatrader, LLC, www.ninjatrader.com.

"NinjaTrader charts visualize all your orders and positions in addition to standard market data. All your working orders, positions, and executions are plotted on the chart with bars and intelligently marked labels. With NinjaTrader Charts, you can instantly see how far or close your stops and targets are relative to key support and resistance levels." From www.ninjatrader.com.

www.equis.com: MetaTrader. Very popular and integrated with many broker-dealer platforms. A common comment on the forums, "I like MetaTrader, but the broker is awful."

www.FOREXtester.com: FOREXTester is also a new kid on the street and trying harder. FOREXTester's software simulates actual market conditions with historical data for strategy testing; think of it as a flight simulator for FOREX traders! It has a great deal of potential because it integrates with a full-featured Pascal-like programming language, Delphi 7, and also C++. Support is superior; a refreshing surprise in this industry. (See Figure 13.9.)

FIGURE 13.9 FOREXTester
Source: FOREXTester Software, www.forextester.com.

```
Condition1 = Low < Low of 1 bar ago;
Condition2 = Close > Close of 1 bar ago;
If Condition1 and Condition2 then Buy;
```

About EasyLanguage

Since its introduction just over a decade ago, EasyLanguage has become an industry standard used by professional traders to test trading strategies.

FIGURE 13.10   Tradestation EasyLanguage
Source: TradeStation Securities, www.tradestation.com.

FOREXTester allows traders to reproduce historical currency rate fluctuations with the regulated speed of price updating. Thus, a trader can make trading decisions on history, manually test trading ideas, and monitor trading results in the form of trading statistics and equity line.

> **www.tradestation.com:** Tradestation's EasyLanguage is very well developed. There is a significant amount of documentation and literature, as well as third-party programmers. You may wish to have someone write a trading method for you from your own basic idea and design. (See Figure 13.10.)

> **www.esignal.com:** The eSignal scripting language is called EFS2; eSignal is a third-party vendor at different levels for several broker-dealers. Some traders love eSignal, some do not. My experience in attempting to gain information about their products from them has been uniformly poor, and I find the web site confusing.

> **www.gordago.com:** An easy to use visual systems-building system although the toolset is not extremely robust. Good for the nonprogrammer who simply desires to manipulate indicator batteries.

> **www.wealth-lab.com:** Advertises for stock traders, but I assume it can be used for currency trading. Lots of documentation and help online but the web site appears somewhat chaotic. Probably worth digging deeper, however.

> **www.strategybuilder.com:** Currently a contender with TradeStation and MetaStock for the most popular venue in this category.

FOREX Managed Accounts

The premise of this book is that you desire to make your own FOREX trading decisions. It is also possible to have your account managed by a professional money manager. Be leery of managed accounts promising too much. Fifty percent a year—consistently—is big money. $10,000 invested is over $75,000 in five years at 50 percent, $320,000 at 100 percent. Look for consistency in performance more than how much a manager made in his or her best year. Generally, the more the manager aims to make, the more risk involved. Carefully analyze a manager's performance, and look for market environments that may be an Achilles' heel. See Chapter 16 for more on market environments. Be sure costs are subtracted from gross performance. Costs will also give you an idea of how frequently the manager trades. Inquire if the manager is participating in the broker's pip spread income. Such an arrangement might encourage a manager to trade frequently.

Managed accounts may be individual or aggregated in a fund. Fund participation typically begins at $5,000 and individual managed accounts at $25,000.

Most of the major broker-dealers offer management services. They have already completed a thorough due diligence, but do not let that stop you from doing your own. The CFTC does not currently require FOREX money managers to register—as they do futures money managers—so it is up to the client to do his or her own research.

Two Approaches to Performance Analysis

Performance analysis asks this core question: "How much can I make for how much risk?"; basically, this is the Risk/Reward Ratio of a money manager.

The conventional approach to performance analysis has become extremely complex, involving numerous mathematical and statistical methods and ratios. The most common is the Sharpe Ratio.

Sharpe Ratio   This popular performance ratio was developed by Nobel laureate William F. Sharpe. The Sharpe ratio typically is calculated by subtracting a risk-free investment rate, such as the 10-year U.S. Treasury bond, from the rate of return for an investment or portfolio, then dividing the result by the standard deviation of the investment or portfolio return. Sortino, Calmar, and Treynor are some of the many alternatives to Sharpe.

ME   I use Market Environments (ME) to analyze performance.

ME divides all markets into functions of Directional Movement (DM) and Volatility (V). If each is rated on a scale of 1 to 10 from very low to very high, it gives a matrix of 100 market environments (10 × 10). Look for money managers who have done well in a broad spectrum of MEs instead of just a scattered few. Performance—good or bad—that clusters in a mostly contiguous area of the matrix can tell you much about the manager's trading

				Table 13.1 A 10 × 10 DP/V ME Matrix					
1	2	3	4	5	6	7	8	9	10
1	1	1	1	1	1	1	1	1	1
1	2	3	4	5	6	7	8	9	10
2	2	2	2	2	2	2	2	2	2
1	2	3	4	5	6	7	8	9	10
3	3	3	3	3	3	3	3	3	3
3	3	3	3	3	3	3	3	3	3
4	4	4	4	4	4	4	4	4	4
1	2	3	4	5	6	7	8	9	10
5	5	5	5	5	5	5	5	5	5
1	2	3	4	5	6	7	8	9	10
6	6	6	6	6	6	6	6	6	6
1	2	3	4	5	6	7	8	9	10
7	7	7	7	7	7	7	7	7	7
1	2	3	4	5	6	7	8	9	10
8	8	8	8	8	8	8	8	8	8
1	2	3	4	5	6	7	8	9	10
9	9	9	9	9	9	9	9	9	9
1	2	3	4	5	6	7	8	9	10
10	10	10	10	10	10	10	10	10	10

methods. See Chapter 16, "Tactics and Strategy," for more on ME applications to trading.

The Big Three all offer a number of money management programs.

- www.gaincapital.com
- www.gftFOREX.com
- www.fxcm.com

Peter Panholzer

One of the most respected names in the managed FOREX business is Peter Panholzer. Mr. Panholzer is the founder of Dynex Corp and commands the fees and account minimums that long-term success in the markets confer. (See Figure 13.11.)

DynexCorp

Dynamic
Currency
Alpha

FIGURE 13.11   DynexCorp
Source: DynexCorp, Ltd, www.dynexcorp.com.

A number of companies track individual and fund FOREX account performance.

- www.parkerglobal.com
- www.managedfutures.com
- www.mainfo.org

Odds and Ends

Spread Betting

It has been said that retail FOREX market makers are essentially bookmakers. You might wish to consider spread betting on currencies. Be sure to check the legality of spread betting where you reside.

www.deltaindex.com: Originally iPan, deltaindex.com offers spread betting on a wide range of financial instruments, including foreign exchange.

www.fxbt.com: This web site offers binary options in a number of markets, including FOREX. You take a yes or no side to a financial question such as, "Will the EUR/USD go over 1.3700?" Or you can speculate on the likelihood of a hurricane. Government regulated and open only to U.S. citizens.

www.hedgestreet.com: Trade the political, financial, and weather events that make up at least part of the fundamental picture for currencies. (See Figure 13.12.)

www.intrade.com: Many retail firms offer contests for clients only. The ones below are free to enter.

MOCK TRADER DAILY MARKETS

 Energy/Metals
Crude Oil, Natural Gas, Gold, Silver

 Currencies
EUR/USD, GBP/USD, USD/YEN and more

 Economic Events/Interest Rates
Initial Claims, Non-farm Payrolls, Core CPI,
Fed Fund Rate

MOCK TRADER INFREQUENT/SEASONAL MARKETS Print

 Housing Prices
Chicago, New York, San Francisco, and more

 Mergers and Acquisitions
Microsoft/Yahoo!, NASDAQ/PHLX, and more

 Hurricanes
Named Atlantic Storms once they form
(During Hurricane Season Only)

FIGURE 13.12 Hedgestreet
Source: HedgeStreet, Inc., www.hedgestreet.com.

www.citytrader.info

www.tradergames.com

FOREX Search Engine

www.search-FOREX.com: A FOREX-specific search engine.

Online Encyclopedias

www.investopedia.com: Superior reference on technical analysis, charting, and other aspects of trading.

www.linnsoft.com

Magazines and Newsletters

Almost every magazine and newsletter today is either online or available online. Gone forever are the good old days of the hardcopy Harry Schultz Letter, Dines Letter, Holt Advisory, and Myer's Energy and Finance.

www.currencybulletin.com: An interesting FOREX Newsletter/ Advisory with a very long track record in FOREX.

www.TradersJournal.com

Online FOREX Magazines

www.currencytradermag.com

www.euromoney.com

www.e-FOREX.net: By subscription, pricey but excellent if you are serious about the inner workings of the FOREX industry.

www.tradersjournal.com: Dickson Yap's *Traders Journal* is not devoted exclusively to FOREX but offers a wealth of information on technical analysis.

These four periodicals offer articles on FOREX and technical analysis. *Futures* is just a shell of its former self; the glory years were when it was edited by Darrell Jobman, but it still offers occasional content of value to currency traders.

www.futuresmag.com

www.activetrader.com

www.traders.com

www.fxweek.com

Books

I would be remiss if I did not accord especial mention to Ed Dobson's Traders Press, www.traderspress.com, which has been around for decades. They carry a number of FOREX-specific books as well as hundreds of newly published and reprinted books on technical analysis.

www.traderspress.com

www.forex-books.com

www.global-view.com

For specific titles and out-of-print books, see www.abebooks.com, www.amazon.com, www.bn.com, www.alibris.com, and, of course, www.ebay.com.

Summary

As I stated at the beginning of the chapter, this is but a small sampling of what is available to the currency market participant. Armed with these links and a reliable bookmark manager, you should be able to navigate to almost anything in the burgeoning FOREX marketplace. Begin with some idea of what you want and need, but be open to new ideas, also.

Part

The Complete FOREX Trader

14

Psychology of Trading

Ten years ago you would find, if you looked, perhaps one or two books written about the psychology of trading. Today there are nearly a dozen on the market. I think this is partly a function of the fact almost everything that can be said about trading methods has been said. I say "almost" because I am constantly peppering my editor with proposals for more books!

There is perhaps another reason. Traders are finally coming to the realization that a trading method—no matter how good—does not in itself lead to consistent success in the market.

When you were a teenager, your mother or father probably accused you at one time or another of having an attitude.

Traders have an attitude also, although probably not of the kind your parents meant. While trading methods are as varied and different as snowflakes, successful traders seem to share a set of attitude traits and money management techniques. In this chapter and Chapter 15, "Money Management Made Simple," I will delineate and discuss these common traits and techniques.

The Trading Pyramid

As I have mentioned previously, there are three components to a trading program: trading method, money management, and psychology or attitude. The vast majority of traders spend almost all of their efforts effecting a trading method. Ninety percent of market books are still trading method tomes. In

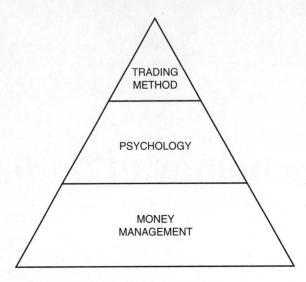

FIGURE 14.1   The Trading Pyramid

fact, most successful traders will tell you, of the three components, the trading method is the least important.

You will be well advised to allocate significant thought and effort to attitude and money management. How much you order their relative importance determines your trading pyramid. (See Figure 14.1.)

Most traders place their trading method at the base as the most important and substantial. Money management is in the middle and psychology of trading gets little attention at the top. To my way of thinking money management is the base, then psychology, and a trading method as a finishing touch. An argument could be made that psychology of trading should be the base. Top traders share more attitude characteristics than anything else.

Fear and Greed, Greed and Fear

Fear and greed are the base emotions that drive every market. They are instinctive to humans and unless you use an automated computer program to trade, your goal can only be to control them and not to eliminate them.

Since economic booms, busts and bubbles keep recurring, year after year, century after century, it is clear evolution isn't going to transfer the skills learned in one generation to another. People have short memories, and fear and greed keep returning; the dot.com bubble was followed by the real estate bubble in less than a decade. A hedge fund bubble may not be far behind.

We tend to get greedy when we are making money and overstay our welcome; we tend to become fearful when we are losing and again overstay our welcome. These emotions cause us to mentally freeze and delay making critical decisions that would be in our own best, rational interest.

One very successful trade may cause overconfidence and lead to what we call the King Kong Syndrome—the warm feeling that we can do no wrong. A large losing trade can lead to enormous self-doubt, leading us to make revolutionary changes in our trading program when, in fact, a little time away from the market and a few evolutionary changes would put us back on track.

The late Pete Rednor, office manager at Peavey and Company where I apprenticed as a commodity trader in the early 1970s, would wait for a trader to get the King Kong Syndrome. When the trader next placed an order, Pete would go to a telephone in the back office and place the identical order—but in reverse. He usually won, and when the trader lost it all and stopped trading, Pete lamented the loss of a meal ticket.

The key is containing the emotions of fear and greed within a relatively slight area. To do that, you must in turn be able to anticipate the onset of fear or greed, and find methods for controlling them before they impact trading decisions.

Never be afraid of the markets but always respect them. Never be hesitant to simply walk away for a few hours or a few days. The markets won't go away; they are happy to wait for you to return. Never trade when you are emotionally distraught.

Profiling

Good records of your trading will help you build profiles you can review from time to time. Often a marked change in profiles will be a leading indicator of a bout of fear or greed. Monitor your trading results on a weekly basis.

Look not only for how much money you are making—you can't win them all—but look also to see the patterns in trade series that went well for you. Profit/Loss ratios, the currency pairs that worked the best for you, the types of markets—trading or tending—that worked well. How often did you move a stop or profit objective?

"Know Thyself," the ages-old Socratic saying, is a trader's watchword. Only you know which factors cause emotional unbalance, and which do not.

The Attitude Heuristic

In Chapter 13 I suggested a heuristic for your trading method. I like to keep a mental chart of my emotions. Imagine a graph going from 0 in the middle to 0 at the bottom and 10 at the bottom. (See Figure 14.2.) Greed is the top half; fear, the bottom half. Sure, it is exciting to make a trade. It is even more satisfying to close out a winner. And it is a disappointment to see a trade go bad.

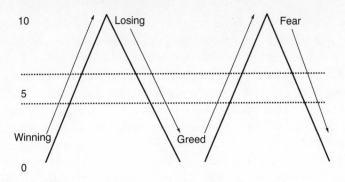

FIGURE 14.2   Charting Fear and Greed

Don't expect your emotions to stay between 4 and 6; you're human. They will not. At least after tracking yourself for a few weeks you will know when you are in the danger zones, perhaps above 8 or below 2. Review these numbers vis-à-vis your performance. You will be surprised how much you learn and the ways you can benefit. If you can eliminate 1-out-of-3 losing trades you'll almost certainly be successful in the long run. The line between winning and losing can be razor thin.

Characteristics of Successful Traders

No one has all these characteristics all of the time. But having known literally hundreds of traders, I can assure you that most of them share most of these characteristics—most of the time. The characteristics of successful traders are:

- Successful traders tend to have control over their emotions—they never get too elated over a win or too despondent over a loss.

- Successful traders do not think of prices as "too high" or "too low." Prices are numbers; zeros are zeros whether there are three of them or seven of them.

- Successful traders don't get emotionally attached to a market or a trade. They don't anthropomorphize about the markets: "They're going after stops now," or, "The market is nervous," or "The market must know something I don't." Just thinking in such terms is an error. The market isn't going, nervous, or seeing anything.

- Successful traders do not panic. They make evolutionary changes to their trading program, not revolutionary changes.

- Successful traders do not flinch at making a decision, pulling the trigger once everything has lined up for a trade.

- Successful traders treat trading as a business, not a hobby or game—even if it is a hobby.
- Successful traders stay physically fit.
- Successful traders do not trade when they are emotionally stressed or under duress.
- Successful traders hang up the DO NOT DISTURB sign when they are trading.
- Successful traders come prepared for all eventualities on any given trading session. They come to work with a plan that includes many contingencies and not just for what they hope will happen.
  - In your trading program you should have predetermined responses to the following, "What happens if . . ." situations: Prices open sharply higher or lower; the market is very quiet; the market is very volatile; the market makes new highs; the market makes new lows; the market opens higher and reverses; the market opens lower and reverses.
- Successful traders trade only with money they can afford to lose. Trading FOREX is speculation, not investment. It can be exciting, exhilarating—and addictive. Being emotionally involved with the money at risk is a formula for losing if ever there was one.
- Successful traders spend as much time on improving their attitude and money management as they do their trading method.
- Successful traders keep a low profile and don't discuss their trading with others.
- Successful traders let the market do its thing and try to take advantage. Unsuccessful traders attempt to impose their will on the markets.
- Successful traders consistently review their trades.

Summary

FOREX trading will greatly magnify any emotional or psychological hang-ups or concerns you bring to the table with you. Trading when not in top form is asking for financial injury in the same way driving drunk is asking for physical injury.

Dismiss the importance of attitude at your own peril. More than any other factor, it is what separates the winners from the losers in FOREX and other trading arenas.

Chapter 15

Money Management Made Simple

For the new trader, money management is the art and science of breaking even. That does not sound very exciting, does it? Not what you expected from the FOREX markets? I am reminded of the person who purchased a one-dollar lottery scratch ticket and won one dollar. "I already had a dollar; if I wanted it I would have kept it!" But the logic here is quite sound. Most new FOREX traders are shown the door quickly. They leave discouraged, never to return, and write pamphlets proclaiming "The FOREX Big Scam!" and such.

Breaking Even—The Belgian Dentist

No, you do not enter a trade just to exit 30 seconds later. Breaking even is about managing your money and staying in the game. It is about thinking in terms of capital preservation and waiting for good trades to present themselves. My mentor, Charles B. Goodman, said it over and over: "You'll make most of your money sitting on your hands." The longer you stay in the game, the more you will learn about it, and the more you will develop your skill set. The longer you stay in the game, the more likely a good trade will find you. If you lose your grubstake, it is over.

Be conservative. Mr. Goodman preached the Belgian Dentist approach to money management. In Europe a Belgian Dentist is a term for an ultraconservative investor. "Even a Belgian Dentist would buy this stock!"

Money management is not difficult to understand. Many new traders find money management rules impossible to live by and are usually the first to leave.

Expectations

Your trading method will tell you when to enter a market. Your money management program will tell you if you should. Money management is also vital to placing stop-loss orders to minimize risk and take-profit orders to capture gains.

Do not expect to hit 80 percent winning trades with a 10:1 ratio of winners-to-losers. Do not expect to make millions trading a $500 account.

Trader Profiles

You will need to set money management parameters and live with them and by them. To do this you must first determine your trader profile.

Although traders are in actuality on a continuum from very short-term traders to very long-term traders, all of them fall into three or at most four distinct classes with specific money management needs.

The Guerilla

The guerilla trader seldom stays in a position for more than a few minutes. Taking 10 to 20 pips from a trade is considered a good deal. Guerillas often trade the news and need very low pip-spread even to survive. When you make 20 trades a session, the pip costs add up very quickly. I do not recommend that the new trader attempt the guerilla style of trading.

The Scalper

One level up from the Guerilla is the scalper. A scalper may extend his profit horizons to perhaps 30 or even 50 pips in a very volatile market. A scalper might trade a pair once or perhaps twice a session. Being a scalper is a reasonable space for the new trader. But, again, costs can be significant. The counterbalancing idea is that you can't (usually!) lose too much money only being in the market or exposed for 30 minutes to an hour.

The Day Trader

The day trader seeks profits in the 50-to-100 pip range. Such a trader must often sit between multiple sessions or seek markets with high directional movement. By seeking larger profits a day trader can afford to make quite a few losing trades; if none of them are very large. The day trader only needs a few good trades a week to make the program effective. By staying longer in the market day traders are exposed to more unforeseen circumstances and market-jarring news events or announcements. I am a day trader. It is a good profile for new traders, also.

The Position Trader

Few retail FOREX traders can afford the heat of staying over not only several sessions but several days in a market. Yes, you can make a killing as the EUR/USD goes from 1.25 to 1.30 in two weeks. You can also lose it all in a single trade. The exposure is enormous over such periods of time. If you perceive a longer-term trend, you can catch most of it—or perhaps even more by trading the intermediate swings—as a day trader. This is certainly not a profile for the new trader.

Now we can examine the primary money management parameters and build out each for the two suggested trader profiles. (See Table 15.1.) These factors are dependent variables. In many instances, one depends on the other. Once you've done a few dozen FOREX calculations, the relationship of these factors will be second nature to you. Practice. Don't be afraid to heat up your Demo account or use an online FOREX calculator such as the ones at www.forexcalc .com or www.oanada.com. Refer to Chapter 6, "The Calculating Trader."

Capital Allocation—Aggregate What is the maximum amount of your total margin capital that you should allocate at any one time? Brokers may require different margins for the same number of units of different pairs—and they change them often, as well. I recommend that the new trader never have more than one position going at a time. You will have a lot of unused margin but a lot of cushion and staying power, also.

Typically, gorillas and scalpers may be often margined at nearly 100 percent. Day traders generally should stay under 75 percent and position traders,

TABLE 15.1 Money Management Parameters	
Trader	*Profiles*
Trader	Profit Objective
Guerilla	10–20 Pips
Scalper	20–50 Pips
Day Trader	50–100 Pips
Position Trader	100+ Pips

50 percent. The more exposure you have, the less total margin you should have in play at any given time.

Capital Allocation—Per Trade If you never want to go over 75 percent margined and a trade takes an average of 25 percent, that's a maximum of three concurrent positions, more than enough simultaneous action for most of us.

Leverage Leverage is the total value of the trade divided by the margin required. Trade Value/Margin. If a trade has a value of $10,000 and it cost you $500 to trade that pair, your margin is 20:1.

Your broker will give you multiple leverage possibilities which can be set on your trading platform. Start at the lowest, usually 10:1 and move up by the smallest increments possible as you have success.

For these next two ratios, it is vitally important that they work together and with your trader profile in harmony.

Profit/Loss Ratio The higher your Winner/Loser Ratio, the lower can be your Profit/Loss Ratio. If you average a $500 profit for every $100 loss you can have a Winner/Loser Ratio of less than 50 percent (more losers than winners) and still do very well.

Winners/Losers Ratio Here's the flip side. The higher your Winner/Loser Ratio, the lower can be your per-trade Profit/Loss Ratio. If you hit 80 percent of your trades, your Profit/Loss ratio can be razor thin, and you will still be successful.

The goal is to have all these work together in harmony, in a realistic structure, in accordance with your trader profile. Note how these last two are inversely proportional to one another.

Parameters for Trader Profiles

We may now set suggested money management parameters for the two recommended Trader Profiles.

Scalper Profile Parameters

Pip Gain Goal	30 pips
Per-Trade Profit/Loss	3:1
Winners/Losers Ratio	1:1

Campaign Scenario: A Scalper makes 12 trades. He wins on six and loses on six. On the winners he nets 30 × 6 pips = 180 pips. On the losers he nets −10 × 6 = 60 pips. He's on fire, but he'll feel cold water if either ratio goes the wrong way for any length of time. Many scalpers would give an arm to maintain a 3:1 per trade ratio.

Day Trader Profile Parameters

Pip Gain Goal	60 pips
Per-Trade Profit/Loss	4:1
Winners/Losers Ratio	2:1

Campaign Scenario: A day trader makes 12 trades. He wins on four and loses on eight. On the winners he makes 60 pips × 4 = 240 pips. On the losers he is −15 × 8 = 120 pips. Life is good, but it depends on keeping the per trade ratio very high.

The success of a trader is always a delicate and precarious thing. You can see from the above how small changes in ratios could turn either one of these traders to the negative side.

When analyzing your performance, use these ratios and observe how they might be changing over time, and how much they vary per trade. It is very important to understand the basic FOREX calculations before actually trading.

I cannot emphasize enough the importance of understanding the basic FOREX calculations. Learn them from this book, then go into your broker-dealer's Demo account and generate as many What If? Campaign scenarios as you possibly can. You will learn not only how FOREX works but perhaps most importantly what is required for it to work for *you*.

The Trade Campaign Method (TCM)

This concept was developed by Bruce Gould in his enormously insightful advisory letter for commodity traders published in the 1970s. Mr. Gould's work is highly recommended to all traders in all markets. For information on his offerings, www.brucegould.com.

In conjunction with the trader profile this method provides an ad hoc method of setting fixed stops and taking profits. Once you have some experience trading, you may wish to discontinue this approach or meld it with a method of stop-loss and take-profits inherent in your trading method.

In Figure 15.1 the moving average stop, below the moving average line, would be much further away than a fixed stop. Either use the fixed, campaign method or pass the trade. The perfect scenario is for a trading method stop to be within the accepted set parameters of the campaign fixed stop. If a method stop is not in the campaign stop, I would reconsider the trade.

Calculating TCM Profit and Loss

Step One. What is your trading capital or grubstake? If you are in the midsection of the bell curve, it is probably between $1,000 and $10,000. You can trade with less (in a mini- or micro-account), or you can trade with more. We are here considering not your micro- or mini-account, which should be funded with no more than $500, but your full-fledged trading account.

Let us assume your stake is $3,000. Remember, this is money you can afford to lose. Your spouse may yell at you if you lose it but at least the kids won't go hungry.

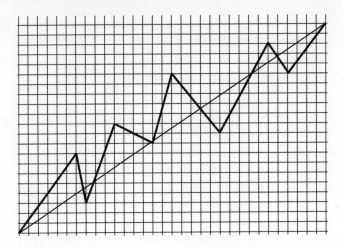

FIGURE 15.1   A Simple Stop-Loss System

Step Two. Allocate your money into three imaginary campaign parcels. You will have three campaigns to get long term traction in the markets. If you lose campaign #1 you can regroup and go on to campaign #2, and so forth. This gives your tradink some basic structure, something almost no new traders have or even think about.

Step Three. Allocate each of your $1,000 pots into ten trades, risking a set $100 per trade. (See Table 15.2.)

Your stop-loss is mechanically calculated in advance as a pip value equal to $100. See, I told you that you would need the calculations in Chapter 9!

Step Four. Refer to the profile parameters above, and work backward. If you are a scalper and seek 3:1 profit to loss ratio, you want to make $300.

Step Five. You only now need to know how many units to buy or sell. Refer to your pip gain in the same profile. The scalper wants to make 30 pips per trade, on average. All you must do now is calculate how many units make $300 on 320 pips, and your trade money management parameters are ready to go.

Do not reset or adjust your campaign schedule until you have made 30 trades and completed all three campaigns.

TABLE 15.2 Allocating Your Account Grubstake		
Trading Capital Day Trader		
$3,000		
Campaign	#1	#2	#3
Trades	10	10	10
Profit Objective	$300	$300	$300
Stop Loss	$100	$100	$100

Before you execute a trade, review these five steps. Together they constitute your money management heuristic.

Stop-Loss Orders—A Brief Discussion

As above you may either set stops using my campaign method or you may set them in accordance with your trading method. Some trading methods generate stop-loss prices, some do not. In the later instance I continue to advise that you pass a trade if the stop-loss your trading method requires is excessive. If you are trading as a scalper, do not take a trade requiring a 75-pip stop-loss. When in doubt, stay out; do not let your trading method overrule common sense.

Tip: Once entered, do not change your stop-loss order. Live with it, good, bad, or ugly. Manipulating stop-losses is for the expert, and even for experts, it is a dicey business. A trade is a process and tinkering with the process once it is in motion is a *bad* idea.

As a new trader be sure your stop order is in the market at all times. Enter it as a pure stop order so that if the price is hit, the stop is executed. A bad fill in a fast market is better than no fill at all.

There is an ongoing discussion among traders, teachers, and researchers as to whether stops should be mental or actually placed in the market. For the new trader I believe the answer is slam-dunk territory. Put them in the market. Whatever you do—don't walk away leaving a position open, unattended, without a stop in the market. New traders have so much sensory and emotional data hitting them from all sides that adding the duty of exiting a trade per one's strategy on the fly is just asking too much.

Selecting Markets

I recommend the novice trader begin by trading the major USD currency pairs only. These pairs usually entail a lower bid/ask pip spread, which increases your profit potential while reducing your transaction costs. While it may not matter for the small trader, they are also the most liquid of all currency pairs. If you venture forth past the majors, stay with combinations of the Euro (EUR), British Pound (GBP), Japanese Yen (JPY), Australian Dollar (AUS), and Canadian Dollar (CND).

Irrespective of currency pair, attempt to trade only markets with modest volatility and high directional movement. Scalpers and guerilla traders prefer high volatility pairs; day traders and position traders prefer markets with high directional movement.

TABLE 15.3 Absolute Range-Pips

Pips	Absolute Range	Range–Pips
10	1.0	10
50	2.0	100
100	3.0	300

Over long periods of time both directional movement and volatility for any given pair changes, but typically the change is gradual. After you trade a pair for a reasonable period of time, you will see that each has its own unique personality. We can often identify an unlabelled pair simply by doing a market environment analysis. See Chapter 16, "Tactics and Strategy."

Table 15.3 is also a useful guide. Absolute range is converted from a decimal value of pips by multiplying by 1,000 (or 10 in some cases) and expressed as pips in the quote (second currency).

Summary

Know your FOREX calculations, and practice with them on a Demo account as much and as often as you can. Play What If? scenarios to sharpen your understanding of the relationships between not only the calculations but the basic money management ideas presented here. Once you are comfortable, factor in your trader profile.

I recommend the campaign method of money management for new traders. You may meld in parameters derived from your trading method as it develops, if you wish. But the basic campaign parameters should always trump anything else, in my humble opinion. If your trading method money management parameters are, too often, too far away from your campaign parameters, it is probably the trading method parameters that need changing.

The best way to learn how a ratio or conversion works is to do multiple scenario calculations, leaving the other numbers unchanged and manipulating the one you are learning.

A very small change in only one or two money management factors can make a big difference in overall trader performance. Keep this in mind especially when evaluating trade performance.

Add the money management heuristic to your trading method and attitude heuristics, and go through all of them before executing a trade. It will take time at first, but after 20 or 30 trades it will require but a few seconds.

Chapter 16

Tactics and Strategy

Here I present a potpourri of tactical and strategic trading ideas culled from countless years of trading.

Screenwriter Lew Hunter claims it is the small touches that make a movie special. It is the same for traders. The small touches you add to your trading program can make it stand out from the crowd—and I know the crowd usually loses. They can also add a personal flavor to your trading, giving it a unique style. It may astound you how a small jiggle can change bottom-line performance in a big way—for better or for worse. Think about your trading program with some perspective; consider the totality of it all, but keep an eye on the details, too. Is it coherent, efficient? Do the various parts work together well, perhaps offer a little the-whole-is-greater-than-the-sum-of-its-parts synergy? Are you pleased and proud of it? Does it have style?

Trending and Trading Markets

Markets have traditionally been classified as trading markets or trending markets, meaning they move predominantly sideways or predominantly up or down. For an excellent modern look at this conventional approach I recommend Ed Ponsi's *FOREX Patterns and Possibilities: Strategies for Trending and Range-Bound Markets* (John Wiley & Sons, 2007).

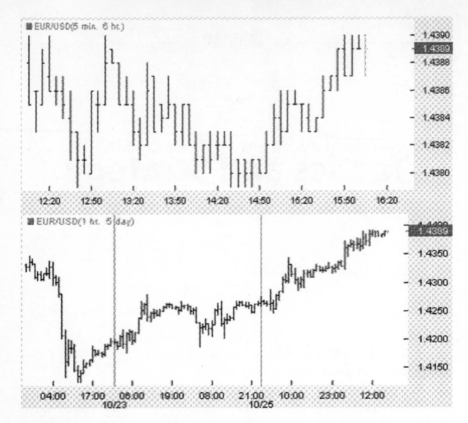

FIGURE 16.1 Trading and Trending Markets
Source: Intellicharts, Inc, www.FXtrek.com.

While this classification is useful, it is limited and very general. Markets are much more than simply trending or trading. Further, trending and trading are relative. A five-minute chart of the EUR/USD may be trading while an hourly chart may be trending. (See Figure 16.1.)

Market Environments (ME)

ME is a method for determining a more meaningful and accurate profile of any market. It is enormously useful as a complement to your trading method, money management, and performance analysis. It can also be used in what is called "quant" in the industry—risk, portfolio, and money manager analysis.

ME also teases out indicator-like information directly off charts without the need for calculation. Bar charts work perfectly. Market Environments was developed by Charles B. Goodman and I have done further development and research. I use it as a primary tool in my Codex approach to trading and include it in my trading method heuristic, money management, and performance evaluations.

There are two primary MEs, two secondary MEs, and a single tertiary ME. Just using the two primaries may add meaningfully to your trading arsenal.

Directional Movement (DP) and Volatility (V)

Directional Movement is the net price change from price-time point A to price-time point B. In Figure 16.2, draw a straight line from the low price at the beginning of the trend to the high price at the end of the trend—the directional movement. This is the net price change. Note that there is price movement on either side of the directional movement line.

There are precise methods for measuring DP, but the core concept is simplicity and avoiding the calculations necessary with indicators.

$$\text{Directional Movement} = P(\text{rice})2 - P(\text{rice})1$$

With A at 0-0 divide the 90 degrees of the chart into five sections. Scale the 90 degrees to equal 100 percent and make each segment 20 percent. Label them 1 through 5.

Volatility is the gross price movement from A to B, given a specified minimum price fluctuation value. You may obtain a ratio with V/DP. Look at a sampling of 50 or 100 charts to get an idea of volatility ranges, then divide the samples into five equal segments as with DP.

In the conventional classification volatility would be similar to trading. (See Figure 16.3.)

You can plot DP and V either on a 10 × 10 matrix or use a continuum from 1 to 25: 1 is lowest V and lowest DP; 25 is highest V and highest DP.

Every market can be defined as one of these 100 MEs or on a continuum. (See Figure 16.4.)

The secondary MEs are Rhythm—Time Rhythm and Price Rhythm—and Thickness.

Price and Time Rhythm (PR and TR)

The markets very often have regular price and time rhythm. But you won't see them if you aren't looking for them.

For time rhythm, measure the length of time (number of time units along the horizontal scale of a bar chart). Measure bottoms to bottoms and tops to tops; make an average of each. The closer the average is to each of the specific instances, the more regular the time rhythm.

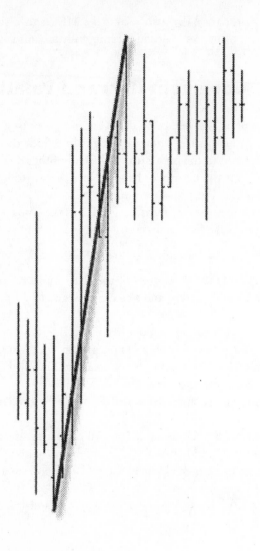

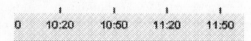

FIGURE 16.2 ME—Directional Movement (DP)

VOLATILITY				
1.5	2.8	3.9	4.0	3.3

AVERAGE
2.4

FIGURE 16.3   ME—Ratios for Trading

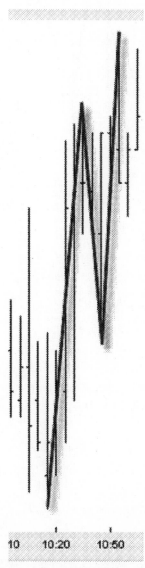

FIGURE 16.4   ME—A Continuum of DP/V

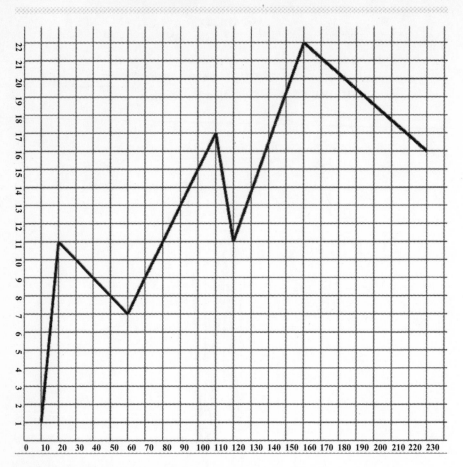

FIGURE 16.5 ME—Price Rhythm

For price rhythm do the same measurements of up trends and down trends. Keep a running record of both values and again, average them. (See Figure 16.5 and Figure 16.6.)

Thickness (T)

Thickness is loosely defined as how much the range from high-to-low of a bar overlaps the previous bar. The more overlap, the thicker the pair or market. Thick markets by definition also possess low volatility and low directional movement. It is enough to define three ranges of thickness—thick, average, and thin. (See Figure 16.7.)

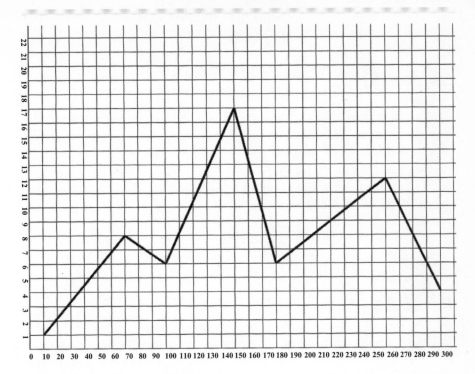

FIGURE 16.6 ME—Time Rhythm

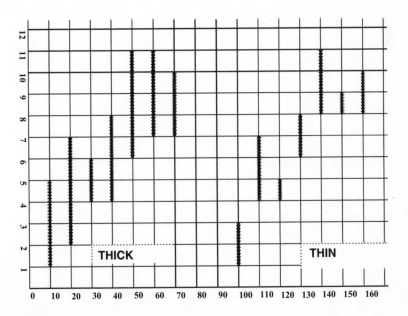

FIGURE 16.7 ME—Thickness

I have found that my trading program works exceptionally well in thick markets. Therefore I seek out such markets to watch on a regular basis.

Shape (S)

To determine shape, draw a line along the significant tops of the market. You may use the same peaks you used for price rhythm. Draw a line along the significant bottoms of the market; you may use the valleys you used for price rhythm, also. (See Figure 16.8.)

The shape forms a rough channel—Mr. Goodman called it a semaphore—in which prices have moved. Average the widths of the channel from top-bottoms.

TIP: You may not want to enter a buy side order near the top of the channel average nor enter a sell side order near the bottom of the channel average.

Pretzels (PZ)

1) Draw a line between the top of a primary swing and the bottom of a primary swing; 2) draw a line between the top of a secondary swing and the bottom of a secondary swing; 3) draw a line connecting the tops and a line connecting the bottoms. These create pretzels, an offshoot of a charting technique invented by the late, great commodity broker Eugene Hartnagle. Somewhat similar to candlesticks, the pretzels yield much information in the angles of the lines, the shapes of the two triangles, and the relative volume of the two triangles. In a unit price chart, pretzels may be made by connecting the high to the low and the open to the close, crossing the tops and the bottoms. (See Figure 16.9.) For more on pretzel charting, see the Currency Codex section of www.fxpraxis.com.

ME Applications

Before initiating a trade, seek to define, even if roughly, directional movement and volatility. What do you see? Do they fit in with the conclusion you reached from the analysis of your other tools? If not, why not? Is it important?

Look at the time rhythm and price rhythm. Is the timing of both rhythms good for a trade? If either the time rhythm average or price rhythm average is off substantially, it may be good to take a bit longer look before pulling the trigger. If both are off, perhaps consider passing the trade. If it is

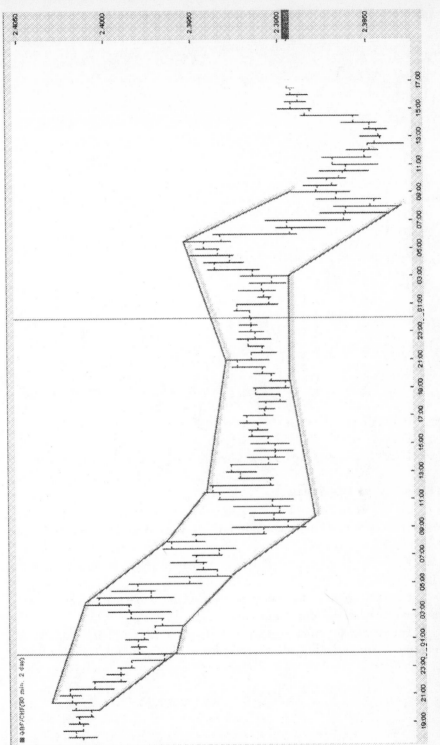

FIGURE 16.8 ME—Shape

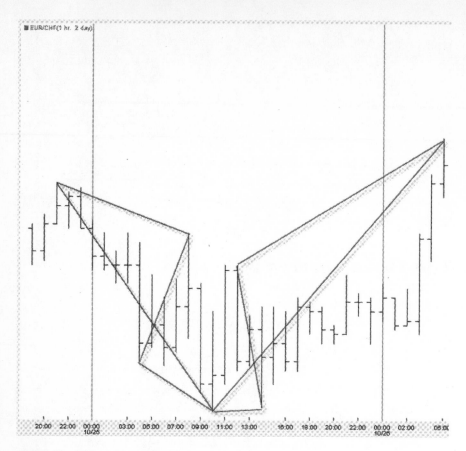

FIGURE 16.9 ME—Pretzels

still on when the rhythms come into line, then you may have a winner. Is the market thick or thin?

A Market Environment Profile is the complete set of MEs for a given chart. (See Table 16.1.)

Specific currency pairs will sometimes exhibit stable market environment profiles over relatively long periods of time.

For each trade you make, keep a short notational record of the directional movement and volatility for that market. Once a month, compare your

TABLE 16.1 ME—Profile
A MARKET PROFILE
DM = 2.2/V = 1.8/PR = 4.4/TR = 3.0

Note: ME Profiles will vary depending on how the individual environments are calculated.

winning trades with your losing trades. Almost all traders find they do better in some primary MEs than in others.

To dig deeper, keep ME profiles for all MEs on your trades, and look for winning patterns and losing patterns.

Mutual and hedge funds, which use multiple managers, may use this last idea to allocate funds to specific managers for specific anticipated long-term MEs; managers receiving more money to trade in markets in which they excel, less in markets in which they do poorly.

Market environments may also be used to back-test systems and methods using historical data. Rather than look for the usual suspects of Sharpe Ratio and so forth, look for methods that did well in a very wide range of market profiles.

The Three Chart System

This is a well-known, popular, and effective tool. Each trader profile should use three FOREX charts with different time unit scales for each currency pair they trade. The middle chart is the analysis chart. The largest unit chart is used for perspective. The smallest scale chart is used for timing.

Guerilla	1-minute	5-minute	30-minute
Scalper	5-minute	30-minute	1-hour
Day Trader	30-minute	1-hour	6-hour
Position Trader	6-hour	12-hour	3-day

I would not trade without the Three Chart System.

The Dagger Entry Principle

This is embarrassing in its simplicity but effective. More often than not, simpler is better.

The principle first appeared in an article, "Conservation with a Gnome," by Michael D. Archer and R. David Van Treuren in *Denver Magazine* (July 1977).

It involves three easy steps:

1. Identify the major trend within the context of your trading profile.

2. Wait for a significant correction, a secondary trend in the opposite direction of the major trend. A significant correction is typically a minimum of 25 percent.

3. Enter your trade as soon as prices resume moving in the direction of the major trend.

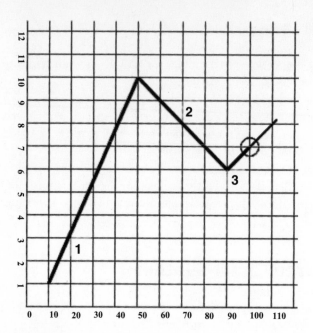

FIGURE 16.10 The Dagger Entry

The Dagger presupposes you have already identified a trade candidate from your trading program work and are watching for an entry point. (See Figure 16.10.)

Sitting on Your Hands

Traders do not particularly enjoy sitting on their hands. It is akin to going to a casino and not throwing a few dollars into a slot machine. The underlying concept is to be patient and wait for trades that really line up for your personal trading program—trading method, attitude, and money management. FOREX provides over 20 highly liquid currency pairs and multiple time frames. The trader is never long without an opportunity. Take your time, pick and choose, then seize the moment! "Wait," as Mr. Goodman would say, "for the sitting ducks."

Be an active watcher; you are sitting on your hands, not covering your eyes. Ask questions, form hypotheses, see how the market reacts, draw conclusions, take notes.

I'd much rather miss a good trade and not win than roll snake-eyes and lose money unnecessarily.

Time Filters

The author has done enormous statistical work on time filters. Some of these studies were published in the now out-of-print and privately published Currency Trader's Companion series. Below is a brief overview of the subject.

Market Opening

Officially the FOREX market opens at 5:30 P.M. EST, though different brokers react differently in different time zones. Keep in mind that over the weekend all currency pairs carry an extra premium in transaction cost. A normal 3-pip bid/ask spread during normal trading hours may increase or balloon to a 10-pip or even 20-pip spread on weekends.

Once the weekend transaction costs return to normal, many pairs exhibit high volatility due to economic influences that occurred over the weekend. The effects of these influences have pent up while traders have been away. Analyzing a set of a number of currency pairs enhances profit opportunities. Frequently a trend emerges in one direction or the other and continues until the weekend influences have been absorbed by the markets. This may entail tracking several more pairs during the early hours of Monday morning than one would normally follow. When opportunity knocks . . .

Market Closing

Many corporations like to clear out last-minute orders on Friday afternoon to avoid possible rollover charges and reduce the risk of holding substantial positions over a weekend. Three-day weekends exacerbate this phenomenon. This equates to increased volatility right before the market closes at 4:20 P.M. on Friday afternoon.

If you trade during the peak period of volatility, always be certain to liquidate your trades before the bid/ask spread jumps to its increased weekend range.

Time of Day

For the most part, the higher volatility periods revolve around banking hours in New York City. This overlaps only slightly with banking hours in London and Frankfurt. Another factor is the time zone in which your broker is located. Taking these three factors into consideration plus your own time zone, you should be able to determine periods of high volatility that increase risk and reward. See Appendix F for details on time zones and banking hours.

Day of Week

The days on which the market opens and closes have already been discussed. Other days of the week may also have special significance. For instance, new interest rates are normally published on Thursdays, which causes immediate changes in USD pairs.

Keep your FOREX calendar computer-side and be aware of pending news for the currencies you trade.

Trading the News

Don't do it!

There are many news traders—those who wait for a news event and try to catch the reaction it invariably entails. I strongly recommend against trading the news for new FOREX participants. Volatility goes into overdrive and although profits can be large and fast, so can losses. Such opportunities do not fit my sitting duck or Belgian Dentist advice for new traders.

I have observed a phenomenon I call shockwave or Price Trace Dispersement (PTD). In many instances the initial reaction to news or an announcement will be a short but sharp price move in one direction. Then occurs the shockwave: a price movement in the opposite direction of the initial reaction, significantly longer in both time and price duration.

All traders should have a daily calendar of pending, scheduled announcements for the currencies they trade. My advice is not to trade these announcements. In fact, I prefer to be on the sidelines just before the announcement and until the shockwave begins.

Watch the market's reaction to the news. Is the reaction as anticipated, or different? Traders sometimes refer to this as "expectation." Expectation, if it is different from reality, can tell you a lot about the technical underpinnings of the market at that particular time. Don't be quick to judge the news reaction; the shockwave may last several hours.

If you must trade the news, do use an execution tool such as www .forexnewsweapon.com. An invaluable reference is James Bickford's *Forex Shockwave Analysis* (McGraw-Hill, 2007).

Going Against the Crowd

There are now quantified daily studies of Contrary Opinion in the currency markets. The most convenient is Jay Meisler's www.global-view.com weekly poll of professional traders. But it isn't difficult to tell from the news where the public (read "retail traders") will be found and on which side of the market they will be trading.

The author's www.fxpraxis.com will soon offer a quantified Contrary Opinion tool for FOREX traders.

The logic of Contrary Opinion is flawless; gathering the information is the difficult part. Once everyone is bullish or bearish, everyone will inevitably be in the market on that side. Where will the money be to take the new positions to continue to drive that trend? Remember, once buyers buy or sellers sell they have functionally no impact on the market until they offset their position.

Trading Methods

I was once bounced from an expert's forum because of my unconventional ideas about trading methods. In a discussion on support and resistance, I proffered the heretical idea that since so many traders used the same methods to calculate support and resistance, they couldn't possibly be of value. I want to find support and resistance areas that other traders ignore. That is where the money is, in my humble and contrary opinion.

This does not mean conventional methods are taboo. It does mean to be aware that many others are using them and have read the same books you have. Conventional chart patterns have been around so long that I find it difficult to believe they can still be the basis of a successful trading program. Those who do use them seem to have found a twist that sets them apart from the crowd.

This also is about expectation. If too many traders expect an indicator or chart pattern to work, it won't; it can't. Markets anticipate events. If everyone anticipates prices going to a certain price to form a head-and-shoulders chart formation, prices will never get there. Traders will anticipate that price and begin buying and selling on that expectation well before prices reach that level.

Markets also discount information. This means that information finds its way into prices before the event. "Buy on the rumor, sell on the news." Stock traders anticipate endless growth from a company. How often have you seen a quarterly report with a large increase in earnings, but the stock price drops? The market anticipated the report, and there is no one left to buy. Worse, while the earnings were good, the rate of earnings was lower than expected.

A weekly hour on the FOREX forums over the weekend will give you a good idea of upcoming expectations. Make a note of them, and see how the market actually reacts. I advise against perusing the forums during the week unless you are seeking specific information; it can be too unsettling.

The Flyer

No, this is not a new trading method. I advise traders—once they have established some basic stability in the markets—to take the occasional flyer.

Yes, I advised you to pick your tools and stick with them. But it is easy to get in a rut. Sometimes we need a self-push to see things from a different perspective, encourage our imagination to find new ideas or joggle the subconscious into freeing an idea or solution tucked deep away.

If you are a scalper, try a day trade. If you use GSCS as a primary trading tool, try DiNapoli Levels. Trade a different pair. I traded FOREX eight years and never gave a second glance at the AUS/USD. One night I took a flyer on it. Now, it is one of my favorite markets.

Even a different look may encourage something good. Change the scale or colors on one of your charts for a day. Pick an indicator you have never studied from your broker-dealer's platform, and add it to a chart for a week.

Bathtub Analysis

Despite the intensive research of the markets using computers over the past 30 years, I am certain there is much yet to find; new methods, chart formations, tactics, and filters. Mr. Goodman used what he called Bathtub Analysis. It is a form of what scientists call hypothesis testing. The logic is that if you aren't looking for something, you won't find it.

Take a few dozen charts with you the next time you bathe or have a few moments of quiet solitude. An hour in the den with classical music in the background and two fingers of a good single-malt scotch also works! Form hypotheses—make them as wild and imaginative as you can; be creative. If the market opens higher and closes lower for three consecutive time units, what happens on the fourth unit? Look for patterns. Keep a notebook.

There are an infinite number of hypotheses to test. Some complex ones would require a computer, but many would not. If your bathtub analysis turns up something promising, drill down on a few dozen charts, and see if it holds up and/or can be quantified in some fashion.

Summary

Market Environments may be used as a trading method, a money management tool, and as a performance analysis method.

Do not encumber your trading program with dozens of small tactical tricks. Stay focused on your primary tools. But do be open to new and promising ideas, especially those that will complement your program. Seek synergy instead of complexity. Test, verify, apply, retest. Or to adapt Hegel, Hypothesis –> Antithesis –> Synthesis.

When and How to Regroup

What do you do if things do not go as planned? Do you regroup or throw in the towel? I assume you used the Campaign Trading Method, and your first and second campaign stakes are gone. You still have another opportunity to succeed.

Take a deep breath. Things do not always go as planned. There is strength in adversity. And learning. It is frustrating to have a losing streak, but even the best traders have them. Famous traders have soared, crashed, soared, and crashed again. I rolled 16 consecutive lemons once in the late 1970s. I was literally a weekend away from throwing in the towel.

Very often small changes or adjustments may make a big difference. But you need to dig deep to find them.

Examine all three areas of your program—trading method, money management, and attitude.

Common Trading Errors

Peruse the list below, and honestly decide if any of these errors might have been a cause:

- **Trading without a stop-loss order:** Neglecting to set a stop-loss order, placed in the market and not a mental stop, is asking for financial disaster. Did you suffer a large loss because of not entering a stop-loss order on a trade?

- **Trading without a take-profit objective:** These, too, should be in the market once you have entered a trade and had it confirmed by your broker. Did a healthy profit deteriorate because you wanted more?

- **Trading too many pairs at one time:** This is usually caused by trading too many pairs concurrently. I recommend only a single trade at any one time for the novice; three at the very most. Did you have too many balls in the air, and one or more of them fell through?

- **Trading in high volatility markets:** Were the pairs traded high volatility markets? The novice should stay with low and midrange volatility pairs.

- **Trading the news:** Did you attempt to trade the news? Or did you incur a large loss because of a news event while you had an open position? Keep your FOREX calendar handy, and try to be flat and out of the market at least until the post-news shockwave has set in for an hour or two.

- **Trading exotic and obscure pairs:** Were you tempted to trade exotic pairs? The liquidity in these markets is poor and fills on orders can be dreadful.

- **Pyramiding:** Did you add to a losing position in hopes of breaking even on a bounce? This is a very common new trader error and can result in a large loss. Pyramiding a winning trade is risky business; pyramiding a losing trade spells disaster.

- **Trade plan:** Did you stick with your predetermined trade plan—or vary from it? Did you follow your trading method, attitude, and money management heuristics for each and every trade?

- **Whipsawing:** Were you whipsawed? This means being caught in a volatile sideways market and constantly reversing your position attempting to catch the trend that never comes. This happens to everyone and is part of the game. If we don't catch our entry after two tries, we move on or go to the sidelines. You should never quickly reverse a position. That implies you have suddenly reversed all of your planning and trade analysis.

- **Overconfidence:** After a couple of winning trades, it is easy to catch the King Kong Syndrome; the warm feeling that everything you touch will turn to gold. It won't. Each trade is a clean slate. The market doesn't know if you are hot or cold.

- **False expectations:** Currency trading offers no guarantees. Do not become discouraged by losses but do not expect to make a fortune overnight. "Take care of the dimes, and the dollars will take care of themselves."

- **Being prepared:** Did you come to the trading session fully prepared with your FOREX calendar and trade plan in hand? Or did you just sit down and decide to make a couple of trades? Currency trading is serious business and requires a serious attitude all of the time.

- **Clouded judgment:** Are you as objective as you can be, keeping fear and greed at bay? The leverage in FOREX is substantial, and losing focus even momentarily can be harmful.

- **Money management:** Did you follow your money management parameters closely? It is easy to stray from one's plan slightly and soon find you are far down the wrong road, unable to turn back easily.

- **Emotional upheaval:** Did you trade at a time when for whatever reasons you were emotionally agitated or worried about something? Bringing sadness or elation to the market will skew your judgment in almost every case. Never trade when under emotional duress or stress.

Review your trades, and see which ones get a checkmark for any of these common errors. Do you see one or two predominate?

Performance Review

Next, look at things from a different perspective—performance. Analyze each campaign separately, then together. You will need the log of your trades. This is available on your broker-dealer's web site on a page named Trade Summary or something similar. You will want at least this information: Date, Pair Traded, Profit/Loss Per Trade, Aggregate Profit/Loss. If your broker hasn't calculated it for you, pick out the highest winner, highest loser, average winner, and average loser. You can use pips or dollars; we are only concerned here with percentages.

Look at the two key profit-loss ratios. Which one needs the least change to move you into the winners' column? Do you need more winners or perhaps a bigger win-lose ratio?

If you stayed with the CTM of money management with a fixed profit-to-loss ratio, at least it is easy to identify the problem: You had too few winners.

If so, it is likely your trading method does need some work. Attempt more long-term perspective before making a trade. Look at the Market Environments of directional movement and volatility. Spend more time studying the long-term perspective chart for your trade profile.

If you strayed from the campaign method, calculate the average profit-to-lose per trade. How far away was it from the suggested parameters for your trading profile? Was it a matter of too few wins or large losses?

Review the trades vis-à-vis all the MEs—directional movement, volatility, thickness, shape, time rhythm, price rhythm. Build an ME Profile for each trade. Do you spot any patterns in the Market Environments or profiles in which you excel, or those in which you struggle?

I have found a high correlation between thick markets and successful trades. In doing ME profiles for other traders I have almost always found some correlation between MEs and trade performance.

Throw out the best trade and the worst, and look again. It is not uncommon for new traders to do well for most of their trades but have one or two losers that destroy overall performance. If this occurred, where was the problem? Near the beginning of the campaign or perhaps toward the end? That may tell you something of value. The CTM does prevent large losses from occurring. You may at least direct your focus to finding more winning trades.

Heuristics Review

The last regrouping step is to study your trade heuristics. Perhaps they are too complex—or too simple? Can you think of a question or two you could have asked about the worst trades that would have stopped you from making them? If so, add it to the appropriate part of the heuristic. Is there a question that would have made you take a trade you passed that would have been a big winner?

When to Say Uncle

We all bring different skills and abilities to the table of life. We cannot all be good at trading. Why some people excel at trading and some do not remains a mystery to me. It may be a situation similar to chess—if you are wired for it, you will succeed; if not, you will not. My hunch is that it has to do with attitude, but I cannot prove it.

But be sure you know when to say Uncle.

Summary

The Campaign Trading Method of money management is designed to give you three solid tries at success in FOREX trading. If you lose all three campaigns, should you try again? That is a question only you can answer. If you have additional risk capital, you may want to take a month away from trading. Make notes while you are away. Start from scratch and rebuild your trading program if small adjustments did not work.

Chapter 18

For the Record

"**W**ould you tell me, please, which way I ought to go from here?" asked Alice in Wonderland. "That depends a great deal on where you want to get to," said the Cheshire Cat.

And, on where you have been before. Keeping good records is a key to success. It is easier to know where you are going when you know where you have been. Good records are critical for reviewing performance and making corrections in your trading program. Since small midcourse corrections can make large differences on your bottom line, good record keeping is necessary in order to find those small changes.

Type of Records

Business Records

These pertain to the business of FOREX trading. They include *all* communication with your broker-dealer, the vendors you use for third-party tools, your Internet bookmarks, and, if you trade as some legal entity, the documentation pertaining thereof.

Accounting Records

These are the records you need for tax purposes. Your broker will supply those pertaining to your trading. You will also need any receipts for the cost of doing business. Your accountant can guide you on what is and what is not a legitimate expense.

If the tax man cometh, cheer—he ignores losers who have no more money. No matter where you live in this world, there is a Caesar unto whom you must render. Good accounting records and a competent accountant will aid you in not rendering more than your fair share. As mentor Charlie Goodman said upon winning a twin-quin for $3,000 at the greyhound races and having 20 percent deducted from his check, "Where were they when I was losing!"

Trade and Performance Records

Your trading platform keeps a record of all your trading activity. Some are better than others, but they all provide the core information.

Most brokers do a fantastic job of this task. Many even offer a statistical page overview of your trading performance. If not, you should definitely calculate and maintain your own. Here is what I suggest at a bare minimum:

- Entry date
- Exit date
- Pair
- Position (buy/sell)
- Entry price
- Exit price
- Net gain (pips and dollars)
- Closed position account balance

The pertinent money management ratios and statistics are also recommended, as are at least the primary market environments for each trade.

Performance records are those for diagnosing errors and keeping you on target with your trading plan. I review performance on a weekly and monthly basis. Plan to spend a few hours a month on this task. You will almost certainly discover small characteristics about your trading. You can use some to minimize losses, others to maximize profits. It does not take much to turn a loser into a winner or vice versa. Think of trading in terms of a process with a continuous feedback loop. Trading is a dynamic, not static enterprise.

Record keeping can be very involved or simple. I like to keep it simple as possible while still recording enough information to evaluate performance on an ongoing basis. You may certainly jiggle the tumblers as you begin trading and see for yourself what information is worth preserving.

FOREX trading is a continuous process—unlike stocks and futures, which begin and end at a set time. No one can trade 24 hours a day. When you begin a new trading session you are bound to have missed something. At the end of a session write a few "pick-up" notes about your thinking on markets you are trading. When you come to the next session, a quick review of those notes will help you get in sync again quickly with the markets. I take 10 minutes before each session for reviewing pick-up notes and 10 minutes at the end of each session to write them.

The Rogers Method

Trader Joe Rogers takes performance recording and the feedback loop to the next level. He uses the Camtasia suite of tools to record just about everything that happens during a trading session. "Smile, You're on FOREX camera!" For an idea of what Joe's method involves, go to www.camtasia.com.

The SnagIt Tool

For a less intensive version of the same concept, use the SnagIt tool (see Figure 18.1). You can annotate charts on the fly to remember what your thoughts were at the time you made a trade or did an analysis. Go to www.techsmith.com for more information. It is great for marking MEs and making short notes. Techsmith is also the maker of Camtasia.

Using SnagIt, you can select and capture anything on your screen, then easily add text, arrows, or effects, and save the screen capture to a file or share it immediately by e-mail or IM.

Capture Anything

Capture an article, image, or Web page directly from your screen. Or, capture windows, menus, icons, and regions from any application that runs on your PC.

Edit and Transform

The SnagIt image editor makes it easy to add creative and professional touches to your screen capture. Transform your images with a full-featured paint tools palette, a variety of edge effects, and practical options for color and size adjustment.

Share Easily

E-mail, copy and paste, print, and IM your screen captures, or upload them to your Web site, SnagIt helps you communicate any way you prefer.

FIGURE 18.1 SnagIt
Source: TechSmith, www.techsmith.

Planning Records

Always come to *every* trading session with a *plan*! A daily or session trade plan is a must; I would not touch my mouse without one in front of me. I also maintain a weekly trade plan because I am primarily a day trader and have a bit longer-term perspective.

The trade plan will vary from trader to trader depending very much on your trading method, your money management parameters, trader profile, and heuristic. The touchstone of any plan, however, is contingency planning. Know what action you will or will not take, given a wide range of possibilities during the trading session.

You will almost certainly include items specific to your personal trading method on the Daily Plan.

Keep a notepad handy for ideas you might have while sitting on your hands.

Summary

View trading as a process with a continuous feedback loop. Strive to review your performance regularly and make evolutionary not revolutionary changes to your trading program. Do not be afraid to dig deep for small factors; even the smallest may make a large difference in performance to the bottom line of a trading campaign. It may sound obvious, but seek to minimize losing trades and maximize winning trades. For many traders it is the big loser or the big winner in a campaign that tells the tale.

5 Part

Extra for Experts

Chapter 19

Options and Exotics

At the Interbank level, options have been an integral part of the FOREX landscape for many years. It is estimated that options may comprise up to 10 percent of FOREX market share, a substantial portion for hedging purposes by banks and corporations.

A bank may be at risk on an international loan for a short period of time. Hedging with currency options can eliminate that risk. Hedging acts as an insurance policy. If the bank is at risk on the long side of the EUR/USD, they can take the opposite position in options. A corporation might do the same while awaiting payment on a large sale. Loss on the business-side transaction is compensated by a profit in the hedge. More on hedging in Chapter 20, "The Final Frontiers."

But for retail currency traders, speculative options trading has been the domain of seedy boiler-room operations until recently. Several reputable broker-dealers now offer FOREX options, and the Philadelphia Options Exchange (www.phlx.com) has gone a long way toward legitimizing currency options and making them available to retail traders. The International Securities Exchange (www.ise.com) is also venturing into the FOREX options space. (See Figure 19.1.)

The PHLX web site has a great deal of information about options, including beginner tutorials. Shani Shamah has written an excellent text reference on the subject, *A Currency Options Primer* (John Wiley & Sons, 2006).

Exotics, currency pairs with the USD, and a small or exotic countries' currency provide exceptional opportunities along with higher risks than the

FX SUMMARY TABLE

CURRENCY NAME	CURRENCY CODE	CONVENTION	SYMBOL	BIN	FX PMM	HISTORICAL RATES
ISE FX British Pound	(GBP)	USD/GBP	BPX	81	Timber Hill LLC	download
ISE FX Canadian Dollar	(CAD)	USD/CAD	CDD	81	Timber Hill LLC	download
ISE FX Euro	(EUR)	USD/EUR	EUI	81	Timber Hill LLC	download
ISE FX Yen	(JPY)	USD/JPY	YUK	81	Timber Hill LLC	download

FIGURE 19.1 ISE FOREX Options

Source: International Securities Exchange, LLC. ISE® is a registered trademark of International Securities Exchange, LLC. Copyright © 2008, International Securities Exchange, LLC. All rights reserved.

majors or top-tier crosses. They offer variety, have trading personalities all their own, and may be attractive if you have some knowledge or insight about the exotic country other traders do not.

Options

Options are not a simple investment vehicle and the terminology can be confusing.

Options may be used for speculation—to make a profit—or as a hedge—to protect a position maintained in the normal course of one's business. If you hedge a speculative spot FOREX position with options, it is considered a speculative hedge. It is only a true hedge if you are hedging a legitimate business transaction that entails currency risk.

For speculation, options may be used as either a trading instrument in and of themselves or as a money management tool paired with spot FOREX trading.

I strongly advise new traders to become fully comfortable in the spot FOREX space before considering options. Because of the additional time value component, the matrix of possibilities and strategies can be enormously complex and mathematically heady.

The value of an option decays over time until it reaches zero. (See Figure 19.2.) The decay is not always linear, nor is its path easily predictable.

In options time is not on your side. It is a constantly deteriorating ("decaying") value. The price of the underlying currency must not just move in your favor to make money, it must move enough to compensate for the time decay.

An Options Primer

An *option* is the right to buy or sell the underlying currency at a specific price for a specified period of time. You may *purchase* an option or *write* an option. For speculative purposes, purchasing is most common.

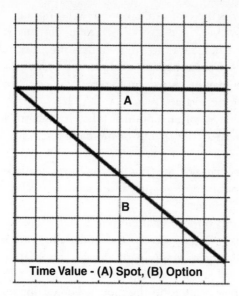

Time Value - (A) Spot, (B) Option

FIGURE 19.2 Options Decay

The right to buy is a *call*. You have the right to *call* the position away from someone holding the spot equivalent.

The right to sell is a *put*. You have the right to *put* a spot position to someone.

You purchase a call if you believe the currency price is headed up. You purchase a put if you believe the currency price is headed down. An option is a contract between a buyer and a seller; the seller is termed the *writer*, the buyer is the purchaser. Let us examine the purchase side first.

Basic Options Terms

The *strike price* is the price at which the call or put may be exercised. It does not make sense to exercise a call or put (exchange it for a spot position) unless the call or put is *in-the-money*—trading above (call) or below (put) the strike price.

You may, of course, *offset* your option, buying it back (a put) or selling it (a call) before the expiration or even if it is not in-the-money. You have effectively transferred your contractual obligation to someone else.

The *expiration* is the time frame of the option. In stocks and commodities, these are normally set for months. An option is said to expire in September, for example. In FOREX the expiration dates are closer since very few traders hold positions for months at a time.

The *premium* is the cost of the option. With options you are paying for the time-value as well as the price values. The underlying value of the option falls as time approaches the expiration—unless the price value increases at a faster rate. Options pricing, because of these twin values, can be complex and unpredictable. You may be correct on the price direction and still lose money because of decaying time values.

The *intrinsic value* of an option is what it is worth if exercised at any given time. When an option is out-of-the-money its only intrinsic worth is time value.

A call is *in-the-money* if the spot price is above the strike price; *out-of-the-money* if below. A put is in-the-money if the spot price is below the strike price; out-of-the-money if above.

The price of an option, or premium, is determined primarily by strike and expiration vis-à-vis the price of the underlying currency. But there are other factors such as liquidity, speculative fervor, and volatility. For example, an out-of-the-money call is more valuable if the underlying currency is volatile; it has a better chance of going to in-the-money. Forecasting option prices—even knowing or inputting the price of the underlying currency—is far from an exact science. A small change in time value or price value may cause the option price to change by an inordinate amount. The various price factors appear to interact in a nonlinear fashion. Mathematic whizzes will find a similarity to the famous *n*-body problem.

Traditionally, currency options have been of two types:

- **American-style:** This type of option may be exercised at any point up until expiration.
- **European-style:** This type of option may be exercised only at the time of expiration.

And they call us crooks!

If you trade with options, consider only American-style. You may find terms for other flavors of options at: http://www.FOREXdirectory.net/exover.html.

The Pros and Cons of Options

Major pro: Buying options limits your exposure. The maximum you can lose is the value of the option; the price you paid for it.

Purchasing options as a speculative vehicle offers limited downside—you cannot lose more than the price you paid for the option—and unlimited upside, at least on a call. If you purchase a put, your profit is technically limited to the underlying currency going to zero.

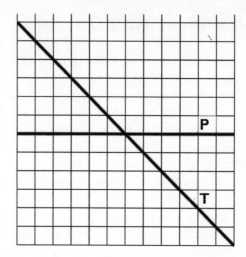

FIGURE 19.3 The Downside of Options

The cost of the option may be less than the margin on the same spot position.

Major con: You pay for the time value of an option. In spot FOREX other than rollover charges (typically very small), you do not pay for time you hold a position.

Forecasting option pricing—even given the price of the underlying currency—is difficult.

If your option expires worthless, you lose your entire purchase price. This can occur from prices moving sideways and the time premium decaying to zero. If prices move sideways for the spot trader, he loses nothing and retains his margin funds. You may find prices of the currency moving in your favor but not fast enough to compensate for the time decay—a discouraging predicament most options traders have experienced more than once. If the time on your option expires and the option is "out-of-the-money," its value is zero. (See Figure 19.3.)

The Four Basic Options Strategies

Terminology note: Be careful not to associate "buying" with calls only. You may also buy or purchase a put.

1. Purchasing a call
2. Purchasing a put
3. Writing a call
4. Writing a put

Purchasing and Writing Options

You may purchase either a call or a put, although it may sound strange to purchase the right to sell.

You may either purchase or write an option—either a call or a put. Remember, an option is a contract between a purchaser and a writer. An option writer collects the premium as income from the purchaser. The writer of a call must be ready to have his spot position called away or purchase a spot position if the buyer exercises his option. The writer of a put must be ready to purchase (or repurchase) the spot position from the buyer of the put.

If a writer holds a spot position when he enters an options contract, he is said to be a *covered writer*. If he does not hold a position, he is said to be *uncovered* or a *naked writer*.

Advanced Options Strategies

As I have mentioned, the mathematics of options is enormously complex. There are many high-level option strategies based on combinations of puts/calls, writing/purchasing, different strikes and expirations. They are not for the new trader!

Some of these have exotic names such as "condor" or "butterfly" derived from the graph of profit/loss calculations for the strategy. (See Figure 19.4.)

The Retail FOREX Options Landscape

There is a substantial Over-the-Counter (OTC) FOREX options market—this has been around for many years. But it is only open to banks, institutions, and large corporations. Fortunately large broker-dealers are beginning to tap into this arena and offer it to their customers.

For listed currency options, the retail trader must look to either the PHLX (www.phlx.com) or the International Securities Exchange (www.ise.com). Both offer listed FX options in a limited number of markets. (See Figure 19.5.) Selection and liquidity is currently low, but listed FOREX options have enormous retail potential.

Some broker-dealers offering options trading: Cfosfx, www.cfosfx.com; and SaxoBank, www.saxobank.com. Oanda, www.oanda.com, offers something called a BoxOption with intriguing possibilities.

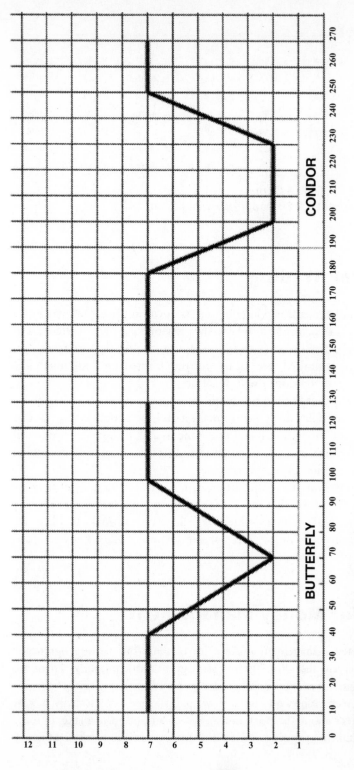

FIGURE 19.4 Exotic Option Strategies

CURRENCY CROSSRATES

	AUD	GBP	CAD	EUR	JPY ·	CHF	USD
AUD	1	0.4590	0.9159	0.6040	97.1800	0.9827	0.8996
GBP	2.1774	1	1.9948	1.3158	211.6700	2.1402	1.9590
CAD	1.0922	0.5014	1	0.6599	106.1000	1.0724	0.9815
EUR	1.6545	0.7598	1.5155	1	160.8800	1.6265	1.4884
JPY	0.0103	0.0047	0.0094	0.0062	1	0.0101	0.0092
CHF	1.0169	0.4667	0.9309	0.6144	98.9000	1	0.9149
USD	1.1117	0.5105	1.0183	0.6718	108.0500	1.0924	1

FIGURE 19.5 PHLX FOREX Options
Source: Philadelphia Stock Exchange, www.phlx.com.

Options for Trading

If you have concluded a currency is going up or down in price, you may buy a call or buy a put on the currency. Today only a few major pairs are offered, but the list is growing; a few brokers are dealing options on exotic currencies. You gain the advantage of limited risk but pay for that limited exposure much like an insurance policy; if you don't use it, it is lost.

Unfortunately, that limited risk tends to lull inexperienced traders into a false sense of security. They don't have to make a decision about getting out of a bad trade because of a margin call and are prone to let a losing trade ride until either the price of the currency is so far away and/or there is so little time value remaining that the option expires worthless.

Always keep in mind the basic options con position. You may see the currency price go in your favor but the time value decays at a faster rate. The net result is your option goes down in value. I experienced this worst case phenomenon in stock options early in my career, and it does not make for anything approaching emotional nirvana!

Options for Money Management

Options for money management make a lot of sense but require significant study, experience, and discipline for the strategy to work properly. There are three basic strategies for money management with options but dozens of permutations on them. Remember, no matter how sophisticated your strategy is, you still must be correct about the price movement of an option to make a profit. There's no magic in the torturing of the numbers, friend. (See Figure 19.6).

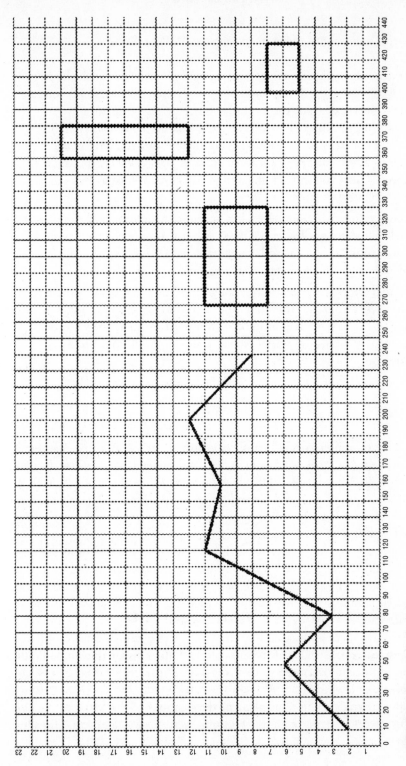

FIGURE 19.6 Box Options

These strategies are all based on long the EUR/USD.

Strategy 1: Perhaps you entered a market with extremely high volatility; long the Euro, short the US Dollar (EUR/USD). You might purchase a put on the Euro. Once prices begin to move in your favor, you can raise your stop to a break-even point and sell the put. Of course, you've lost money on the put, but you have bought time to allow your position to stabilize in your favor. If the trade moves against you instead, the option will cover at least a large portion of your spot trade loss.

Strategy 2: Perhaps you have a long-term trade in mind and plan to hold the position over several days. A put helps anchor your position against the risks and vagrancies of a long-term hold. In FOREX the risks associated with long hold periods is substantial.

Strategy 3: In this scenario of a long-term hold, you could write a call against your position and collect income during the holding time from the purchaser of the call. You must calculate the value of the income versus the risk of having your spot position called away from you.

Exotics

Although the terminology is not consistent throughout the industry: A *major* is a pair consisting of currencies from the United States (USD), Great Britain (GBP), Japan (JPY), Europe (EUR), Australia (AUD), and Canada (CAD). A minor pair consists of one of these and an exotic. An *exotic* is a pair with two exotics. Exotics may also be called *emerging*, although there is not a strict one-to-one relationship between the two. (See Table 19.1.)

Exotics are *illiquid*—there is much less trading in them than in the majors or minors. The degree varies; the Polish Zloty is relatively liquid while the Thai Baht is very illiquid. The lack of liquidity means that pip spreads are high and large orders may be difficult to execute. Risks are greater but so is profit potential.

Given a news event in an exotic country, prices may soar or dive, and exiting at any reasonable price may be difficult. Devaluations are uncommon, but when they do occur, overnight price changes of 20 percent or more can be either a disaster or a windfall.

Old-time traders will remember the devaluations of the Mexican Peso in the 1970s of 50 percent or more. Fortunes were made—and lost—literally overnight.

TABLE 19.1 Exotic Pairs

Currency	Name	Symbol
BRAZIL	REAL	BRL
CHILE	PESO	CLP
CZECH REPUBLIC	KORUNA	CZK
HUNGARY	FORINT	HUF
ICELAND	KRONA	ISK
INDIA	RUPEE	INR
LATVIA	LAT	LVL
LITHUANIA	LITAS	LTL
MEXICO	MEXICAN PESO	MXN
MOLDOVA	LEU	MDL
POLAND	ZLOTY	PLN
SOUTH AFRICA	RAND	ZAR
THAILAND	BAHT	THB
TURKEY	LIRA	TRY
TURKMENISTAN	MANAT	TMM
URUGUAY	PESO	UYU
YUGOSLAVIA	NEW DINAR	YUD

Trading Exotics

If you are interested in trading the exotics, buying call or put options may be an excellent idea. The disadvantages of options trading probably outweigh the risks involved in spot trading. Nonetheless, I believe the new trader should first gain experience in the spot FOREX arena before attempting options, exotics, or both.

GFT FOREX, www.GFTFOREX.com is a trailblazer in offering exotics to retail customers, but most other major brokers offer at least a few exotics. Notable are Gain Capital, www.gaincapital.com and Saxo Bank, www.saxobank.com. Visit web sites for a list of currencies traded by each broker-dealer. The brokers who offer options also tend to be stronger in exotics.

I must repeat: Be very mindful of liquidity in exotics. If you think liquidity in the AUS/USD is poor at 9:00 pm, wait until you see the Thai Baht spreads! There is also the potential instability of these counties, causing their currencies to move suddenly and sharply. Requoting and ballooning spreads could be an issue, even for small traders. If you use an ECN broker instead of a market maker to trade exotics, be doubly cautious. Remember, an ECN must find an order to match yours and does not act as a counterparty to your trades.

Begin trading exotics in very small lots of perhaps 5,000 or 10,000 to get a feel for liquidity and other potential execution issues.

Summary

Options and exotics offer new possibilities for traders and open many doors to new and exciting trade opportunities. My advice is that there is enough action in the major pairs and the top-tier crosses spot market to satisfy most traders. Consider options as a money management tool more than as a substitute for spot FOREX. Trade exotics and options as speculative vehicles only after you have become experienced in the spot market of the major pairs and crosses.

The Final Frontiers

This chapter is optional for the novice currency trader, although investors with some trading experience will find it informative. All traders should at least be aware of advanced FOREX techniques and ongoing market research.

Rollovers

A rollover is the process whereby the settlement of an open trade is rolled forward to another value date. The cost of this process is based on the interest rate differential of the two currencies.

In the spot FOREX market, trades must be settled within two business days. For example, if a trader sells a certain number of currency units on Wednesday, he must deliver an equivalent number of units on Friday. Yet currency trading systems may allow for a rollover, with which open positions can be swapped forward to the next settlement date (giving an extension of two additional business days). The interest rate for such a swap is predetermined, and, in fact, these swaps are actually financial instruments that can also be traded on the currency market.

In any spot rollover transaction, the difference between the interest rates of the base and counter currencies is reflected as an overnight loan. If the trader holds a long position in the currency with the higher interest rate, he would gain on the spot rollover. The amount of such a gain would fluctuate from day to day according to the precise interest-rate differential between the base and the counter currency. Such rollover rates are quoted in dollars and are shown in the interest column of the FOREX trading system. Rollovers, however, will not affect traders who never hold a position overnight, since the rollover is exclusively a day-to-day phenomenon.

Some brokers will automatically roll over open trades while others may liquidate orders that exceed the two-day limitation. Also some dealers may append a rollover charge in addition to the interest differential. Rollover credits or debits are reflected in the unrealized profit-and-loss column of the open position.

If you intend to maintain open positions longer than two days, carefully read your dealer's policy agreement, or consult their customer service department. Also note that rollover costs may affect margin requirements.

Hedging

A hedge is a position or combination of positions in one security that reduces the risk of your primary position in the same security.

An example of hedging in commodity futures is the Midwest farmer who grows #1 Soft Red Wheat and intends to take his harvest physically to market for September delivery. After tilling the soil and planting the seeds in late spring, the farmer initiates a short (sell) commodity futures contract for September Wheat at the Chicago Board of Trade at what he feels is a fair price. If the price of wheat declines dramatically in September, the farmer will suffer losses on his physical delivery but will make profits on his futures contract. If the price of wheat rises substantially in the fall, the farmer will make profits on his physical delivery but will suffer losses on his futures contract. Thus, hedging not only reduces risk but can also be used to lock in predetermined profits in some situations.

Normally when you have an open position to buy or sell at your FOREX dealer, and you open a new position in the opposite direction, the two positions will close each other out. If you had a position for USD/CHF to buy and you opened a new position USD/CHF to sell, both positions would close, since you cannot be buying and selling currencies at the same time. The feature of hedging however, allows you to do exactly that if your FOREX dealer offers this trading feature.

When you open a hedge position, both positions (the original and the newly hedged one) will remain open. You will have two positions, going in the opposite direction of each other in the same currency pair. This is basically used to lock your current loss or win, until you have a better understanding of where the market is moving. Theoretically, profit is to be gained by skillful timing of the liquidation orders. If liquidated at the same time, the trader will automatically lose the transaction cost.

Brokers who offer hedging do not normally require additional margin for the second hedged position. Consult your broker for details before attempting to apply this rather esoteric trading strategy. You can hedge a speculative position, but it remains speculative and is not considered a legitimate hedge.

Arbitrage

In general, arbitrage is the purchase or sale of any financial instrument and simultaneous taking of an equal and opposite position in a related market in order to take advantage of small price differentials between markets. Essentially, arbitrage opportunities arise when currency prices go out of sync with each other. There are numerous forms of arbitrage involving multiple markets, future deliveries, options, and other complex derivatives. A less sophisticated example of a two-currency, two-location arbitrage transaction follows:

Bank ABC offers 170 Japanese Yen for one US Dollar and Bank XYZ offers only 150 Yen for one Dollar. Go to Bank ABC and purchase 170 Yen. Next go to Bank XYZ and sell the Yen for $1.13. In a little more than the time it took to cross the street that separates the two banks, you earned a 13 percent return on your original investment. If the anomaly between the two banks' exchange rates persists, repeat the transactions. After exchanging currencies at both banks six times, you will have more than doubled your investment.

Within the FOREX market, triangular arbitrage is a specific trading strategy that involves three currencies, their correlation, and any discrepancy in their parity rates. Thus, there are no arbitrage opportunities when dealing with just two currencies in a single market. Their fluctuations are simply the trading range of their exchange rate.

In the subsequent examples, I will refer to Tables 20.1 to 20.4 of currency pairs consisting of the five most frequently traded pairs (USD, EUR, JPY, GBP, and CHF) with recent bid/ask rates.

We omitted the other two majors, CAD and AUD, for the sake of simplicity and not because of lack of arbitrage opportunities in these two majors.

TABLE 20.1 Combinations of the Five Most Frequently Traded Currencies

Currency	Bid	Ask	Pip Spread
CHF/JPY	0.8514	0.8519	4
EUR/CHF	1.5676	1.5678	2
EUR/GBP	0.6915	0.6917	2
EUR/JPY	133.51	133.54	3
EUR/USD	1.2638	1.2640	2
GBP/CHF	2.2666	2.6674	8
GBP/JPY	193.02	193.10	8
GBP/USD	1.8275	1.8278	3
USD/CHF	1.2402	1.2405	3
USD/JPY	105.61	105.64	3

EXAMPLE 1: Two USD pairs and one cross pair (multiply).

First we must identify certain characteristics and distinguish the following categories:

USD is the base currency (leftmost currency in the pair):

USD/CHF	1.2402/05
USD/JPY	105.61/64

USD is the quote currency (rightmost currency in the pair):

EUR/USD	1.2638/40
GBP/USD	1.8275/78

Cross Rates (non-USD currency pairs):

CHF/JPY	85.14/19
EUR/CHF	1.5676/78
EUR/GBP	0.6915/17
EUR/JPY	133.51/54
GBP/CHF	2.2666/74
GBP/JPY	193.02/10

The fact that the USD is the base currency in two of the pairs (USD/CHF and USD/JPY) and is the quote currency in two other pairs (EUR/USD and GBP/USD) plays an important role in the arithmetic of arbitrage. We begin our investigation with just the bid prices. (See Table 20.2.)

The criterion whether to multiply or divide the USD pairs in order to calculate the cross rate is simple:

If the USD is the base currency in both pairs, then divide the USD pairs.

If the USD is the quote currency in both pairs, then divide the USD pairs.

Otherwise multiply the USD pairs.

To determine the deviation from parity for each cross pair, subtract the exchange rate from the calculated rate and convert the floating point decimals to pip values. (See Table 20.3.)

TABLE 20.2 Formulas for Cross Currencies

CHFJPY	= USDJPY / USDCHF	85.14 = 105.61 / 1.2402	85.1556
EURCHF	= EURUSD × USDCHF	1.5676 = 1.2638 × 1.2402	1.567365
EURGBP	= EURUSD / GBPUSD	0.6915 = 1.2638 / 1.8275	0.691546
EURJPY	= EURUSD × USDJPY	133.51 = 1.2638 × 105.61	133.4699
GBPCHF	= GBPUSD × USDCHF	2.2666 = 1.8275 × 1.2402	2.266466
GBPJPY	= GBPUSD × USDJPY	193.02 = 1.8275 × 105.61	193.0023

TABLE 20.3	Calculations for Cross Currencies			
Pair	Rate	Calculation	Deviation	Pip Values
CHFJPY	85.1556	−85.14	= +0.0156	+1.56 pips
EURCHF	1.567365	−1.5676	= −0.000235	−2.35 pips
EURGBP	0.691546	−0.6915	= +0.000046	+0.46 pips
EURJPY	133.4699	−133.51	= −0.0401	−4.01 pips
GBPCHF	2.266466	−2.2666	= +0.000134	+1.34 pips
GBPJPY	193.0023	−193.02	= −0.0177	−1.77 pips

From Table 20.3, we can see that the EUR/JPY is out of parity by 4 pips. To determine if an arbitrage opportunity is profitable, we must first calculate the total transaction cost by adding the three bid/ask spreads of the corresponding pairs. (See Table 20.4.)

An 8-pip transaction cost to earn a 4-pip profit is counterproductive (it amounts to a 4-pip loss). If the parity deviation (the number of pips by which the three currency pairs are out of alignment) were greater, say 30 pips, then a definite arbitrage opportunity exists.

The trading mechanism to take advantage of this anomaly requires some consideration. First, determine what market actions are necessary to correct this anomaly. Assume that the EUR/JPY rate is currently trading at 133.51 and the calculated rate using the current EUR/USD and USD/JPY pairs is 133.81 (a 30-pip deviation). Parity between the three currencies will be restored if the following price action occurs:

- The EUR/JPY pair rises to 133.81, or
- The product of the EUR/USD and USD/JPY pairs drops to 133.51.

Therefore the following trades are required to "lock" in the 30-pip profit:

- Buy one lot of the EUR/JPY pair
- Sell one lot of the EUR/USD pair

TABLE 20.4 Transaction Cost	
EUR/USD	2
USD/JPY	+3
EUR/JPY	+3
	8

- Sell one lot of the USD/JPY pair
- Liquidate all three trades simultaneously when parity is re-established

Warning: Executing only one, or even two, legs of the three trades required in an arbitrage package does not guarantee a profit and may be quite dangerous. All three trades must be executed simultaneously before the locked-in profit can be realized.

EXAMPLE 2: Two USD pairs and one cross pair (divide)

The above example uses the product of the two USD currencies to calculate the cross rate. An example of the ratio of the two USD currencies follows. Assume the EUR/GBP cross pair is currently trading at 0.6992 and that the ratio between the EUR/USD and GBP/USD pairs is calculated as 0.6952, a 40-pip deviation. Parity will be restored when the following price actions occur:

- The EUR/GBP pair drops to 0.6952, or
- The ratio of the EUR/USD and GBP/USD pairs rises to 0.6992.

In order for the second action to rise, either the EUR/USD pair must also rise or the GBP/USD pair must decline (this differs in the previous example). Therefore the following trades are required to realize a 40-pip profit:

- Sell one lot of the EUR/GBP pair
- Buy one lot of the EUR/USD pair
- Sell one lot of the GBP/USD pair
- Liquidate all three trades the moment parity is re-established

EXAMPLE 3: Three non-USD cross pairs

Technically the arbitrage strategy can be performed on three non-USD currency pairs also. In this example, we will examine a straddle between the three European majors (EUR, GBP, CHF) where we focus on the EUR/CHF pair in respect to the two GBP currency pairs (GBP/CHF and EUR/GBP).

Assume the current rates of exchange are:

EUR/CHF = 1.5676/78
EUR/GBP = 0.6915/17
GBP/CHF = 2.2604/12

and their relationship is:

$$EUR/CHF = EUR/GBP \times GBP/CHF$$

Thus the calculated value for the EUR/CHF rate is 0.6915×2.2604 or 1.5631. The deviation from parity is $-.0045$ ($1.5631 - 1.5676$) or 45 CHF pips since CHF is the pip currency in the EUR/CHF pair. The trading strategy is:

- Sell one lot of EUR/CHF
- Buy one lot of EUR/GBP
- Buy one lot of GBP/CHF
- Liquidate all three when parity is re-established

If all three trades are executed successfully, a profit of 45 CHF pips is realized. Subtract the three bid/ask spreads for the transaction costs ($2 + 2 + 8 = 12$) to see a net profit of 33 CHF pips. Now convert CHF pips to dollars (33 divided by USD/CHF rate 1.2402) to obtain 27 USD pips.

It should be noted in all the examples presented above that only three currencies are analyzed simultaneously. It is possible to add a fourth, or even a fifth, currency to the mix though this is normally left to the very serious arbitrage strategists.

The methodology for examining four (or even five or six) currencies at one time is to calculate every possible 3-currency combination among the currencies selected. Rearrange them in magnitude of deviation from parity. Examine the deviations closely to see if there is a single anomaly or possibly even a double anomaly among the four currencies. This type of scrutiny will then determine if a 4-currency arbitrage opportunity exists.

Specialized software is definitely required when dealing with four or more currencies in a single arbitrage package.

Pros and Cons of Arbitrage

Using triangular arbitrage strategies on the FOREX market has one very salient advantage: predetermined profits can be realized if the trades execute smoothly. Unfortunately, the disadvantages of this strategy are numerous:

1. Higher transactions costs. The trader must pay the bid/ask spreads on three separate trades.
2. Higher margin requirements. Roughly three times the margin is necessary to execute the arbitrage strategy and odd-lot trading may be required for the small capital investor.
3. Precision timing is required. Arbitrage opportunities are usually short lived.

4. Multiple dimensions. The trader must thoroughly understand the arbitrage mechanism in order to determine which currency pairs to buy and which to sell. Each arbitrage package consists of two buys and one sell or one buy and two sells. Miscalculating any one of the three trades can cause disaster.

5. Advanced monitoring techniques are usually required. This means calculating the above analysis on several pairs simultaneously in real-time and will involve a software program that analyzes streaming quotes continually. It is possible to perform these tasks manually but the trader must have a high tolerance for tedium.

I must also mention that in the examples above, I intentionally simplified calculations by using only the bid price throughout. When executing an actual arbitrage trade, the investor must supply both bid and ask rate where applicable.

Artificial Intelligence

Although it has lost some luster in this century, application of artificial intelligence methods have been seen in the FOREX arena. The three primary approaches are: expert systems, neural networks, and genetic algorithms.

I developed an expert system-neural network hybrid in the early 1980s, Jonathan's Wave, and used it successfully in the futures markets for a number of years. I moved on to exploring a cellular automata–based model, The Trend Machine. (See below.) But the possibility of revamping Jonathan's Wave with modern techniques and computer firepower has rekindled my interest in artificial intelligence. The entire AI approach may have a second wind.

Although there is intense disagreement on this subject, I feel these methods are still linear or conventional. Past market prices and data are manipulated to make forecasts, and curve-fitting remains the theoretical backbone involved.

Complexity Theory Models

The search for a Philosopher's Stone—a method that will consistently beat the market—has been afoot from the very inception of the markets themselves. In the mid-1900s many traders published (usually privately) small volumes with techniques to beat the markets. They typically looked good on paper—but failed when applied to real-time trading. Most were tested on simplistic market environments (trading markets, trending markets) and failed when the real-time market morphed into a different environment. (See Back-testing and Market Environments, Currency Codex, www.fxpraxis.com.)

I am reminded of the secret system used by a trader I met in Hawaii in the 1980s. He believed the random spread of ink spots from the news printer was actually hidden buy and sell signals from the floor traders. To each his own.

The advent of computer analysis in the 1970s and automated trading in the 1990s encouraged traders to use this new tool to find the trading method over the rainbow. Much of the effort has been directed to using vast batteries of conventional techniques with deep mathematical and statistical twists. It is clear, after 30 years of effort, no linear method is going to beat the market, at least not consistently in all markets.

The Trend Machine

There is however exciting and promising research using nonlinear methods and modeling techniques culled from the science of complexity. The underlying hypothesis is this: While the basic input datum of the markets—primarily prices—may be simple, the output can only be forecast with nonlinear methods derived from complexity theory. They do not use back-fit data or curve-fitting as do all conventional technical analysis methods. These include chaos theory, catastrophe theory, and cellular automata. Whether it is possible to beat the markets with them remains to be seen. For an example, see "Is the Market a Computer?" discussing The Trend Machine, a cellular automata approach on www.fxpraxis.

See a 5-hour noninterpreted forecast for the EUR/USD in 5-minute increments from The Trend Machine. (See Figure 20.1.) The top row is Up (1) or Down (0) from the previous 5-minute High. The bottom row is Up (1) or Down (0) from the previous 5-minute Low. The interpreted forecast generates an ordinal bar chart.

Automated Trading and Robots

Many hedge funds now use "algorithmic trading" (a term I coined in 1991), which is fully automated order entry based on a computer trading model. Individual traders are also now fishing in the same waters. I certainly do not recommend this approach for new traders, but the approach is very interesting. Ninjatrader, www.ninjatrader.com, is a software suite that includes robot or bot trading functionality. Many broker-dealers are also adding the feature to their platforms for advanced traders.

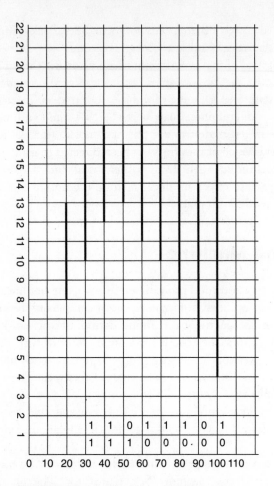

FIGURE 20.1 Trend Machine Forecast

FOREX traders may ponder this commentary from "A Bust to the Markets" by Michael D. Archer (*Source:* Currency Codex, April 1996).

The investment markets will evolve into a war between several powerful computer programs, each seeking to develop new rules and information coding mechanisms and growing forecasts to "keep up" with the market's parallel behavior.

But each computer will need to deal with another factor as well; a factor already noted in the markets. That is: What are the other players doing, or thinking of doing? What rules do they use to find the market's rules?

Trading decisions will be made not on just what one concludes the market will do, but on what one concludes other systems "on-line" are likely to do. This becomes a problem for GAME THEORY, a field of study likely to be soon dominated by self-organizing and evolutionary computing techniques such as cellular automata and Agent computing.

Computers in the market will make false moves to deflect the ability of other computers to know what it is planning to do and how it makes its decisions. (This will not sound at all futuristic to commodity floor traders who see the big interests routinely throw in false orders to deflect true intentions.)

This multi-dimensional game theory scenario, with a single technique periodically busting a market will, I predict, be the hallmark of the investment arena not long into the 21st Century.

This image of the market may not be to everyone's liking; especially old-timers like this writer who fondly remembers customer boardrooms alive with the comforting din of ticker tapes and clacker boards. But the fact remains, the markets will continue to exist even when a single technique dominates the action from time to time. Trading will become even more difficult and undemocratic, but also much more profitable for the few.

A Last Word

Whether you trade with a two-moving average crossover calculated daily on a ten-dollar calculator or a bot executing a catastrophe model with an agent-driven genetic algorithm subroutine, I wish you success in the FOREX market.

How the FOREX Game Is Played

There are two types of retail FOREX brokers: market maker and ECNs (Electronic Communications Network).

ECN is similar in method to how the Interbank foreign exchange market works—orders are matched on a client-to-client basis. A large network of banks, institutions, and traders connect to the network, and orders are matched; there is no central clearinghouse for orders. If you wish to sell 50 million US Dollars (USD) against the Euro (EUR), you place your order and wait for someone who wants to buy. Typically, because of the huge volume of foreign exchange business, transactions are instantaneous. The market is said to be liquid. Nevertheless, your order technically requires a counterparty to be executed.

ECN retail FOREX brokers build their own network and often tap in to the Interbank ECN.

Market Makers

Most retail brokers—especially the smaller ones accepting so-called mini-accounts—are market makers. Market makers act as a de facto central clearing-house for their clients. If you look closely at Market Maker web sites and their account documentation you will see a statement such as, "XYZ-FOREX is the counterparty to all trades."

Market makers typically guarantee execution at the price you want, assuming their data stream touches that price. There are exceptions, however, as discussed below.

Market makers sometimes trade against their own clients. There is inherently nothing wrong with this; that is how they play the game. Trading against their clients performs several useful functions: (1) It provides liquidity; (2) it helps maintain an orderly market; and (3) it keeps their book from becoming too unbalanced. Because they are the counterparty to all trades, if they have 500 million USD on the buy side and only 50 million USD on the sell side (this is an exaggeration to make the point—balance is rarely off more than 5 percent) market makers are at risk if the USD should fall sharply. Market makers often hand off large orders to an ECN or the Interbank market to maintain balance.

Market makers are effectively bookmakers. In choosing a Market Maker broker, it is good to know how much net worth or liquidity they have in case they do suffer from an order imbalance. The CFTC (Commodity Futures Trading Commission) is working to set minimum net worth/liquidity requirements for market makers. But this is a work-in-progress, and FOREX today remains very much a caveat emptor enterprise.

Market makers are often accused of "running" or "harvesting" stop-loss orders. To a limited extent this is in pursuit of the three legitimate functions listed above. However, if a broker-dealer harvests stops primarily as a profit center, traders are not happy. It is very difficult, if not impossible, to tell if a market maker is running stops at all and—if they are—the motive. Such is the capitalist experience. Because of the lax regulatory environment the inner workings of retail brokers is more opaque than it is transparent.

If you have access to multiple data streams, you can watch for stop harvesting. If one of the streams shows a sharp price spike resulting in a price several pips from the maximum or minimum of all the other streams, it is possibly a case of stop harvesting, especially if it is in an active market with good liquidity.

FOREX markets are said to be "fast" especially after the release of a major news announcement. This means there is a dramatic increase in price movement and/or volatility. Market makers often dramatically increase their pip spreads ("ballooning") for a short period of time under these conditions to maintain order balance. Pip spreads have been know to balloon from 2 pips to as much as 30 pips for one or two minutes after a Federal Reserve announcement. There are horror stories of ballooning 100 to 200 pips. Spreads also balloon during inactive market periods when liquidity is low. Traders should either avoid trading during these times or at least be aware of this phenomenon. Ballooning spreads should be a legitimate Market Maker function, but many traders believe some market makers use it as a profit center technique. Again, caveat emptor.

Although not as big a problem as it once was, requoting (or "dealer intervention") has been the bane of market makers. In requoting, a broker gives you a fill at a price not seen on their official streaming data feed. More than any other factor, requoting has driven traders away from specific brokers and from FOREX generally.

Another form of dealer intervention that has frustrated retail FOREX traders is being "put on manual." This means that your orders are executed by hand at the dealing desk. Some reviews claim traders have been put on manual when they are making too much money (remember the market maker is the counterparty to your trader). Some traders have claimed to have had their accounts frozen or closed for the same reason.

Brokers do seem to be getting the message. Requoting is much less an issue than it was in the past. But to a large extent, the damage is done and the term "market maker" has negative connotations to traders. To this end many brokers now advertise they have no dealing desk (NDD) implying they are not market makers. What "no dealing desk" actually means and its functional affect is not clear. At the very least the line between market makers and ECNs is blurring, but the trend is certainly toward ECNs today. An NDD may simply refer to a fully automated dealing desk. It is certainly possible to imagine a broker profiting from traders without a dealing desk, by running them through an ECN of some kind.

Dukascopy, www.dukascopy.com, promotes a third-way called a "centralized-decentralized" clearing system. An interesting article on this approach may be found on www.e-forex.com in the January 2007 edition.

If you trade the news—and I recommend against it for the beginning trader—use an execution tool such as www.secretnewsweapon.com.

Even on an ECN platform, executions in fast markets may be off your price by many pips. A 5-pips slippage might not dramatically affect a day trader or a position trader, but it is a very significant cost to the guerilla trader or the scalper.

At the highest level of foreign exchange trading, there are two games being played simultaneously. The first is simply attempting to determine what prices are going to do. There is a second, tactical level that is less visible, but very real.

The tactical level demands that the trader (1) know what the other players are doing or planning to do; (2) keep the other players from knowing what you are going to do; and, perhaps most interesting, (3) feed the other players false information so their conclusions about what you are going to do or planning to do are incorrect. The typical retail FOREX trader need not concern himself with this tactical level, but should be aware of its existence.

Most of the regulatory and order execution issues of interest to the retail FOREX trader stem from the fact there is no central clearinghouse for currency trading. It is difficult, if not impossible, to regulate an industry with no central locus. Consider the Internet as an example of that paradigm.

Many web sites offer broker-dealer reviews. When reading these reviews keep in mind: (1) satisfied traders generally post less than unsatisfied traders; (2) the larger the broker-dealer, the larger its volume of complaints; (3) a small sample of reviews may not be meaningful; (4) seeing similar complaints on multiple web sites over several months increases the chances that the complaints are legitimate; and (5) small traders complain the most—and loudest—and the largest broker-dealers get the overwhelming share of newbies.

For reviews, see www.forexpeacearmy.com, www.forexrealm.com www.moneytec.com, www.goforex.net, www.forex-ratings.com, and www.forexreview.org. For others, see Google "FOREX broker reviews," "currency dealer reviews," "FOREX broker complaints," and permutations thereof.

FOREX trading remains a very laissez-faire industry; *caveat emptor* is the watchword.

Retail FOREX Regulations—CFTC Reauthorization Act of 2005

To reauthorize and amend the Commodity Exchange Act to promote legal certainty, enhance competition, and reduce systemic risk in markets for futures and over-the-counter derivatives, and for other purposes.

Be it enacted by the Senate and House of Representatives of the United States of America in Congress assembled,

SECTION 1. SHORT TITLE.

This Act may be cited as the "CFTC Reauthorization Act of 2005".

TITLE I—GENERAL PROVISIONS

SEC. 101. COMMISSION AUTHORITY OVER AGREEMENTS, CONTRACTS OR TRANSACTIONS IN FOREIGN CURRENCY.

(a) In General—Section 2(c)(2) of the Commodity Exchange Act (7 U.S.C. 2(c)(2)) is amended by striking subparagraphs (B) and (C) and inserting the following:

(B) AGREEMENTS, CONTRACTS, AND TRANSACTIONS IN RETAIL FOREIGN CURRENCY—

'(i) This Act applies to, and the Commission shall have jurisdiction over, an agreement, contract, or transaction in foreign currency that—

'(I) is a contract of sale of a commodity for future delivery (or an option on such a contract) or an option (other than an option executed or traded on a national securities exchange registered pursuant to section 6(a) of the Securities Exchange Act of 1934 (15 U.S.C. 78f(a))); and

'(II) is offered to, or entered into with, a person that is not an eligible contract participant, unless the counterparty, or the person offering to be the counterparty, of the person is—

'(aa) a financial institution;

'(bb)(AA) a broker or dealer registered under section 15(b) (except paragraph (11) thereof) or 15C of the Securities Exchange Act of 1934 (15 U.S.C. 78o(b), 78o-5); or

'(BB)an associated person of a broker or dealer registered under section 15(b) (except paragraph (11) thereof) or 15C of the Securities Exchange Act of 1934 (15 U.S.C. 78o(b), 78o-5) concerning the financial or securities activities of which the broker or dealer makes and keeps records under section 15C(b) or 17(h) of the Securities Exchange Act of 1934 (15 U.S.C. 78o-5(b), 78q(h));

'(cc) a futures commission merchant registered under this Act (that is not also a person described in item (bb)), or an affiliated person of such a futures commission merchant (that is not also a person described in item (bb)) if such futures commission merchant makes and keeps records under section 4f(c)(2)(B) of this Act concerning the futures and other financial activities of such affiliated person;

'(dd) an insurance company described in section 1a(12)(A)(ii) of this Act, or a regulated subsidiary or affiliate of such an insurance company;

'(ee) a financial holding company (as defined in section 2 of the Bank Holding Company Act of 1956); or

'(ff) an investment bank holding company (as defined in section 17(i) of the Securities Exchange Act of 1934 (15 U.S.C. 78q(i))).

'(ii) Notwithstanding item (cc) of clause (i)(II) of this subparagraph, agreements, contracts, or transactions described in clause (i) of this subparagraph shall be subject to subsection (a)(1)(B) of this section and sections 4(b), 4b, 4c(b), 4o, 6(c) and 6(d) (except to the extent that sections 6(c) and 6(d) prohibit manipulation of the market price of any commodity in interstate commerce, or for future delivery on or subject to the rules of any market), 6c, 6d,

8(a), 13(a), and 13(b) if the agreements, contracts, or transactions are offered, or entered into, by a person that is registered as a futures commission merchant or an affiliated person of a futures commission merchant registered under this Act that is not also a person described in any of item (aa), (bb), (dd), (ee), or (ff) of clause (i) of this subparagraph.

'(iii)(I) Notwithstanding item (cc) of clause (i)(II), a particular person shall not participate in the solicitation or recommendation of any agreement, contract, or transaction described in clause (i) entered into with or to be entered into with a person described in such item, unless the particular person—

'(aa) is registered in such capacity as the Commission by rule, regulation, or order shall determine; and

'(bb) is a member of a futures association registered under section 17.

'(II) Subclause (I) shall not apply to—

'(aa) any person described in any of item (aa), (bb), (dd), (ee), or (ff) of subparagraph (B)(i)(II); or

'(bb) any such person's associated persons.

'(C)(i)(I) This subparagraph shall apply to any agreement, contract, or transaction in foreign currency that is—

'(aa) offered to, or entered into with, a person that is not an eligible contract participant (except that this subparagraph shall not apply if the counterparty, or the person offering to be the counterparty, of the person that is not an eligible contract participant is a person described in any of item (aa), (bb), (dd), (ee), or (ff) of subparagraph (B)(i)(II)); and

'(bb) offered, or entered into, on a leveraged or margined basis, or financed by the offeror, the counterparty, or a person acting in concert with the offeror or counterparty on a similar basis.

'(II) Subclause (I) shall not apply to—

'(aa) a security that is not a security futures product; or

'(bb) a contract of sale that—

'(AA) results in actual delivery within 2 days; or

'(BB) creates an enforceable obligation to deliver between a seller and buyer that have the ability to deliver and accept delivery, respectively, in connection with their line of business.

'(ii)(I) Agreements, contracts, or transactions described in clause (i) of this subparagraph shall be subject to subsection (a)(1)(B) of this section and sections 4(b), 4b, 4c(b), 4o, 6(c) and 6(d) (except to the extent that sections 6(c) and 6(d) prohibit manipulation of the market price of any commodity in interstate commerce, or for future delivery on or subject to the rules of any market), 6c, 6d, 8(a), 13(a), and 13(b).

'(II) Subclause (I) of this clause shall not apply to—

'(aa) any person described in any of item (aa), (bb), (dd), (ee), or (ff) of subparagraph (B)(i)(II); or

'(bb) any such person's associated persons.

'(iii)(I) A person shall not participate in the solicitation or recommendation of any agreement, contract, or transaction described in clause (i) of this subparagraph unless the person is registered in such capacity as the Commission by rule, regulation or order shall determine, and is a member of a futures association registered under section 17.

'(II) Subclause (I) shall not apply to any person—

'(aa) any person described in any of item (aa), (bb), (dd), (ee), or (ff) of subparagraph (B)(i)(II); or

'(bb) any such person's associated persons.

'(iv) Sections 4(b) and 4b shall apply to any agreement, contract, or transaction described in clause (i) of this subparagraph as if the agreement, contract, or transaction were a contract of sale of a commodity for future delivery.

'(v) This subparagraph shall not be construed to limit any jurisdiction that the Commission may otherwise have under any other provision of this Act over an agreement, contract, or transaction that is a contract of sale of a commodity for future delivery.

'(vi) This subparagraph shall not be construed to limit any jurisdiction that the Commission or the Securities and Exchange Commission may otherwise have under any other provision of this Act with respect to security futures products and persons effecting transactions in security futures products.'.

(b) Effective Date—Clause (iii) of section 2(c)(2)(B) and clause (iii) of section 2(c)(2)(C) of the Commodity Exchange Act, as amended by subsection (a) of this section, shall be effective 120 days after the date of the enactment of this Act or such other time as the Commodity Futures Trading Commission shall determine.

SEC. 102. ANTIFRAUD AUTHORITY.

Section 4b of the Commodity Exchange Act (7 U.S.C. 6b) is amended—

(1) by redesignating subsections (b) and (c) as subsections (c) and (d), respectively; and

(2) by striking `SEC. 4b.' and all that follows through the end of subsection (a) and inserting the following:

'SEC. 4b. CONTRACTS DESIGNED TO DEFRAUD OR MISLEAD.

(a) Unlawful Actions—It shall be unlawful—

'(1) for any person, in or in connection with any order to make, or the making of, any contract of sale of any commodity in interstate commerce or for future delivery that is made, or to be made, on or subject to the rules of a designated contract market, for or on behalf of any other person; or

'(2) for any person, in or in connection with any order to make, or the making of, any contract of sale of any commodity for future delivery, or other agreement, contract, or transaction subject to paragraphs (1) and (2) of section 5a(g), that is made, or to be made, for or on behalf of, or with, any other person, other than on or subject to the rules of a designated contract market—

'(A) to cheat or defraud or attempt to cheat or defraud the other person;

'(B) willfully to make or cause to be made to the other person any false report or statement or willfully to enter or cause to be entered for the other person any false record;

'(C) willfully to deceive or attempt to deceive the other person by any means whatsoever in regard to any order or contract or the disposition or execution of any order or contract, or in regard to any act of agency performed, with respect to any order or contract for or, in the case of paragraph (2), with the other person; or

'(D)(i) to bucket an order if the order is represented by the person as an order to be executed, or is required to be executed, on or subject to the rules of a designated contract market; or

'(ii) to fill an order by offset against the order or orders of any other person, or willfully and knowingly and without the prior consent of the other person to become the buyer in respect to any selling order of the other person, or become the seller in respect to any buying order of the other person, if the order is represented by the person as an order to be executed, or is required to be executed, on or subject to the rules of a designated contract market unless the order is executed in accordance with the rules of the designated contract market.

'(b) Clarification—Subsection (a)(2) of this section shall not obligate any person, in or in connection with a transaction in a contract of sale of a commodity for future delivery, or other agreement, contract or transaction subject to paragraphs (1) and (2) of section 5a(g), with another person, to disclose to the other person nonpublic information that may be material to the market price, rate, or level of the commodity or transaction, except as necessary to make any statement made to the other person in or in connection with the transaction, not misleading in any material respect.'.

List of World Currencies and Symbols

Table C.1 is a list of global currencies and the three-character currency codes that we have found are generally used to represent them. Often, but not always, this code is the same as the ISO 4217 standard. (The ISO, or International Organization for Standardization, is a worldwide federation of national standards.)

In most cases, the currency code is composed of the country's two-character Internet country code plus an extra character to denote the currency unit. For example, the code for Canadian dollars is simply Canada's two-character Internet code ("CA") plus a one-character currency designator ("D").

I have endeavored to list the codes that, in my experience, are actually in general industry use to represent the currencies. Currency names are given in the plural form. This list does not contain obsolete Euro-zone currencies.

TABLE C.1 Symbol, Place, Currency Name		
AED	United Arab Emirates	Dirhams
AFA	Afghanistan	Afghanis
ALL	Albania	Leke
AMD	Armenia	Drams
ANG	Netherlands Antilles	Guilders
AOA	Angola	Kwanza

(continued on next page)

TABLE C.1 *(continued)*

ARS	Argentina	Pesos
AUD	Australia	Dollars
AWG	Aruba	Guilders
AZM	Azerbaijan	Manats
BAM	Bosnia, Herzegovina	Convertible Marka
BBD	Barbados	Dollars
BDT	Bangladesh	Taka
BGN	Bulgaria	Leva
BHD	Bahrain	Dinars
BIF	Burundi	Francs
BMD	Bermuda	Dollars
BND	Brunei Darussalam	Dollars
BOB	Bolivia	Bolivianos
BRL	Brazil	Brazil Real
BSD	Bahamas	Dollars
BTN	Bhutan	Ngultrum
BWP	Botswana	Pulas
BYR	Belarus	Rubles
BZD	Belize	Dollars
CAD	Canada	Dollars
CDF	Congo/Kinshasa	Congolese Francs
CHF	Switzerland	Francs
CLP	Chile	Pesos
CNY	China	Renminbi
COP	Colombia	Pesos
CRC	Costa Rica	Colones
CUP	Cuba	Pesos
CVE	Cape Verde	Escudos
CYP	Cyprus	Pounds
CZK	Czech Republic	Koruny
DJF	Djibouti	Francs
DKK	Denmark	Kroner
DOP	Dominican Republic	Pesos
DZD	Algeria	Algeria Dinars
EEK	Estonia	Krooni

TABLE C.1 *(continued)*

EGP	Egypt	Pounds
ERN	Eritrea	Nakfa
ETB	Ethiopia	Birr
EUR	Euro Member Countries	Euro
FJD	Fiji	Dollars
FKP	Falkland Islands	Pounds
GBP	United Kingdom	Pounds
GEL	Georgia	Lari
GGP	Guernsey	Pounds
GHC	Ghana	Cedis
GIP	Gibraltar	Pounds
GMD	Gambia	Dalasi
GNF	Guinea	Francs
GTQ	Guatemala	Quetzales
GYD	Guyana	Dollars
HKD	Hong Kong	Dollars
HNL	Honduras	Lempiras
HRK	Croatia	Kuna
HTG	Haiti	Gourdes
HUF	Hungary	Forint
IDR	Indonesia	Rupiahs
ILS	Israel	New Shekels
IMP	Isle of Man	Pounds
INR	India	Rupees
IQD	Iraq	Dinars
IRR	Iran	Rials
ISK	Iceland	Kronur
JEP	Jersey	Pounds
JMD	Jamaica	Dollars
JOD	Jordan	Dinars
JPY	Japan	Yen
KES	Kenya	Shillings
KGS	Kyrgyzstan	Soms
KHR	Cambodia	Riels
KMF	Comoros	Francs

(continued on next page)

TABLE C.1 *(continued)*

KPW	Korea (North)	Won
KRW	Korea (South)	Won
KWD	Kuwait	Dinars
KYD	Cayman Islands	Dollars
KZT	Kazakstan	Tenge
LAK	Laos	Kips
LBP	Lebanon	Pounds
LKR	Sri Lanka	Rupees
LRD	Liberia	Dollars
LSL	Lesotho	Maloti
LTL	Lithuania	Litai
LVL	Latvia	Lati
LYD	Libya	Dinars
MAD	Morocco	Dirhams
MDL	Moldova	Lei
MGA	Madagascar	Ariary
MKD	Macedonia	Denars
MMK	Myanmar (Burma)	Kyats
MNT	Mongolia	Tugriks
MOP	Macau	Patacas
MRO	Mauritania	Ouguiyas
MTL	Malta	Liri
MUR	Mauritius	Rupees
MVR	Maldives	Rufiyaa
MWK	Malawi	Kwachas
MXN	Mexico	Pesos
MYR	Malaysia	Ringgits
MZM	Mozambique	Meticais
NAD	Namibia	Dollars
NGN	Nigeria	Nairas
NIO	Nicaragua	Gold Cordobas
NOK	Norway	Krone
NPR	Nepal	Nepal Rupees
NZD	New Zealand	Dollars
OMR	Oman	Rials

	TABLE C.1 *(continued)*	
PAB	Panama	Balboa
PEN	Peru	Nuevos Soles
PGK	Papua New Guinea	Kina
PHP	Philippines	Pesos
PKR	Pakistan	Rupees
PLN	Poland	Zlotych
PYG	Paraguay	Guarani
QAR	Qatar	Rials
ROL	Romania	Lei
RUR	Russia	Rubles
RWF	Rwanda	Rwanda Francs
SAR	Saudi Arabia	Riyals
SBD	Solomon Islands	Dollars
SCR	Seychelles	Rupees
SDD	Sudan	Dinars
SEK	Sweden	Kronor
SGD	Singapore	Dollars
SHP	Saint Helena	Pounds
SIT	Slovenia	Tolars
SKK	Slovakia	Koruny
SLL	Sierra Leone	Leones
SOS	Somalia	Shillings
SPL	Seborga	Luigini
SRG	Suriname	Guilders
STD	São Tome, Principe	Dobras
SVC	El Salvador	Colones
SYP	Syria	Pounds
SZL	Swaziland	Emalangeni
THB	Thailand	Baht
TJS	Tajikistan	Somoni
TMM	Turkmenistan	Manats
TND	Tunisia	Dinars
TOP	Tonga	Pa'anga
TRL	Turkey	Liras
TTD	Trinidad, Tobago	Dollars

(continued on next page)

	TABLE C.1 *(continued)*	
TVD	Tuvalu	Tuvalu Dollars
TWD	Taiwan	New Dollars
TZS	Tanzania	Shillings
UAH	Ukraine	Hryvnia
UGX	Uganda	Shillings
USD	United States of America	Dollars
UYU	Uruguay	Pesos
UZS	Uzbekistan	Sums
VEB	Venezuela	Bolivares
VND	Viet Nam	Dong
VUV	Vanuatu	Vatu
WST	Samoa	Tala
XAF	Communauté Financière Africaine	Francs
XCD	East Caribbean	Dollars
XDR	International Monetary Fund	Special Drawing Rights
XOF	Communauté Financière Africaine	Francs
XPF	Comptoirs Français du Pacifique	Francs
YER	Yemen	Rials
YUM	Yugoslavia	New Dinars
ZAR	South Africa	Rand
ZMK	Zambia	Kwacha
ZWD	Zimbabwe	Zimbabwe Dollars

Major Currency
Cross Rates

Table D.1 shows the major currency cross rates on April 7, 2008.

TABLE D.1 MAJOR CURRENCY CROSS RATES

CURRENCY	UK Pound	CANADIAN Dollar	EURO	JAPANESE Yen	SWISS Franc	US US Dollar	AUSTRALIAN Dollar	NEW ZEALAND Dollar
UK Pound	1.0000	0.4984	0.7947	0.004936	0.4995	0.5052	0.4682	0.4018
CANADIAN Dollar	2.0056	1.0000	1.5941	0.009901	1.0018	1.0133	0.9391	0.8060
EURO	1.2581	0.6271	1.0000	0.006211	0.6285	0.6356	0.5891	0.5056
JAPANESE Yen	202.536	100.956	160.989	1.0000	101.180	102.335	94.8371	81.4001
SWISS Franc	2.0015	0.9976	1.5909	0.009881	1.0000	1.0112	0.9371	0.8044
US Dollar	1.9792	0.9865	1.5731	0.009770	0.9886	1.0000	0.9268	0.7954
AUSTRALIAN Dollar	2.1352	1.0643	1.6970	0.010540	1.0666	1.0788	1.0000	0.8580
NEW ZEALAND Dollar	2.4870	1.2396	1.9767	0.01228	1.2423	1.2566	1.1647	1.0000

Euro Currency Unit

On January 1, 1999, eleven of the countries in the European Economic and Monetary Union (EMU) decided to give up their own currencies and adopt the new Euro (EUR) currency: Austria, Belgium, Finland, France, Germany, Ireland, Italy, Luxembourg, the Netherlands, Portugal, and Spain. Greece followed suit on January 1, 2001. The Vatican City also participated in the changeover. This changeover is now complete.

It is worth noting that any place that previously used one or more of the currencies listed below has now also adopted the Euro. This applies to the Principality of Andorra, the Principality of Monaco, and the Republic of San Marino. This of course applies automatically to any territories, departments, possessions, or collectivities of Euro-zone countries, such as the Azores, Balearic Islands, the Canary Islands, Europa Island, French Guiana, Guadeloupe, Juan de Nova, the Madeira Islands, Martinique, Mayotte, Réunion, Saint-Martin, Saint Pierre, and Miquelon, to name just a few.

Euro bank notes and coins began circulating in the above countries on January 1, 2002. At that time, all transactions in those countries were valued in Euro, and the "old" notes and coins of these countries were gradually withdrawn from circulation. The precise dates that each "old" currency ceased being legal tender are noted in Table E.1.

For convenience, and because their values are now irrevocably set against the Euro as listed in Table E.1, the XE.com Universal Currency Converter will continue to support these units even after their withdrawal from circulation. In

TABLE E.1 Official Fixed Euro Rates for Participating Countries

Legacy (Old) Currency			Conversion to Euro	Conversion from Euro
ATS	Austria	Schilling	ATS / 13.7603 = EUR	EUR × 13.7603 = ATS
BEF	Belgium	Franc	BEF / 40.3399 = EUR	EUR × 40.3399 = BEF
DEM	Germany	Mark	DEM / 1.95583 = EUR	EUR × 1.95583 = DEM
ESP	Spain	Peseta	ESP / 166.386 = EUR	EUR × 166.386 = ESP
FIM	Finland	Markka	FIM / 5.94573 = EUR	EUR × 5.94573 = FIM
FRF	France	Franc	FRF / 6.55957 = EUR	EUR × 6.55957 = FRF
GRD	Greece	Drachma	GRD / 340.750 = EUR	EUR × 340.750 = GRD
IEP	Ireland	Punt	IEP / 0.787564 = EUR	EUR × 0.787564 = IEP
ITL	Italy	Lira	ITL / 1936.27 = EUR	EUR × 1936.27 = ITL
LUF	Luxembourg	Franc	LUF / 40.3399 = EUR	EUR × 40.3399 = LUF
NLG	Netherlands	Guilder	NLG / 2.20371 = EUR	EUR × 2.20371 = NLG
PTE	Portugal	Escudo	PTE / 200.482 = EUR	EUR × 200.482 = PTE
VAL	Vatican City	Lira	VAL / 1936.27 = EUR	EUR × 1936.27 = VAL

addition, most outgoing Euro currencies will still be physically convertible at special locations for a period of several years. For details, refer to the official Euro site, www.europa.eu.int/euro.

Also note that the Euro is not just the same thing as the former European Currency Unit (or "ECU"), which used to be listed as "XEU." The ECU was a theoretical "basket" of currencies rather than a currency itself, and no "ECU" bank notes or coins ever existed. At any rate, the ECU has been replaced by the Euro, which is a bona fide currency.

A note about spelling and capitalization: the official spelling of the EUR currency unit in the English language is "euro," with a lower case "e." However, the overwhelmingly prevailing industry practice is to spell it "Euro," with a capital "E." Since other currency names are capitalized in general use, doing so helps differentiate the noun "Euro," meaning EUR currency, from the more general adjective "euro," meaning anything even remotely having to do with Europe.

Time Zones and Global Banking Hours

The following table emphasizes the importance of the effect of time of day on FOREX market activity and volatility based on hours of operation around the globe. The top row is Greenwich Mean Time expressed in 24-hour military format. Banking hours are arbitrarily assumed to be 9:00 am to 4:00 pm around the globe. See Figure F.1.

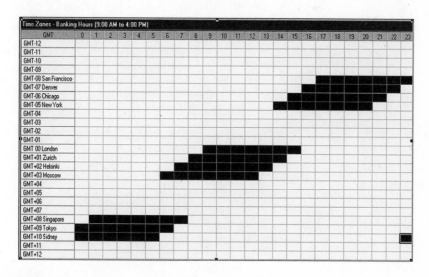

FIGURE F.1 Global Banking Hours

Examples of chart usage are:

- Locate Denver (row 6, or GMT less 7 hours). The first darkened cell in this row indicates when Denver banks open relative to other world banks.

- Move upward to top row to see that the concurrent time in London is 17:00 or 5:00 P.M., where British banks are now closed.

- A FOREX trader in New York must trade between 3:00 A.M. and 11:00 A.M. Eastern Standard Time in order to follow the heightened activity in central European markets (GMT+1: Zurich, Frankfurt, Vienna, Copenhagen).

- San Francisco banks are closing while Sidney banks are opening, and so on.

The darkened areas in Figure F.1 accentuate the major banking centers. FOREX is a 24-hour market. You can trade 24 hours a day. TOD (Time of Day) can strongly influence trading volume, liquidity, and volatility.

Central Banks and Regulatory Agencies

A brief history of currency regulation is provided in Chapter 2 of this book. Traders interested in more details may visit the web sites listed in Table G.1.

The complete text of the "Commodity Futures Modernization Act 2000" in Adobe PDF format can be accessed at the following web site: www. cftc.gov/files/ogc/ogchr5660.pdf.

Table G.2 is a list of affiliated central banks by country.

TABLE G.1 Regulatory Agencies	
Federal Reserve System	www.federalreserve.gov
Federal Reserve Bank	www.ny.frb.org
Securities and Exchange Commission	www.sec.gov
Commodity Futures Trading Commission	www.cftc.gov
National Futures Association	www.nfa.futures.org
Financial Services Authority	www.fsa.gov.uk
Australian Securities & Investments Commission	www.asic.gov.au/asic/asic.nsf
Bank of International Settlements	www.bis.org
Regulation in Canada	www.ida.ca/Investors/SecRegulation_en.asp

TABLE G.2   Central Banks

Argentina	Banco Central de la Republica Argentina
Armenia	Central Bank of Armenia
Aruba	Centrale Bank van Aruba
Australia	Reserve Bank of Australia
Austria	Oesterreichische Nationalbank
Bahrain	Bahrain Monetary Agency
Belgium	Banque Nationale de Belgique
Benin	Banque Centrale des Etats de l'Afrique de l'Ouest
Bolivia	Banco Central de Bolivia
Bosnia	Central Bank of Bosnia and Herzegovina
Botswana	Bank of Botswana
Brazil	Banco Central do Brasil
Bulgaria	Bulgarian National Bank
Burkina Faso	Banque Centrale des Etats de l'Afrique de l'Ouest
Canada	Bank of Canada
Chile	Banco Central de Chil
China	Peoples Bank of China
Colombia	Banco de la Republic
Costa Rica	Banco Central de Costa Rica
Côte d'Ivoire	Banque Centrale des Etats de l'Afrique de l'Ouest
Croatia	Croatian National Bank
Cyprus	Central Bank of Cyprus
Czech Republic	Ceska Narodni Banka
Denmark	Danmarks Nationalbank
East Caribbean	The East Caribbean Central Bank
Ecuador	Banco Central del Ecuador
Egypt	Central Bank of Egypt
El Salvador	The Central Reserve Bank of El Salvador
Estonia	Eesti Pank
European Union	European Central Bank
Finland	Suomen Pankki
France	Banque de France
Germany	Deutsche Bundesbank
Greece	Bank of Greece

TABLE G.2 *(continued)*

Guatemala	Banco de Guatemala
Guinea Bissau	Banque Centrale des Etats de l'Afrique de l'Ouest
Hong Kong	Hong Kong Monetary Authority
Hungary	National Bank of Hungary
Iceland	Central Bank of Iceland
India	Reserve Bank of India
Indonesia	Bank of Indonesia
Ireland	Central Bank of Ireland
Israel	Bank of Israel
Italy	Banca d'Italia
Jamaica	Bank of Jamaica
Japan	Bank of Japan
Jordan	Central Bank of Jordan
Kenya	Central Bank of Kenya
Korea	Bank of Korea
Kuwait	Central Bank of Kuwait
Latvia	Bank of Latvia
Lebanon	Banque du Liban
Lithuania	Lietuvos Bankas
Luxembourg	Banque Centrale du Luxemburg
Macedonia	National Bank of the Republic of Macedonia
Malaysia	Bank Negara Malaysia
Mali	Banque Centrale des Etats de l'Afrique de l'Ouest
Malta	Central Bank of Malta
Mauritius	Bank of Mauritius
Mexico	Banco de Mexico
Moldova	The National Bank of Moldova
Mozambique	Bank of Mozambique
Namibia	Bank of Namibia
Netherlands	De Nederlandsche Bank
Netherlands Antilles	Bank van de Nederlandse Antillen
New Zealand	Reserve Bank of New Zealand
Niger	Banque Centrale des Etats de l'Afrique de l'Ouest
Norway	Norges Bank

(continued on next page)

TABLE G.2 *(continued)*

Paraguay	Banco Central del Paraguay
Peru	Banco Central de Reserva del Peru
Poland	National Bank of Poland
Portugal	Banco de Portugal
Qatar	Qatar Central Bank
Romania	National Bank of Romania
Russia	Central Bank of Russia
Saudi Arabia	Saudi Arabian Monetary Agency
Senegal	Banque Centrale des Etats de l'Afrique de l'Ouest
Singapore	Monetary Authority of Singapore
Slovakia	National Bank of Slovakia
Slovenia	Bank of Slovenia
South Africa	The South African Reserve Bank
Spain	Banco de España
Sri Lanka	Central Bank of Sri Lanka
Sweden	Sveriges Riksbank
Switzerland	Schweizerische Nationalbank
Tanzania	Bank of Tanzania
Thailand	Bank of Thailand
Togo	Banque Centrale des Etats de l'Afrique de l'Ouest
Trinidad and Tobago	Central Bank of Trinidad and Tobago
Tunisia	Banque Centrale de Tunisie
Turkey	Türkiye Cumhuriyet Merkez Bankasi
Ukraine	National Bank of Ukraine
United Kingdom	Bank of England
United States	Board of Governors of the Federal Reserve System
Zambia	Bank of Zambia
Zimbabwe	Reserve Bank of Zimbabwe

Central bank web sites may be found at www.bis.org/cbanks.htm.

Resources

Periodicals

Though the following monthly magazines focus on very specific material, each frequently prints very informative and timely articles on the FOREX marketplace:

Active Trader (TechInfo, Inc.)—www.activetradermag.com

Currency Trader (Online)—www.currencytradermag.com

E-FOREX (Quarterly)—www.e-forex.net

Futures (Futures Magazine, Inc.)—www.futuresmag.com

FX Week—www.fxweek.com

Technical Analysis of Stocks & Commodities (Technical Analysis, Inc.)—www.traders.com

Books

The following list, though in no way complete, provides traders with FOREX library essentials:

Archer, Michael. *Getting Started in Forex Trading Strategies.* John Wiley & Sons, 2007.

Archer, Michael D. *The Goodman Swing Count System Codex.* FxPraxis, 2007.

Archer, Michael D., and James Lauren Bickford. *The FOREX Chartist Companion.* John Wiley & Sons, 2006.

Booker, Rob. *Adventures of a Currency Trader.* John Wiley & Sons, 2007.

Evans, Lewis, and Olga Sheean. *Left Brain Thinking: The Right Mindset and Technique for Success in Forex.* Inside Out Media, 2006.

Henderson, Callum. *Currency Strategy.* John Wiley & Sons, 2002.

Horner, Raghee. *Thirty Days of Forex Trading.* John Wiley & Sons, 2005.

Klopfenstein, Gary. *Trading Currency Cross Rates.* John Wiley & Sons, 1993.

Lein, Kathy. *Day Trading the Currency Market.* John Wiley & Sons, 2005.

Louw, G. N. *Begin Forex.* FXTrader, 2003.

Luca, Cornelius. *Technical Analysis Applications in the Global Currency Markets.* Prentice Hall, 2000.

Luca, Cornelius. *Trading in the Global Currency Markets.* Prentice Hall, 2000.

Murphy, John. *Intermarket Financial Analysis.* John Wiley & Sons, 1999.

Murphy, John. *Technical Analysis of the Financial Markets.* Prentice Hall, 1999.

Person, John L. *Forex Conquered.* John Wiley & Sons, 2007.

Reuters Limited. *An Introduction to Foreign Exchange and Money Markets.* Reuters Financial Training, 1999.

Shamah, Shani. *A Foreign Exchange Primer.* John Wiley & Sons, 2003.

There are hundreds (if not thousands) of books pertaining specifically to technical analysis. A few of the most well-known are:

Aby, Carroll D., Jr., PhD. *Point and Figure Charting.* Traders Press, 1996.

Aronson, David R. *Evidence-Based Technical Analysis.* John Wiley & Sons, 2007.

Bickford, Jim. *Chart Plotting Algorithms for Technical Analysts.* Syzygy, 2002.

Bulkowski, Thomas N. *Encyclopedia of Chart Patterns.* John Wiley & Sons, 2005.

DiNapoli, Joe. *Trading with DiNapoli Levels.* Coast Investment, 1998.

Kaufman, Perry J. *New Trading Systems and Methods.* John Wiley & Sons, 2005.

McGee, John. *Technical Analysis of Stock Trends.* American Management Association, 2001.

Nison, Steve. *Japanese Candlestick Charting Techniques*. Hall, 2001.

Wilder, J. Welles Jr. *New Concepts in Technical Trading Systems*. Trend Research, 1978.

A fine resource for finding more titles is http://www.traderspress.com.

Web Sites

I encourage the trader to visit the following web sites for additional information on trading currencies. These sites are provided for research purposes. The amount of information on currency trading now on the Internet is enormous: A Google search finds over 2.2 million entries for "forex." Inclusion herein *does not* represent an endorsement of any kind. Suggested key words: "forex" and "currency trading."

Online Brokers and Dealers

www.cbfx.com

www.ac-markets.com

www.saxobank.com

www.gftforex.com

www.hotspotfx.com

www.cmc-forex.com

www.cms-forex.com

www.oanda.com

www.fxall.com

www.efxgroup.com

www.dukascopy.com

www.gaincapital.com

www.forex.com

www.dbfx.com

www.currenex.com

www.hawaiiforex.com

www.fxcm.com

www.fxsol.com

Data

ozforex.tradesecuring.com/misc/ozchart.asp

www.csidata.com

www.forexcapital.com/database.htm

www.olsendata.com

disktrading.is99.com/disktrading

www.cqg.com/products/datafactory.cfm

www.datastream.com/

www.tenfore.com/index.php?T4_Session=9b7d26531b2829babdb317083f8fe994

www.dukascopy.com

www.netdania.com

www.pctrader.com

Charts

www.esignal.com

www.dynexcorp.com/charts/eu1h.shtml

www.forex-markets.com/javacharts.htm

www.fxstreet.com/nou/graph/senseframeschartsnetdania.asp

www.forexcharts.com/

www.fxtrek.com

www.moneytec.com

www.global-view.com/beta/

System Development

www.ninjatrader.com

www.forextester.com

www.strategybuilder.com

www.tradestation.com

www.esignal.com

www.fxstreet.com

www.forexdirectory.net

www.forex-markets.com

www.hantec.com.hk

www.business.com/directory/financial_services/investment_banking_and_ brokerage/sales_and_trading/foreign_exchange

Portals and Forums

www.global-view.com

www.forexbastards.com

www.goforex.net

www.moneytec.com

www.investorsresource.info

www.fxstreet.com

www.forexdirectory.net

www.forexvision.com

Software Development

www.snapdragon.co.uk

www.fxpraxis.com

Link Pages

www.global-view.com

www.go-forex.net

www.dynexcorp.com/links.shtml

www.forexdirectory.net

www.forex-brokers-list.com

www.investorsresource.info/portal.htm

Glossary

algorithmic trading   Trading by means of an automated computer program. Sometimes called Program Trading.

API (Application Program Interface)   Computer code or routines for integrating trading programs to a broker-dealer's trading platform, most commonly used to allow a proprietary trading program to read and process a broker-dealers data feed.

appreciation   A currency is said to "appreciate" when it strengthens in price in response to market demand.

arbitrage   The purchase or sale of an instrument and simultaneous taking of an equal and opposite position in a related market, in order to take advantage of small price differentials between markets.

ask price   The price at which the market is prepared to sell a specific currency in a foreign exchange contract or cross-currency contract. At this price, the trader can buy the base currency. It is shown on the right side of the quotation. For example, in the quote USD/CHF 1.4527/32, the ask price is 1.4532; meaning you can buy one US dollar for 1.4532 Swiss francs.

at best   An instruction given to a dealer to buy or sell at the best rate that can be obtained.

at or better   An order to deal at a specific rate or better.

balance of trade   The value of a country's exports minus its imports.

ballooning   The practice by market makers of increasing pip spreads during fast or illiquid markets.

bar chart   A type of chart that consists of four significant points: the high and the low prices, which form the vertical bar; the opening price, which is marked with a little horizontal line to the left of the bar; and the closing price, which is marked with a little horizontal line of the right of the bar.

base currency   The first currency in a currency pair. It shows how much the base currency is worth as measured against the second currency. For example, if the USD/CHF rate equals 1.6215 then one USD is worth CHF 1.6215 In the foreign exchange markets, the US Dollar is normally considered the "base" currency for quotes, meaning that quotes are expressed as a unit of one USD per the other currency quoted in the pair. The primary exceptions to this rule are the British Pound, the Euro, and the Australian Dollar.

bear market   A market distinguished by declining prices.

bid price The bid is the price at which the market is prepared to buy a specific currency in a foreign exchange contract or cross-currency contract. At this price, the trader can sell the base currency. It is shown on the left side of the quotation. For example, in the quote USD/CHF 1.4527/32, the bid price is 1.4527; meaning you can sell one US dollar for 1.4527 Swiss francs.

bid/ask spread The difference between the bid and offer price.

big figure quote Dealer expression referring to the first few digits of an exchange rate. These digits are often omitted in dealer quotes. For example, a USD/JPY rate might be 117.30/117.35, but would be quoted verbally without the first three digits, that is "30/35."

BLS Bureau of Labor Statistics.

book In a professional trading environment, a "book" is the summary of a trader's or desk's total positions.

Bretton Woods Agreement of 1944 An agreement that established fixed foreign exchange rates for major currencies, provided for central bank intervention in the currency markets, and pegged the price of gold at US $35 per ounce. The agreement lasted until 1971, when President Nixon overturned the Bretton Woods agreement and established a floating exchange rate for the major currencies.

broker An individual or firm that acts as an intermediary, putting together buyers and sellers for a fee or commission. In contrast, a dealer commits capital and takes one side of a position, hoping to earn a spread (profit) by closing out the position in a subsequent trade with another party.

bull market A market distinguished by rising prices.

Bundesbank Germany's central bank.

cable Trader jargon referring to the Sterling/US Dollar exchange rate. So called because the rate was originally transmitted via a transatlantic cable beginning in the mid-1800's.

call An option to purchase a currency.

cambist An expert trader who rapidly buys and sells currency throughout the day.

candlestick chart A chart that indicates the trading range for the day as well as the opening and closing price. If the open price is higher than the close price, the rectangle between the open and close price is shaded. If the close price is higher than the open price, that area of the chart is not shaded.

cash market The market in the actual financial instrument on which a futures or options contract is based.

central bank A government or quasi-governmental organization that manages a country's monetary policy. For example, the U.S. central bank is the Federal Reserve, and the German central bank is the Bundesbank.

centralized market Any market where all orders are routed to one central exchange. FOREX is not a centralized market.

CFTC   Commodity Futures Trading Commission.

chartist   An individual who uses charts and graphs and interprets historical data to find trends and predict future movements. Also referred to as a technical trader.

cleared funds   Funds that are freely available, sent in to settle a trade.

closed position   Exposures in foreign currencies that no longer exist. The process to close a position is to sell or buy a certain amount of currency to offset an equal amount of the open position. This will "square" the position.

clearing   The process of settling a trade.

CME   Chicago Mercantile Exchange.

collateral   Something given to secure a loan or as a guarantee of performance.

commission   A transaction fee charged by a broker.

confirmation   A document exchanged by counterparts to a transaction that states the terms of said transaction.

Consumer Price Index (CPI)   A weighted average of prices of a basket of consumer goods and services, such as food, medical, and transportation. The CPI is calculated by taking price changes for each item in a specified basket of goods and averaging them according to their estimated importance.

contagion   The tendency of an economic crisis to spread from one market to another. In 1997, political instability in Indonesia caused high volatility in their domestic currency, the Rupiah. From there, the contagion spread to other Asian emerging currencies, and then to Latin America, and is now referred to as the "Asian Contagion."

contract   The standard unit of trading in futures and options.

counter-currency   The second listed currency in a currency pair. See also *quote currency*.

counterparty   One of the participants in a financial transaction.

country risk   Risk associated with a cross-border transaction, including but not limited to legal and political conditions.

cross-currency pair   A foreign exchange transaction in which one foreign currency is traded against a second foreign currency. For example, EUR/GBP.

cross rate   Same as *cross-currency pair*.

currency   Any form of money issued by a government or central bank and used as legal tender and a basis for trade.

currency pair   The two currencies that make up a foreign exchange rate. For example, EUR/USD.

currency risk   The probability of an adverse change in exchange rates.

day trader   A speculator who takes positions in currencies that are then liquidated prior to the close of the same trading session or day.

dealer   An individual or firm that acts as a principal or counterpart to a transaction. Principals take one side of a position, hoping to earn a spread (profit) by closing out the position in a subsequent trade with another party. In contrast, a broker is an individual or firm that acts as an intermediary, putting together buyers and sellers for a fee or commission.

deficit A negative balance of trade or payments.

delivery A FOREX trade where both sides make and take actual delivery of the currencies traded.

depreciation A fall in the value of a currency due to market forces.

derivative A contract that changes in value in relation to the price movements of a related or underlying security, future, or other physical instrument. An Option is the most common derivative instrument.

devaluation The deliberate downward adjustment of a currency's price, normally by official announcement.

directional movement In technical analysis the net price change from one specified time unit to another specified time unit.

downtick A new price quote at a price lower than the preceding quote.

econometric analysis Using mathematical formulas or models to make trading decisions with fundamental information and data.

economic indicator A government-issued statistic that indicates current economic growth and stability. Common indicators include employment rates, Gross Domestic Product (GDP), inflation, retail sales, and so forth.

ECN (Electronic Communications Network) A system in which orders to buy and sell are matched through a network of banks and/or dealers. See *market maker*, the other widely used method of order execution and *NDD*, a hybrid.

ECU European Currency Unit; see *EMU*.

end of day order (EOD) An order to buy or sell at a specified price. This order remains open until the end of the trading day which is typically 5 P.M. EST.

European Monetary Union (EMU) The principal goal of the EMU is to establish a single European currency called the Euro, which officially replaced the national currencies of most member EU countries in 2002. On Janaury 1, 1999, the transitional phase to introduce the Euro began. The Euro now exists as a banking currency, and paper financial transactions and foreign exchange are made in Euros. This transition period lasted for three years, at which time Euro notes and coins entered circulation. On July 1, 2002, only Euros became legal tender for EMU participants; the national currencies of the member countries ceased to exist. The original members of the EMU were Germany, France, Belgium, Luxembourg, Austria, Finland, Ireland, the Netherlands, Italy, Spain, and Portugal. As of February 2008, 27 countries belonged to the EMU.

Euro The currency of the European Monetary Union (EMU). A replacement for the European Currency Unit (ECU).

European Central Bank (ECB) The central bank for the new European Monetary Union.

exotics A currency pair with the USD and a lesser traded currency such as the Thai Baht or the Chilean Peso. Considered riskier to trade than the majors or minors.

fast market A market is fast when it is hit with a large volume of orders over a short period of time. Markets are often fast after an unexpected news announcement.

Federal Deposit Insurance Corporation (FDIC) The regulatory agency responsible for administering bank depository insurance in the United States.

Federal Reserve (Fed) The central bank for the United States.

first in first out (FIFO) Open positions are closed according to the FIFO accounting rule. All positions opened within a particular currency pair are liquidated in the order in which they were originally opened.

flat/square A trader on the sidelines with no position.

floating stop An automated Trailing Stop.

foreign exchange (FOREX, FX) The simultaneous buying of one currency and selling of another.

FOREX futures FOREX traded as a futures contract.

forward The prespecified exchange rate for a foreign exchange contract settling at some agreed future date, based upon the interest rate differential between the two currencies involved.

forward points The pips added to or subtracted from the current exchange rate to calculate a forward price.

fundamental analysis Analysis of economic and political information with the objective of determining future movements in a financial market.

futures contract An obligation to exchange a good or instrument at a set price on a future date. The primary difference between a future and a forward is that futures are typically traded over an exchange (exchange-traded contracts—ETC), versus forwards, which are considered over the counter (OTC) contracts. An OTC is any contract *not* traded on an exchange.

FX Foreign Exchange.

G7 The seven leading industrial countries: the United States, Germany, Japan, France, UK, Canada, Italy.

going long The purchase of a stock, commodity, or currency for investment or speculation.

going short The selling of a currency or instrument not owned by the seller.

gold standard A monetary system whereby a country allows its monetary unit to be freely converted into fixed amounts of gold and vice versa.

Gross Domestic Product (GDP) Total value of a country's output, income, or expenditure produced within the country's physical borders.

Gross National Product (GNP) Gross domestic product plus income earned from investment or work abroad.

good till cancelled order (GTC)   An order to buy or sell at a specified price. This order remains open until filled or until the client cancels.

guerilla trader   Similar to a *scalper* but trades in bursts of several trades then recedes to the sidelines. Sometimes called a *sniper*.

hedge   A position or combination of positions that reduces the risk of a primary position.

high-frequency trading   Trading very frequently; scalping. A high-frequency trader uses tick data. See *ultra-high-frequency trading*.

hit the bid   Acceptance of purchasing at the offer or selling at the bid.

IMM   International Monetary Market.

inflation   An economic condition in which prices for consumer goods rise, eroding purchasing power.

initial margin   The initial deposit of collateral required to enter into a position as a guarantee on future performance.

Interbank rates   The foreign exchange rates at which large international banks quote other large international banks.

intervention   Action by a central bank to affect the value of its currency by entering the market. Concerted intervention refers to action by a number of central banks to control exchange rates.

Introducing Broker   Generally a small broker who relies on a larger broker-dealer to execute his trades and hold fiduciary responsibility for client funds.

King Kong syndrome   The emotional high that overtakes a trader when he or she does exceptionally well for a period of time, such as making a dozen consecutive winning trades. Usually followed by a large losing trade and a reality check.

Kiwi   Slang for the New Zealand dollar.

leading indicators   Statistics that are considered to predict future economic activity.

leverage   Also called margin. The ratio of the amount used in a transaction to the required security deposit.

LIBOR   The London Inter-Bank Offered Rate. Banks use LIBOR when borrowing from another bank.

limit order   An order with restrictions on the maximum price to be paid or the minimum price to be received. As an example, if the current price of USD/YEN is 117.00/05, then a limit order to buy USD would be at a price below 102 (that is, 116.50).

liquidation   The closing of an existing position through the execution of an offsetting transaction.

liquidity   The ability of a market to accept large transactions with minimal to no impact on price stability; also the ability to enter and exit a market quickly.

long position   A position that appreciates in value if market prices increase. When the base currency in the pair is bought, the position is said to be long.

Loonie Slang for the Canadian Dollar.

lot A unit to measure the amount of the deal. The value of the deal always corresponds to an integer number of lots.

major currency Any of the following: Euro, Pound Sterling, Australian Dollar, New Zealand Dollar, U.S. Dollar, Canadian Dollar, Swiss Franc, Japanese Yen. See also *minor currency*.

managed account Having a third party such as a professional money manager make trading decisions for you. Also called a discretionary account.

margin The required equity that an investor must deposit to collateralize a position.

margin call A request from a broker or dealer for additional funds or other collateral to guarantee performance on a position that has moved against the customer.

market maker A dealer who regularly quotes both bid and ask prices and is ready to make a two-sided market for any financial instrument. Most retail FOREX dealers are market makers. A market maker is said to have a dealing desk.

market risk Exposure to changes in market prices.

market-to-market Process of re-evaluating all open positions with the current market prices. These new values then determine margin requirements.

maturity The date for settlement or expiry of a financial instrument.

mercury chart A modified bar chart used in commodity futures. Each bar shows the price range for a time unit and changes in open interest and volume from the previous time unit.

minor currency Any of the currencies between a major currency and an exotic. The Italian Lira and Swedish Krona are minor currencies.

money management The techniques a trader utilizes to manage his money both in the aggregate and for specific trades.

money supply The aggregate quantity of coins, bills, loans, credit, and any other liquid monetary instruments or equivalents within a given country's economy.

Mundo A synthetic global currency calculated as the average of multiple ISO currency pairs. See Michael Archer and James Bickford, *Forex Chartist Companion* (John Wiley & Sons, 2006). The Mundo is useful for creating indices for currency-to-currency or pair-to-pair analysis.

NDD A no dealing desk broker. Provides a platform where liquidity providers such as banks can offer prices to the NDD platform. Incoming orders are routed to the best available bid or offer. See also *market maker* and *ECN*.

net position The amount of currency bought or sold that have not yet been offset by opposite transactions.

NFA National Futures Association.

offer The rate at which a dealer is willing to sell a currency. See *Ask Price*.

offsetting transaction   A trade that serves to cancel or offset some or all of the market risk of an open position.

one cancels the other order (OCO)   A designation for two orders whereby when one part of the two orders is executed the other is automatically cancelled.

open order   An order that will be executed when a market moves to its designated price. Normally associated with *good till cancelled orders*.

open position   An active trade with corresponding unrealized P&L, which has not been offset by an equal and opposite deal.

option   A FOREX option is the right to purchase or sell a currency at a specified price for a specified time period.

over the counter (OTC)   Used to describe any transaction that is not conducted over an exchange.

overnight position   A trade that remains open until the next business day.

order   An instruction to execute a trade at a specified rate.

P & L   Profit and Loss; often used in reference to an account statement.

pips   The smallest unit of price for any foreign currency. Digits added to or subtracted from the fourth decimal place, that is, 0.001, for example.

point   100 pips.

point and figure charts   Similar to swing charts but use Xs to denote upward moving prices and Os to denote downward moving prices.

political risk   Exposure to changes in governmental policy that will have an adverse effect on an investor's position.

position   The netted total holdings of a given currency.

position trader   A trader who holds positions over multiple trading sessions.

premium   In the currency markets, describes the amount by which the forward or futures price exceed the spot price.

pretzel chart   A price chart connecting the open, high, low, and close in such a fashion that it resembles a pretzel with two closed three-sided spaces connected through a center point.

price transparency   Describes quotes to which every market participant has equal access.

profit/loss or p/l or gain/loss   The actual realized gain or loss resulting from trading activities on closed positions, plus the theoretical "unrealized" gain or loss on open positions that have been market-to-market.

programmed trading   See *algorithmic trading*.

put   An option to sell a currency.

pyramiding   Adding to a position as the market moves up or down. Pyramiding a winning position is risky; pyramiding a losing position is suicide.

quote   An indicative market price, normally used for information purposes only.

quote currency   The second currency quoted in a FOREX currency pair. In a direct quote, the quote currency is the foreign currency itself. In an indirect quote, the quote currency is the domestic currency. See also *base currency* and *counter-currency*.

rally   A recovery in price after a period of decline.

range   The difference between the highest and lowest price of a future recorded during a given trading session.

rate   The price of one currency in terms of another, typically used for dealing purposes.

requoting   The practice of a broker-dealer filling an order at a price not seen on their public price feed. Like *ballooning* and *running stops* most typical of *market makers* and frowned upon by traders.

resistance levels   A term used in technical analysis indicating a specific price level at which analysis concludes that people will sell.

revaluation   An increase in the exchange rate for a currency as a result of central bank intervention. Opposite of *devaluation*.

risk   Exposure to uncertain change, most often used with a negative connotation of adverse change.

risk management   The employment of financial analysis and trading techniques to reduce and control exposure to various types of risk.

rollover   Process whereby the settlement of a deal is rolled forward to another value date. The cost of this process is based on the interest rate differential of the two currencies.

round trip   Buying and selling of a specified amount of currency.

running stops   The practice of market makers entering orders for the purpose of hitting customer stop-loss orders. Also called harvesting stops. Like *ballooning*, considered a negative practice by traders.

scalper   Someone who trades very often. Trades are typically measured in minutes but sometimes seconds.

SEC   Securities Exchange Commission.

settlement   The process by which a trade is entered into the books and records of the counterparts to a transaction. The settlement of currency trades may or may not involve the actual physical exchange of one currency for another.

short position   An investment position that benefits from a decline in market price. When the base currency in the pair is sold, the position is said to be short.

slippage   The difference in pips between the order price approved by the client and the price at which the order is actually executed.

spot price   The current market price. Settlement of spot transactions usually occurs within two business days.

spread   The difference between the bid and offer prices.

Sterling   Slang for British Pound.

stop-loss order   Order type whereby an open position is automatically liquidated at a specific price. Often used to minimize exposure to losses if the market moves against an investor's position. As an example, if an investor is long USD at 156.27, he might wish to put in a stop-loss order for 155.49, which would limit losses should the dollar depreciate, possibly below 155.49.

support levels   A technique used in technical analysis that indicates a specific price ceiling and floor at which a given exchange rate will automatically correct itself. Opposite of resistance.

swap   A currency swap is the simultaneous sale and purchase of the same amount of a given currency at a forward exchange rate.

swing chart   A form of charting connecting prices filtered by a minimum increment. Similar to point and figure charts. Pugh swing charts use vertical lines connected by short horizontal lines. Line swing charts use angular lines connecting price to price. Swing charts are said to be price-functional; the time frame is not a parameter.

Swissy   Market slang for Swiss Franc.

technical analysis   An effort to forecast prices by analyzing market data, that is, historical price trends and averages, volumes, open interest, and so forth.

tick   A minimum change in time required for the price to change, up or down.

trading session   Most commonly means one of the three 8-hour sessions for trading FOREX over a 24-hour period: Asian, European, and North American. Technically there are five sessions between Sunday evening and Friday evening: The New York exchange trades from 7:30 A.M. to 5 P.M. EST. The Sydney, Auckland, and Wellington exchanges trade from 3 P.M. to 11 P.M. EST. The Tokyo Exchange trades from 6 P.M. to 11 P.M., stopping for an hour-long lunch break then trading again until 4 A.M. EST. The Hong Kong and Singapore exchanges trade from 7 P.M. to 3 A.M. EST. The last exchanges trading are the Munich, Zurich, Paris, Frankfurt, Brussels, Amsterdam, and London exchanges. These all trade from 2:30 P.M. to 11:30 A.M. EST.

trailing stop   The practice of moving a stop-loss in the direction of the markets movement. Used primarily to protect profits. See also *floating stop*.

transaction cost   The cost of buying or selling a financial instrument.

transaction date   The date on which a trade occurs.

turnover   The total money value of all executed transactions in a given time period; volume.

two-way price   When both a bid and offer rate is quoted for a FOREX transaction.

ultra-high-frequency trading   Trading extremely frequently; limited only by how fast you can click the mouse. Called "churning the customer's account" in the old days.

unrealized gain/loss   The theoretical gain or loss on open positions valued at current market rates, as determined by the broker in its sole discretion. Unrealized gains' losses become profits/losses when the position is closed.

uptick   A new price quote at a price higher than the preceding quote.

uptick rule   In the United States, a regulation whereby a security may not be sold short unless the last trade prior to the short sale was at a price lower than the price at which the short sale is executed.

U.S. prime rate   The interest rate at which U.S. banks will lend to their prime corporate customers.

value date   The date on which counterparts to a financial transaction agree to settle their respective obligations, that is, exchanging payments. For spot currency transactions, the value date is normally two business days forward. Also known as maturity date.

variation margin   Funds a broker must request from the client to have the required margin deposited. The term usually refers to additional funds that must be deposited as a result of unfavorable price movements.

volatility   A statistical measure of a market's price movements over time characterized by deviations from a predetermined central value (usually the arithmetic mean). Also, the gross price movement over a specified period of time given a minimum value unit. See also *directional movement* for net price movement.

whipsaw   Slang for a condition where any securities market begins moving laterally exhibiting very little volatility.

yard   Slang for a billion.

Index

Account deposit, 80
Accounts:
  demo, 56, 83–89
  deposits and withdrawals, 65
  financial information, 79
  minimums, 64–65
  opening, 77–82
  order execution and accounting, 60
  personal information, 79
  selection of type, 79
  types, 78
Account summary balance, calculating, 50–52
Albania, 96
Algorithmic trading, 261
Announcement services, 154–156
Application Program Interface (API), 63, 261
Appreciation, 261
Arbitrage, 223–228
  definition, 265
  pros and cons, 227–228
Argentina, 99
Artificial intelligence, 228
Ask/bid spread, 266
Ask price, 32, 265
At best, definition, 265
At/better, definition, 265
Australia, 96, 99
  currency contract specifications, 20
  foreign exchange currency, 4
Australian dollar (AUD), 4
Australian Securities and Investment Commission
  (ASIC), 28
Austria, 16, 96, 252
Automatic trend lines, 59
Avail Trading Corporation (ATC), 72

Balance of trade, 94–96, 261
Ballooning, 265
Banks:
  central banks and regulatory agencies, 255–258,
    268
  global banking hours, 253–254
  interest rates, 94

Bar charts, 108–110
  bull and bear, 109
  continuous line, 110
  definition, 265
  open/high/low/close (OHLC), 108
  with support and resistance lines, 111
  with trend lines, 110–111
  vertical, 109
Base currency, 30, 41–42, 267
Bear market, 265
Belgian dentist. *See* Money management
Belgium, 16, 96, 252
Better, definition, 265
*Beyond Candlesticks: More Japanese Charting
  Techniques Revealed* (Nison), 116
Bickford, James, 195
Bid/ask spread, 32, 266
Bid price, 32, 266
Big figure quote, 266
Bollinger, John, 123
Bollinger bands, 123–126
Bollinger on Bollinger Bands (Bollinger), 123
Bookmark Buddy, 146
Books, 166, 266
Box-Top, 86
Brazil, 99, 219
Bretton Woods Agreement of 1944, 14–15
British pound sterling (GBP), 4
  currency contract specifications, 20
  U.S. dollar index, 22
Broker-dealers, 69–73
  common orders, 84
  due diligence, 74–76
Brokers, 69–73
  definition, 262
  due diligence, 55–56
  platform capabilities, 58
  selection, 55–76
  trading platform, 61
  Web sites, 261
Bull market, 266
Bundesbank, 266
Bureau of Labor Statistics (BLS), 262

Cable, 266
Calendars, 154–156
Call, definition, 266
Cambist, 266
Camtasia, 205
Canada, 95, 99
    foreign exchange currency, 4
Canadian dollar (CAD), 4
    currency contract specifications, 20
    U.S. dollar index, 22
Candlestick charts, 115–116, 266
Carnegie, Andrew, 117
Cash market, 266
Cellular Antomata, 128
Central bank, 266
Centralized market, 266
CFTC Reauthorization Act of 2005, 27–28
Charting, 150–152
Chartist, 267
Chat rooms, 60
Chicago Board of Trade, 3
Chicago Mercantile Exchange (CME), 15–16, 20,
    263
Chile, 219
China, 95, 99
Ching, Derek, 128
Cleared funds, 267
Clearing, definition, 267
Closed position, 267
Collateral, 267
Combination orders, 86
Commissions, 8, 267
Commodity Exchange Act, 237–242
Commodity Futures Modernization Act of 2000,
    27, 68–69
Commodity Futures Trading Commission (CFTC),
    9, 18, 25, 234, 267
Commodity Trading with Stops (Maxwell), 88
Confirmation, definition, 267
Consumer Price Index (CPI), 101, 104, 267
Contagion, definition, 267
Continuation patterns, 113–114
Contracts, 241–242, 267
Contrary Opinion, 196–197
Counter-currency, 267
Counterparty, 267
Country risk, 267
Covered writer, 214
Crash (1929), 14
Cross-currency pair, 30, 224
    calculations, 225
    definition, 267
Crosses, 65
Cross rates, 42–44, 267
Currency. *See also* Euro dollar (EUR)

calculating units available, 44–46
calculations, 225
combinations of most frequently traded, 223
contract specifications, 20
costs, 8
definition, 267
fixed Euro rates for participating currencies,
    252
foreign exchange, 4
formulas for cross currencies, 224
history of trading, 11–18
list of world currencies and symbols,
    243–248
major and minor, 29
purchasing power parity, 98
risk, 267
timeline of foreign exchange, 17
tools, 8
trading volume, 21–22
types, 212
Currency futures, 20
A Currency Options Primer (Shamah), 209
Currency pairs, 29, 267
Curve-fit data, 126
Customer service, 66–67
Cycle analysis, 128, 129
Czech Republic, 96, 219

Dagger entry principle, 193–194
Day of week, 196
Day trader, 177, 267
Dealers, 69–73
    definition, 267–268
    due diligence, 55–56
    platform capabilities, 58
    trading platform, 61
    Web sites, 261
Deficit, 268
Delivery, definition, 268
Demo account, 56, 83–89. *See also* Account
Denmark, 96
Deposits, 65
Depreciation, definition, 268
Derivative, definition, 268
Deutsches Bank, 73
Devaluation, definition, 268
DiNapoli, Joe, 58, 128, 198
Directional movement, 184, 185, 268
Documentation, 68
Dorsey, Thomas J., 119
Dow, Charles, 117
Downtick, definition, 268
Drummond, Charles, 128
Due diligence, 55–56, 67
    broker-dealer, 74–76

Dukascopy, 72
Durable goods, 101
Econometric analysis, 268
Economic indicators, 100–101, 105
  definition, 268
  lagging, 105–106
The Economist, 98
Education, 152–153
EFX Group, 71
Electronic Communications Network (ECN),
  55–56, 233–236, 264
Elliott, Ralph N., 127, 128
Employment cost index, 101
Encyclopedias, 165
End of day order (EOD), 268
Equal Credit Opportunity Act, 13
Euro dollar (EUR), 4
  currency contract specifications, 20
  currency unit, 251–253
  definition, 268
  fixed Euro rates for participating countries,
    252
  U.S. dollar index, 22
Euro members, foreign exchange currency, 4
European Central Bank (ECB), 268
European Currency Unit (ECU), 268
European Economic and Monetary Union (EMU),
  251
European Monetary Union (EMU), 16–17, 268
European Union, 99
Exotics, 30, 65, 200, 218–220
  definition, 269
  option strategies, 215
  pairs, 219
  trading, 219–220
Expiration, 211

Fast market, 269
Fear, 170–171, 172
Federal Deposit Insurance Corporation (FDIC),
  269
Federal Open Market Committee (FOMC),
  13
Federal Reserve Board (FRB), 13–14
Federal Reserve (Fed), 12–14, 269
  Board of Governors, 12
Fibonacci, Leonardo, 127–128
50 percent rule, 133, 134, 136–137
Financial Markets Association (ACI), 28
Financial Services Authority (FSA), 28
Finland, 16, 96, 252
First in first out (FIFO), 269
Fixed lot size, 8
Flat/square, definition, 269
Floating stop, definition, 269

Forecasting, 102–106
  models, 102
Foreign exchange (FOREX, FX). *See also* Technical
    analysis; Web sites
  broker-dealers, 69–73
  currencies, 4
  currencies traded, 4
  currency price determination, 5
  definition, 271
  education, 152–153
  forecasting, 102–106
  foreign currencies, 5–8
  fundamental analysis, 93–96
  versus futures, 9
  hedging, 222
  managed accounts, 161–163
  market makers, 233–236
  marketplace, 145–166
  online access, 6
  opening an account, 77–82
  options and exotics, 209–220
  overview, 3
  records, 203–206
  regrouping, 199–202
  regulatory environment, 25–28
  retail regulations, 237–242
  rollovers, 221–222
  search engine, 165
  spot market, 19–22
  versus stock market, 6–7, 8–9
  tactics and strategy, 183–198
  three chart system, 193
  timeline, 17
  traders, 4–5
FOREX Capital Markets, 73–74
FOREX Capital Trading, 72
FOREX futures, 269
*FOREX Patterns and Possibilities: Strategies for
    Trending and Range-Bound Markets* (Ponsi),
    183
Forums, 60, 147–150, 263
Forward, definition, 271
Forward points, definition, 271
France, 16, 96, 99, 252
Fraud, 74, 241
Fundamental analysis, 93–106
  balance of trade, 94–96
  definition, 271
  forecasting, 102–106
  gross domestic product, 98–100
  interest rates, 94
  intervention, 100
  puchasing power parity, 97–98
  supply and demand, 93–94
  technical analysis and, 107–130

Futures:
  currencies trading volume, 21
  currency, 20
  versus foreign exchange, 9
  traders, 52
Futures Commission Merchants (FCMs), 26
Futures contract, 269

G7, definition, 269
Gain Capital, 73
Gann, William D., 127
Germany, 16, 95, 99, 252
Getting Started in Futures (Lofton), 22
GFT, 73
Going long, 269
Going short, 269
Gold standard, 12, 269
Good for the day order, 85
Goodman, Charles B., 128, 134, 175, 184–185
Goodman Swing Count System (GSCS), 128,
      133–136
  50 percent rule, 133, 134, 136–137
  measure move rule, 133–134
  3C rule, 135–136
  wave propagation rule, 134–135
Good till cancelled order (GTC), 85, 270
Gould, Bruce, 179
Great Britain, foreign exchange currency, 4
Greece, 16, 96, 252
Greed, 170–171, 172
Gross domestic product (GDP), 98–100, 104, 264,
      271
Gross national product (GNP), 269
Guerilla trader, 270

Hedge, 222, 270
Heuristics, 143–144, 171–172
  review, 202
High-frequency trading, 270
History of currency trading, 11–18
  ancient times, 11
  arrival of the euro, 16–17
  Bretton Woods System, 14–15
  current perspective, 16
  end of Bretton Woods and floating exchange
      rates, 15
  Federal Reserve System, 12–14
  gold standard, 12
  International Monetary market, 15–16
  Securities and Exchange Commission, 14
  timeline of foreign exchange, 17
Hit the bid, definition, 270
Home Mortgage Disclosure Act, 13
Hong Kong, 96

Hotspot FX, 70–71
Hours:
  for banking, 253–254
  for trading, 66
Housing starts, 101
Hungary, 96, 219

Iceland, 96, 219
Ikon GM Royal Division, 72
Illiquid, 218
India, 96, 99, 219
Indicators, 120
Indonesia, 96, 99
Industrial production (IP), 100
Inflation, 270
Initial margin, 270
Insider trading, 7
Institute for Supply Management, 100
Interbank rates, 7, 270
Interest, 69
  open, 142–143
  rates, 94
International Monetary Market (IMM), 15–16, 20,
      270
Internet, 62, 154
Intervention, 100, 270
In-the-money, 211, 212
Intrinsic value, 212
Introducing Brokers (IBs), 26, 28, 57–58, 270
Investors, 14
Iran, 99
Ireland, 16, 252
Israel, 96
Italy, 16, 95, 99, 252

Japan, 95, 99
  foreign exchange currency, 4
Japanese Candlestick Charting Techniques (Nison),
      116
Japanese yen (JPY), 4
  currency contract specifications, 20
  U.S. dollar index, 22
Java, 62

Keene, James R., 117
King Kong syndrome, 171, 270
Kiwi, definition, 270
Kuwait, 96

Latvia, 219
Leading indicators, 270
Legislation:
  Bretton Woods Agreement of 1944, 266
  CFTC Reauthorization Act of 2005, 27–28

Commodity Exchange Act, 237–242
Commodity Futures Modernization Act of 2000,
27, 68–69
Equal Credit Opportunity Act, 13
Securities Exchange Act, 14
Leverage, 8, 32, 36, 178, 270
Lichtenstein, 96
Limit on close (LOC) order, 86
Limit on open (LOO) order, 86
Limit orders, 84–85, 270
LinkStash, 146
Liquidation, definition, 270
Liquidity, 6, 270
Lithuania, 219
Live data streams, 157
Lofton, Todd, 22
London Inter-Bank Offered Rate (LIBOR), 270
Long position, 270
Loonie, definition, 271
Lot, definition, 271
Luxembourg, 16, 96, 252

Magazines, 165–166
Major currency, 29, 218, 271
Major currency cross rate, 249–250
Managed accounts, 161–163, 271
Margin, 8, 31, 34
   availability, 44–46
   calculating requirements, 46–47
   definition, 271
   requirements, 64
Margin call, 271
Margin percent, 36
Market Environments (ME), 162–163, 184–185
   applications, 190, 192–193
Market makers, 55–56, 56–57, 233–236, 271
Market orders, 84
Market risk, 271
Markets:
   closing, 195
   cornering, 7
   opening, 195
   trending and trading, 183–184, 229
   24-hour, 6
Market-to-market, definition, 271
Maturity, definition, 271
Maxwell, Joseph, 88
Meisler, Jay, 196
Mercury chart, 271
Merrill Lynch, 115
Mexican peso, currency contract specifications, 20
Mexico, 95, 99, 219
MF Global, 72
Middlemen, 8

Minor currency, 29, 271
Moldovo, 219
Momentum analysis, 121–123
Money management, 175–182, 201
   allocation, 180
   breaking even, 175–176
   capital allocation, 177–178
   definition, 271
   expectations, 176
   market selection, 181–182
   options, 216–218
   parameters, 177
   parameters for trader profiles, 178–179
   stop-loss orders, 181
   trade campaign method (TCM), 179–181
   trader profiles, 174–176
Money supply, 271
Moving average (MA), 123, 140–142
Moxham, Steve, 148
Mundo, definition, 271

Naked writer, 214
NASDAQ market, 7
National Association of Purchasing Managers
   (NAPM), 100
National Futures Association (NFA), 18, 25,
   26–27, 271
Netherlands, 16, 96, 99, 252
Net position, 271
News, 60, 154–156, 200
Newsletters, 165–166
New York Federal Reserve Bank, 103
New Zealand, 14
   currency contract specifications, 20
NinjaTrader, 159–161, 229
Nison, Steven, 115, 116
No dealing desk broker (NDD), 57, 235, 271
Nofri, Egene, 138–139
Norlin, George, 11
North Korea, 96
Norway, 96

Oanda, 71, 214
Obscure pairs, 200
Offer:
   definition, 271
   third-party, 63
Off-exchange, 74
Offsetting transaction, 211, 272
One cancels the other order (OCO), definition, 272
Onfolio, 146
Online trading, 7
Open interest, 142–143
Open order, 272

Options, 210–218
  decay, 211
  definition, 272
  for money management, 216–218
  open, 272
  overview, 210–211
  pros and cons, 212–213
  purchasing and writing, 214
  retail FOREX landscape, 214–216
  strategies, 213, 214, 216
  terminology, 211–212
  for trading, 216
Orders, 63, 83–89
  backup, 64
  confirmation, 87
  definition, 272
  execution and accounting, 60, 86–87
  placement walk-through, 86
Oscillators, 120
Overnight position, 272
Over the counter (OTC), 7, 214, 272
Pairs, 65
Panholzer, Peter, 163–164
Patriot Act, 27
Paypal, 65
Performance review, 201–202
Philippines, 96
Philosopher's Stone, 228–229
Pips, 30, 66
  absolute range, 182
  definition, 272
  full values, 37
  pip-tick relationship, 31
  single values, 36
Platforms. *See also* Java; Windows
  capabilities, 58
  stability, 62
Point and figure charts (P&F), 117–119
  advantages, 119
  algorithm, 118
  definition, 272
Point & Figure Charting (Dorsey), 119
Points, 272. *See also* Pips
Poland, 96, 99, 219
Political risk, definition, 272
Ponsi, Ed, 183
Portals, 147–150, 263
Portugal, 16, 96, 252
Position, definition, 272
Position trader, 177–178, 272
Premium, 212, 272
Pretzel chart, 272
Pretzels (PZ), 190, 192
Price and time rhythm (PR and TR), 185,
    186, 188

Price Trace Dispersement (PTD), 154
Price transparency, 272
Producer price index (PPI), 100, 104
Profiling, 171
Profit and loss (P & L), 178
  calculating, 37–44
  definition, 274
Programmed trading. *See* Algorithmic trading
Pugh, Bertram, 109, 139–140
Purchasing managers index, 100
Purchasing power parity (PPP), 97–98
Put, definition, 272
Pyramiding, 200, 272

Quote, definition, 275
Quote convention, 32–33
Quote currency, 30, 38–41, 273

Rally, 273
Range, 273
Rate:
  definition, 273
  interbank, 7, 270
  interest, 94
Records, 203–206
  accounting, 203–204
  business, 203
  planning, 206
  trade and performance, 204–205
REFCO, 25
Regrouping, 199–202
Regulation, 7
Regulatory agencies, 255–258
Relative strength indicator (RSI), 120–121
  calculating, 121
Requoting, 68, 273
Resistance levels, 273
Resources, 259–263
Retail sales, 101
Revaluation, 273
Reversal patterns, 112–113
Reviews, 147–150
Risk, definition, 273
Risk management, 273
Robots, 229–231
Rollovers, 33, 69, 221–222, 273
Round trip, definition, 273
Running stops, 273
Russia, 99
Russian ruble, 96
  currency contract specifications, 20

Sales, 101
Saudi Arabia, 96
Scalper, definition, 273

Scams, 74

Securities and Exchange Commission (SEC), 14, 273

Securities Exchange Act, 14

Settlement, definition, 273

Shamah, Shani, 209

Shape (S), 190, 191

Sharpe, William F., 162

Short position, 273

Singapore, 96

Slippage, definition, 273

SnagIt, 205

Software, 153–154

South Africa, 96, 99, 219
   rand, currency contract specifications, 20

South Korea, 96, 99

Spain, 16, 96, 99, 252

Specialty orders, 86

Spot market, 19–22
   overview, 3–4

Spot price, 273

Spread, definition, 273

Spread betting, 164–165

Sterling, definition, 273

Stock market, versus foreign exchange market, 6–7, 8–9

Stop-loss order, 85–86, 181, 199, 200, 274

Strike price, 211

Success in Commodities (Nofri), 138

Support levels, definition, 274

Swap, definition, 274

Sweden, 96

Swedish krona, U.S. dollar index, 22

Swing analysis, 126–128

Swing chart, definition, 274

Swiss franc (CHF), 4
   currency contract specifications, 20
   U.S. dollar index, 22

Swissy, definition, 274

Switzerland, 96
   foreign exchange currency, 4

Taiwan, 95, 99

Take-profit objective, 200

Technical analysis, 107–130. *See also* Foreign exchange (FOREX, FX)
   advanced studies, 128
   bar charts, 108–110
   Bollinger bands, 123–126
   candlestick charts, 115–117
   chart pattern recognition, 111
   continuation patterns, 113–114
   curve-fit data, 126
   cycle analysis, 128, 130
   definition, 274

double intersection, 136–137
falt/complex trade, 138
general principles, 131–132
Goodman Swing Count system (GSCS), 133–136
heuristics, 143–144
indicators and oscillators, 120
momentum analysis, 121–123
moving averages, 123, 140–142
Nofri congestion phase method, 138–139
open interest, 142–143
overview, 107
point and figure charts, 117–119
Pugh swing chart formations, 139–140
relative strength indicator, 120–121
return trend or swing, 137
reversal patterns, 112–113
support and resistance, 111
swing analysis, 126–128
technical services and, 150–151
trend lines, 110–111
volume, 142

Thailand, 96, 99, 219

Thickness (t), 188–190

Third parties, 7–8
   offerings, 63

Three chart system, 193

3C rule, 135–136

Ticks, 31
   definition, 276
   pip-tick relationship, 31

Time-of-day (TOD), 65–66, 195

Time zones, 253–254

Trade campaign method (TCM), 179–181

Trade plan, 200

Traders Journal, 166

TradeStation, 73

Trading, 33–34
   automated and robots, 229–231
   calculations, 35–53
   characteristics of successful traders, 172–173
   with clouded judgment, 201
   combinations of most frequently traded currencies, 223
   customer service, 66–67
   documentation, 68
   with emotional upheaval, 201
   with false expectations, 200
   flat/complex trade, 138
   futures, 52
   heuristics, 143–144
   historical data, 62, 157–158
   history, 11–18
   hours, 66
   methods, 197

Trading, (*Continued*)
  in the news, 196
  options, 216
  with overconfidence, 200
  preparedness, 201
  psychology of, 169–173
  ratios, 187
  regrouping, 199–202
  requoting, 68
  tools, 58–60
  trader profiles, 174–175
  trends, 229
Trading markets, 183–184
Trading pyramid, 169–170
Trading session, definition, 274
Trading signals, 153–154
Trading system, development tools,
    159–161
Trailing stop, 274
Transaction costs, 8, 33, 65–66, 225
  calculating, 47–49
  definition, 274
Transaction date, 274
Transaction exposure, 87–88
Trend lines, 110–111
Trend machine, 229, 230
Truth in Lending Act, 13
Truth in Savings Act, 13
Turkey, 96, 99, 219
Turkmenistan, 219
Turnover, definition, 274
Two-way price, definition, 274

Ultra-high-frequency trading, 274
Uncovered writer, 214
United Kingdom, 96, 99
United States:
  Dollar, 4
  foreign exchange currency, 4
  gross domestic product, 99
  index, 22
  interest rates, 95
  prime rate, 275
Unrealized gain/loss, 274
Uptick, definition, 274
Uptick rule, definition, 275
Uruguay, 219

U.S. dollar (USD), 4
  index, 22
U.S. prime rate, definition, 275
U.S. Steel, 117
Value date, definition, 275
Van Treuren, R. David, 193
Variation margin, 275
Vatican City, 252
Volatility, 185, 200
  definition, 275
Volume, 142

Wall Street Journal, 117
Wave propagation rule, 134–135
Web sites:
  bookmarks, 146
  brokers, 261
  charts, 150–152, 262–263
  data, 262
  dealers, 261
  education, 152–153
  FOREX magazines, 166
  forums, 148–149
  historical data, 157–158
  link pages, 263
  live data streams, 157
  for news trading, 70, 156
  New York Federal Reserve Bank, 103
  online brokers and dealers, 261
  online encyclopedias, 165
  on options, 209
  periodicals, 259
  portals and forums, 263
  regulatory agencies, 255
  reviews, 236
  software development, 263
  spread betting, 164–165
  system development tools, 159–161
Whipsaw, 200, 275
Windows, 62
Withdrawals, 65
World War I, 12
World War II, 12, 14–15

Yap, Dickson, 166
Yard, definition, 275
Yugoslavia, 219